DANCE AND SOCIETY IN EASTERN AFRICA 1890–1970

THE BENI *NGOMA*

Dance and Society in Eastern Africa 1890–1970

THE BENI *NGOMA*

T. O. RANGER
Professor of Modern History
University of Manchester

UNIVERSITY OF CALIFORNIA PRESS

BERKELEY AND LOS ANGELES, 1975

UNIVERSITY OF CALIFORNIA PRESS
BERKELEY AND LOS ANGELES, CALIFORNIA

ISBN: 0-520-02729-9
Library of Congress Catalog Card Number: 74-76389

Printed in Great Britain

Contents

Preface

During the six years in which I taught at the University of Dar es Salaam I was mainly concerned in trying to grasp the reality of the colonial experience in eastern Africa. I soon discovered that this was not an easy or straightforward thing to do, and that illuminations often came from very unexpected sources and from following up interests which at first sight seemed peripheral.

One of my side interests was in the *ngomas*, or team dances, which were regularly performed in Dar es Salaam. There were many different kinds of *ngoma*, but one in particular puzzled and intrigued me. This was a dance performance called *Mganda*, which was regularly danced at the University itself by a team of domestic servants who had migrated to Dar es Salaam from the Tanzanian shore of Lake Malawi. It was a most enjoyable dance to watch and to listen to; performed with un-flagging vigour and disciplined precision to the steady booming of a large military drum and to the drone of *kazoos* made out of gourds. At the same time it raised obvious questions about its origin and function. The dance was performed by a team which was organized on the basis of rank. Its leader was known as the 'King' and he wore appropriately dignified clothes, with a cap of rank, with shoulder badges, with a row of fountain pens in his breast pocket. He paraded up and down the ranks of his men, determining by his signals the development of the dance. The dancers themselves were dressed in a uniform of white shorts and shirts and their movements seemed at once a parody and a consummation of military drill.

I said to myself that it would be interesting to know the origins and history of this dance but at that time I had little intention of following it up. But my attention continued to be attracted to the *ngoma* and its predecessors. I learnt that *Mganda* was the most popular of 'traditional' *ngomas* with the students of the University and I attended a contest in which a student team danced against a team of workers from the city. When I visited Songea district I saw the dance in progress at the secondary school in Songea. Meanwhile my colleague, Dr John Lonsdale, had discovered a file in the National Archives, Dar es Salaam, which had been compiled by the British Censor in 1919 and which contained a mass of fascinating information about dance societies which seemed clearly to be related to the *ngoma* I had been watching. These 1919 dance societies were known as Beni, after the English word 'band'.

After that my attention was drawn to any reference to Beni or to *Mganda* in the government and missionary archives on which I was working. I found material relating to the dances not only in the National Archives of Tanzania but also in the National Archives of Kenya and Zambia. Students and colleagues began to pass on to me oral recollections of Beni and *Mganda* which they had collected during their field research. Gradually, and to my surprise, I began to realize that the dance form had a very long and complex history which I could begin to piece together. Even more gradually, and even more to my surprise, I began to realize that this dance history illuminated some aspects of the colonial experience in eastern Africa.

This book, then, draws upon the work of very many other people. I am grateful to John Lonsdale both for bringing Beni to my attention and then for graciously ceding it to me as a topic of research. Emmanuel Dube worked for me on the Beni material in the National Archives, Dar es Salaam. Oral field research was carried out on my behalf by B. J. Chijumba in Dar es Salaam, by O. R. Khamsini in Ufipa, by C. Mbeya and B. Ndomba in Songea, by Sylvia Maira and M. Mchawala in Masasi, by N. K. M. Mwambene in Rungwe, by E. L. K. Kabbembo in Ujiji, and by G. Mkangi in Mombasa. I was much assisted in my own collection of oral data by Douglas Werner, who arranged for and taped my interview with a Beni 'captain' in the Mbala district of Zambia; by Jim Allen, who put his great knowledge of Lamu at my disposal; by Abdu Ahmed Haffidh, who was as much a fellow researcher as an interpreter in Lamu; by Omari Bwana, who accompanied me to Faza and acted there as my host and guide; and by Ahmed S. M. Nabahani, who introduced me to the Beni history of Malindi. John Iliffe has fed me with a constant stream of tit-bits from the German sources; Lorne Larson has allowed me to make use of his material on Beni in Ulanga; Margaret Strobel has made available to me her notes on Beni from the Mombasa Municipal archives; Jaap Van Velsen allowed me to extract the Eastern African references from his notes on the files relating to Beni in the Malawi National Archives.

Other researchers have drawn my attention to Beni references or given me pieces of evidence so generously but they will have to rest content with this collective mention. What I have done with all these pieces of the jigsaw is very much my own responsibility. I can only hope that it will interest and entertain all those who helped me to find the pieces.

T. O. RANGER

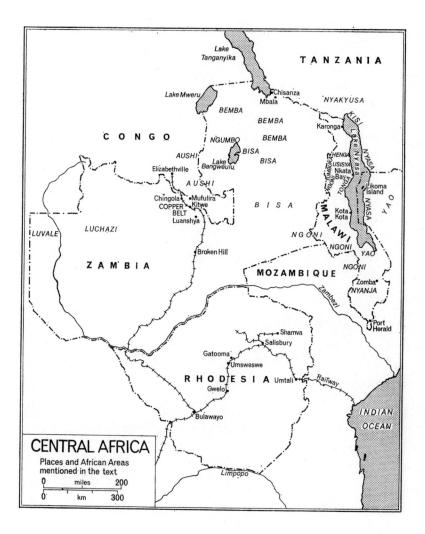

CENTRAL AFRICA

Places and African Areas
mentioned in the text

0   miles   200
0   km   300

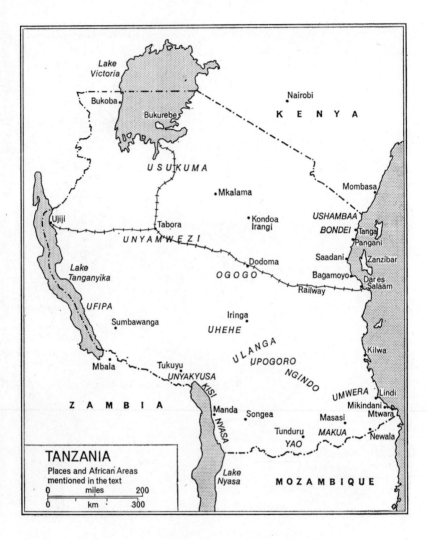

Lake
Victoria

Bukoba

Bukurebe

USUKUMA

Mkalama

Kondoa
Irangi

Dodoma

Nairobi

K E N Y A

Mombasa

USHAMBAA
BONDEI Tanga
Pangani

Ujiji

Tabora

UNYAMWEZI

Saadani

Zanzibar

Bagamoyo

Dar es
Salaam

Railway

OGOGO

Lake
Tanganyika

UFIPA

Iringa

Sumbawanga

UHEHE

ULANGA

UPOGORO

NGINDO

Kilwa

UMWERA

Lindi

Mbala

Tukuyu

UNYAKYUSA

KISI

NYASA

Manda

Songea

Mikindani

Mtwara

Masasi

Z A M B I A

Tunduru

YAO

MAKUA

Newala

TANZANIA
Places and African Areas
mentioned in the text

0   miles   200

0   km   300

Lake
Nyasa

M O Z A M B I Q U E

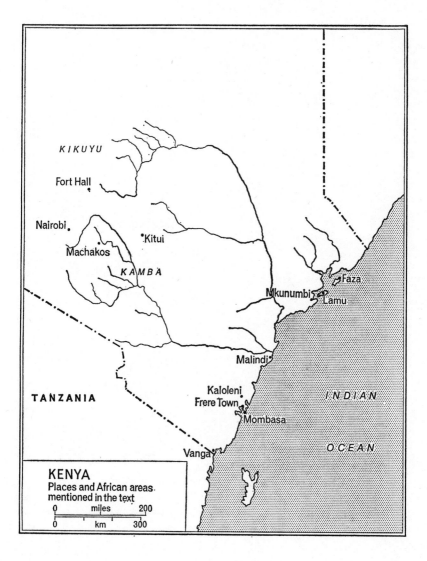

KIKUYU

Fort Hall

Nairobi

Machakos

Kitui

KAMBA

Mkunumbi

Faza

Lamu

Malindi

TANZANIA

Kaloleni
Frere Town

Mombasa

INDIAN

Vanga

OCEAN

KENYA
Places and African areas.
mentioned in the text

0   miles   200

0   km   300

Introduction

The 'colonial situation' in eastern Africa is extraordinarily complex and difficult to grasp. It can be comprehended at the very local microcosmic level through studies of the experience under colonialism of a 'tribe'. It can be comprehended at the formal centre through studies of the making of colonial policy or of the career of a colonial governor. It can be comprehended at a high level of generality in terms of the theory of the underdevelopment of Africa. Comprehended in this way there is even a sense in which the colonial situation is simple – brutally simple. It can be seen to consist of the use of effective power – military and technological – to extract from eastern Africa what was necessary to the developed economies of the world without creating in eastern Africa itself the foundations of a developed economy. It can be seen as an effort to proletarianize Africans without creating a working class; to make them peasants without creating a yeomanry; to equip them with a minimum of skills without equipping them with intellectual tools that could be used creatively.

But what is difficult is to grasp the unevenness and variety which characterized each colonial territory within these brutal simplicities, and especially to grasp the experiences of Africans who moved through these levels and variations. Before colonialism, developments in eastern Africa had been very uneven in any case; the Swahili economy of the coast was very different indeed from the economies of the Yao, or Nyamwezi, or Kamba peoples who were linked with it, and still more different from the 'inward' economies of other eastern African peoples. Under colonialism these very different systems were lumped together by the common predicament of colonial rule, and communication between them was increased through the flow of migrant labour to the coast or to the south and the flow of African administrative, proselytizing, and entrepreneurial talents to the interior. Communications by road and rail and a patch-work system of western education also aided a more even flow of people and ideas. But it was by no means the intention of the colonialists to produce homogeneous colonial societies: 'traditional' unevenness was valued because it allowed for divide and rule or produced a localized focus for protest which was easy to deal with. Above all the working out of colonial policies produced an even greater unevenness. Great divides opened up between areas with much missionary education and areas with little or none; areas with vigorously developed cash crop agriculture or African peasant production and areas designated as labour reserves; areas close to the new urban centres and areas very remote from them.

Colonialism *can* be seen as a single coherent system, but built into that very system – and systematically developed – was a giddy variety of existential experience. It thus becomes very difficult indeed to answer with general formulae such questions as the extent to which any genuine initiative remained to 'Africans' under colonialism or the extent to which 'Africans' were conceptually emasculated by the colonial experience. Somehow one has to find a way of grasping all this unevenness and variety, not merely by cataloguing it, but by seeing it as a process, by studying the movement of men, and ideas, and forms from one level to another.

No doubt there are a number of ways of trying to do this. I seek in this book to use a very informal and impressionistic method. I seek to make use of data on the origins, development, and diffusion of certain elements in the popular culture of colonial eastern Africa in order to throw light on some of the realities of the 'colonial situation'.

This has not been much attempted in African historiography but there are many recent precedents for such an approach in European historical studies. Thus, for example, Natalie Zemon Davies has analysed youth groups and *charivaris* in sixteenth-century France, demonstrating how an examination of the 'festive life' can illumine the strains put upon the relationships of young and old as a result of the developments of Renaissance society.[1] Sally Alexander has described the growth of St Giles's Fair in nineteenth-century Oxford and set out the ways in which the fair met the needs of men and women living in an industrialized society.[2] Eugen Weber has described the rise of gymnastics and of competitive sports in late nineteenth-century France, showing that these two different types of physical activity were seen as sharply contrasting, perhaps irreconcilable, ways of developing manliness among French youths.[3]

These historians have made large, but I believe justified, claims for

[1] Natalie Zemon Davies, 'The Reasons of Misrule: Youth Groups and *Charivaris* in Sixteenth-Century France', *Past and Present*, no. 50, February 1971, pp. 41–75.

[2] Sally Alexander, *St Giles's Fair, 1830–1914, Popular Culture and the Industrial Revolution in 19th century Oxford*, History Workshop Pamphlets, no. 2, Ruskin College, Oxford, 1970.

[3] Eugen Weber, 'Gymnastics and Sports in Fin-de-Siècle France', *The American Historical Review*, vol. 76, no. 1, February 1971, pp. 70–98.

the significance of their studies. Davies emphasizes the need to uncover 'the real uses of popular recreation' and argues that 'festive life' can 'perpetuate certain values of the community, even guarantee its survival, and . . . criticize political order'.[1] Raphael Samuel, introducing Sally Alexander's study, claims for 'street ballads' or 'fairground drama' that 'they alone give us a guide to how men felt about their lives, and what they thought about their times'.[2] And Weber suggests that 'physical exercise and the role that men attribute to it . . . can document times and mentalities as suggestively as can their industrial enterprises'.[3]

In recent European historiography the study of recreation, carnival, etc. has often illuminated shifts of upper-class consciousness, as in the case of Weber's study. But it seems to be agreed that studies of popular culture are especially valuable for getting at the experience and attitudes of the 'masses' and for giving expression to the reactions of the inarticulate. Put crudely the assumption is that the 'masses' did not control formal means of articulating their desires – the universities, the pulpit, the press, the theatre, the political pronouncement – and that when spokesmen did emerge they were at instant risk. For this reason we have to look at the informal, the festive, the apparently escapist, in order to see evidence of real experience and real response; to see how far 'the people' have had to make use, even for this informal vocabulary, of the idioms of the masters; to see how far, on the other hand, creativity and spontaneity survive.

It has seemed to me that in eastern Africa too, it might be illuminating to take this informal approach to the unriddling of the 'colonial situation'; to use the festive song as an index of feeling and to balance the elements of derivation and creativity within eastern African popular culture. And this is what I have tried to do, concentrating particularly on an element in popular culture which was very widely diffused so that one can use it to traverse the unevenness.

But there is one difficulty in doing this which needs to be faced at the outset. Some studies *have* been made in the past of aspects of eastern African urban culture, the most famous of which is Clyde Mitchell's *The Kalela Dance*, in which he gave an elegant demonstration of how a single event – the performance of a dance by a group of young men in a Northern Rhodesian township – could serve as an analogue or metaphor for the essential pattern of urban social relations.[4]

[1] Davies, op. cit., p. 41.   [2] Alexander, op. cit., p. iii.   [3] Weber, op. cit., p. 70.
[4] J. C. Mitchell, *The Kalela Dance, Aspects of social relationships among urban Africans in Northern Rhodesia*, The Rhodes–Livingstone Papers, no. 27, Manchester, 1956.

Recently, however, these studies have come under heavy criticism. In Bernard Magubane's attack on Central African sociology, for example, some sharp things are said about the relevance and validity of concentrating on a phenomenon like the *Kalela* dance at all. Magubane objects to the triviality of the topic; to the impressionistic way in which it is treated; then to what he regards as the condescending and unsympathetic way in which alleged African aspirations to European dress are made crucial to the analysis; and above all to the synchronic emphasis which in his view means that the young men dancing *Kalela* are seen as though self-created, the product of their own taste and choice, rather than as the end result of the long process of colonial violence, colonial compulsion, colonial emasculation. One should study the *real* experience of Africans in Zambia, urges Magubane, not ephemeral and insignificant products of it. This real experience is a matter of colonial invasion, of resistance, of accommodation, of protest and the repression of protest.[1]

I am not here concerned with these criticisms of Mitchell. I am concerned to scrutinize my own enterprise to try to ensure that it does not become in effect trivial, worthlessly impressionistic, condescending, and obscuring of reality. Naturally it is not my aim to be all or any of these things. My own work in the past has stressed resistance, and compulsion, and protest and in this book I hope to illuminate them from some unexpected angles rather than to abandon them as topics altogether. As far as the question of triviality is concerned I am inclined to appeal back to the estimates already cited of the significance of recreational history in Europe. There is a distinction to be made between the ludic and the ludicrous, between the festive and the futile. Thus, I do not believe that an examination of eastern African popular culture will turn out to be trivial though it will certainly have to be impressionistic. Above all, my examination will be diachronic; the dance mode which is the object of my study will be seen over very nearly a hundred years in its relation to the great crises of eastern African history – in relation to colonial occupation and to the overwhelming display of European military power, in relation to the devastation of the First World War, to the Great Depression of the 1930s, to the development of strike action and protest politics. I believe that the dance mode acts throughout all this as an admittedly very impressionistic scale of balance of emulation and creativity, of accommodation and independence. Moreover, because the popular cultural

[1] Bernard Magubane, 'A critical look at Indices used in the study of social change in Colonial Africa,' *Current Anthropology*, vol. 12, nos. 4–5.

form I have chosen was so widely diffused the diachronic treatment has to be wedded to broad geographical sweep and this enables us to move across the unevenness of colonial society in the dimensions of both time and space.

The Beni mode as an object of study

The particular form of popular culture on which I have chosen to focus is the Beni *ngoma*. The *ngoma* takes its name from its essential musical feature – the attempt to reproduce the effect of a military brass-band, though the elaboration of this attempt might vary from the provision of a full bugle, pipe, and drum detachment to the beating of a single big drum in some rural variants of Beni. The dances done to this Beni music have also varied considerably but all have been based on the idea of military drill. Sometimes the dance took the form of a parade, a procession, a march past; sometimes it took the form of a dance in platoon form; sometimes it took the form of a circling drill step. Singing was always an important part of Beni performances. Almost universally the language of Beni songs was Swahili and they normally took the form of simple rhyming commentaries on current affairs. Invariably the music and the dance were merely one part of the activity of Beni members. The Beni *ngomas* had a hierarchy of male and female officers, with elaborate ranks, uniforms, and titles of honour. These dignitaries certainly did participate in and were honoured at the dance. But they also carried out administrative and welfare functions among the membership.

These features of Beni – the sound of a brass band, the military drill, the hierarchies of officers with European titles – made it instantly recognizable wherever it went. In addition, however, the Beni societies founded branches subordinate to them so that the diffusion of Beni was not merely a matter of similar styles or a coincidence of names. The mode was popular for a very long time and in very many places. Its popularity lasted at least sixty years, though during that time Beni changed in many ways. It was popular in 'traditional' Swahili towns, in the new ports and industrial cities, and in rural environments all over eastern Africa. Whatever may be concluded about its origins it ended up by being an integral part of African popular culture, and it gave rise to variant forms – *Mganda*, *Kalela*, *Malipenga*, and the rest – which extended both the chronological and geographical scope of the mode's popularity.

Eastern African Beni can be regarded as one of a series of brass-band responses by people in a transitional period from pre-industrial to industrial society. It can be compared with the brass-band competitions of the Lancashire industrial villages; with the band processions of the 'sets' in eighteenth-century Jamaica, or with the 'marching bands' of Brazil. At the same time, as we shall see, Beni was very much an eastern African phenomenon and drew upon traditions of dance competition which long antedated the specific musical and dance forms involved.

Beni offers many advantages to the researcher who wishes to use it as a 'trace element' in the cultural history of eastern Africa. It was easily and much remarked on by European observers and there are abundant administrative and missionary reports about the dance. There is also a lively oral tradition concerning Beni. I have collected this tradition myself in places as far apart as Lamu on the northern coast of Kenya and the lakeside villages of the Zambian shore of Lake Tanganyika. Students have collected it for me in Mombasa and Dar es Salaam, Ufipa and Rungwe, Songea and Masasi. Other scholars have come across the oral tradition of Beni in Ukambani in Kenya, in the Mahenge district of Tanzania, and in the Zambian industrial town of Kabwe.

Moreover, although Beni songs and the oral memories that go with them illuminate otherwise 'inarticulate' responses, the Beni societies themselves originated in a highly literate coastal tradition. At many times and in many places they produced their own records – poems to celebrate the victory of one society over another, bulletins addressed to the Swahili press, membership lists, correspondence between the officers of one branch of a particular society and another. Much of this is lost but a good deal of it survives.

Beni, then, is very richly documented. On the other hand, by its very character it raises the questions posed by Magubane in an acute form. Beni was in fact the parent form to Mitchell's *Kalela*; like *Kalela* it involved 'imitation' of European dress and conduct. Much of the European evidence about Beni takes the form of mockery and at first sight an extended treatment of the Beni mode would indeed seem an exercise in insensitive triviality. To my mind, however, it is in the end an advantage that Beni forces these issues upon us. Whether one likes or dislikes the fact, the question of what Africans should wear *was* an issue of importance to both blacks and whites and the history of Beni throws a good deal of light on why this should be so. Above all, Beni, with its apparently overwhelmingly imitative character, turns out in the end to be deeply rooted in pre-colonial dance and competitive modes. In this it serves to remind us that judgements of derivation or creativity need to be more subtle than a mere assumption that everything 'modern' comes from the whites.

In this context the question of the origin of Beni becomes particularly important and it is to this that I turn in the first chapter of this book.

1 *The Origins of Beni*

In its region of origin Beni was co-existent with colonial rule. In Lamu, for example, the Beni associations first emerged in the 1890s, soon after the establishment of British control, and came to an end in the early 1960s with the achievement of Kenyan independence. This co-existence was not accidental. There was the closest connection between Beni and colonialism. But the problem is to define precisely what that connection was.

One explanation which has been advanced sees Beni in terms of an 'adjustment to absolute power'.[1] This interpretation draws upon the work of Bruno Bettelheim, as used by Stanley Elkins in his study of the slave mentality in America. Bettelheim found evidence to show that Jewish prisoners in German concentration camps came to imitate the S.S. in the style of their uniforms, to take pride in standing 'really well at attention' during roll-call and, in some cases, even to adopt the intense German nationalism of their oppressors.[2] Elkins used these findings as a metaphor for the slave experience in America. On the surface there seems just as much reason to apply them to Beni. Beni dancers copied European military and ceremonial uniforms; took pride in their skill at drill; and often put on lavish displays of loyalty to the British Crown.

Some descriptions of Beni seem to beg for Bettelheim's sort of interpretation. A European traveller witnesses a Beni march through the streets of Mombasa in the early 1920s, for example. In his account he stresses the degrading aspect of the tattered European clothing worn by the marchers, 'dressed in whatever came to hand', in 'khaki trousers with orange belts, and felt hats trimmed with peacock feathers', in bathing trunks and tennis rigs. He stresses also the assertive 'loyalty' of the procession's climax. 'We found ourselves near an open square where the marchers were assembling around a tall tree. The savage

---

[1] This suggestion was made during the discussion of a paper on the uses of the military mode in eastern Africa which I presented to Professor Boniface Obichere's colloquium on African military history at U.C.L.A. in Spring, 1972.

[2] Bruno Bettelheim, 'Individual and Mass Behaviour in Extreme Situations', *Journal of Abnormal Psychology*, XXXVIII, October 1943.

music came to a sudden stop. When the bands started again it was to play "God Save the King". Every hat came off . . . "Impressive, isn't it?" the [Senior Medical Officer] said.'[1]

Beni themes and the nineteenth-century mission context

There is, in fact, a good deal of evidence which might be used to support this idea of the 'imprinting' of the notions and forms of Beni as a result of the traumatic experiences of eastern Africans. If we are looking for the source of the Beni fascination with uniform, especially with naval uniform; of the Beni pride in the music of the brass band; of the models of battleships which the Beni associations pulled through the streets of Mombasa – then we can most obviously find it in the experience of a particular group of eastern Africans. These were the men and women whose nineteenth-century experiences most closely approximated to the traumatic ordeal of the Jewish prisoners who made their submission to absolute power. These were the men and women who were first taken out of their own communities into slavery; then carried to the coast; then loaded aboard the slave ships; then intercepted by the anti-slave cruisers of the British navy, almost always in circumstances of profound confusion and alarm; then placed in the care of missionaries whose absolute power was made all the more absolute by their benevolence; then taught that their original customs were wrong; and finally offered selected European customs as a new mode of life.

If we look at the 'freed slave' settlements we find the themes of Beni most strikingly enunciated. We find that both the missionaries and the freed slaves regarded European-style drill and uniforms and above all European-style military music as important symbols of progress towards the desired new life. The most vivid account of all this is the story of one of the freed slaves of Freretown, the Church Missionary Society settlement near Mombasa. This man, Mbotela, later told his adventures to his son, who wrote them down. He told of his youth in what is now Malawi; of his capture by slavers; of the horrors of the march to the coast; of the interception of the slave ship by a British man-of-war. He described the day of bewilderment, and fear, and eventual relief on which he first heard the brass band.

One day, being a special day, the slaves were given a treat. There was very sweet food and many nice things to eat, and also a band to

[1] Herman Norden, *White and Black in East Africa*, London, 1924, pp. 47–8.

play for them. The captain and his officers were all dressed in their clothes of honour. The sailors brought those cruel trees that the slaves had borne on their necks, and piled them up in their presence; then the flag of the Union Jack was placed by them. At the sight of these bonds, which they had thought had been thrown away before, some feared that the British intended to cast their bodies into the sea, as the cruel slave-traders had sometimes done for no apparent reason.

But it was the bonds that were thrown into the sea in their presence. All the white people clapped their hands for joy, and the released slaves did the same. Then they were certain that they were safe.[1]

It is only a very small exaggeration to describe the rest of Mbotela's story as the account of how the freed slaves, through their children, obtained a brass band of their own. The first Christmas after their landing at Freretown, the freed slaves performed their own 'different kinds of native dances'. But 'unfortunately these dances excited the performers with memories of evil practices and beliefs. They decorated themselves . . . some even cut themselves on their faces as they had done at home. And the sight was dreadful to behold'. So 'the missionaries . . . forbade the playing of the wicked drums'.[2]

If their own 'wicked' drums were prohibited, could the freed slaves adopt the 'good' drums of the whites? Perhaps so, for they were being taught the other things that went with the brass band. 'Chokamba, who was the head of the Freed Slaves Force, started giving commands in English when he was taking drill . . . Besides drill they were taught all kinds of gymnastics and games . . . The sailors in the man-of-war were ready to help by showing them games, and everyone who was clever in games used to get a red coat with big buttons.' In this way the idea of drill and of uniform was intimately connected with the idea of learning 'civilization' and 'English, the language of Bwana Mzuri, [the naval captain] who had set them free'.[3]

Mbotela's story ends with the acquisition of that supreme symbol of English civilization, a brass band of their own. His account has so many echoes of Beni that it is worth quoting in full:

When Bwana Mzuri knew that he would soon leave the harbour for good, he invited the boys and girls of the freed slaves to his feast . . . The boys and girls were filled with wonder when they

[1] James Juma Mbotela, *The Freeing of the Slaves in East Africa*, London, 1956, p. 47.
[2] ibid., pp. 59–60.   [3] ibid., pp. 57–8.

boarded the man-of-war and saw how it was decorated. They were shown so many things . . . During the meal they sat with Bwana Mzuri at the table, while the Band entertained them and even played their favourite hymn, which they all knew well, 'Once in Royal David's City'. They told the captain that they wished they had a band of their own . . . Before they went, they were told to sing their favourite hymn, while the band played it again. So they sang with all their might . . . the sailors clapped their hands to cheer them . . . As he said good-bye, Bwana Mzuri told them, 'I have not forgotten your need of a band, and I will do my utmost to arrange for you to have one of your own'. All the boys and girls left the man-of-war feeling happy and content, and hoping that they would soon have their own music.

The missionaries were pleased to give them musical instruments for a band, knowing that they were better than their drums. While they waited for these instruments to arrive, the band from the man-of-war, by order of Bwana Mzuri, entertained them every evening. . . . There was great excitement when everything necessary for the band arrived. At first they were taught to play flutes in tonic sol-fa. They tried to do their best . . . It did not take them long to play properly, and to learn a good many of the hymns. On feasts, like Christmas, and on half-term holidays, they used to go to Nyale and Mkung'ombe with their band. And they played at farewell parties for prominent people such as the Bishop of Mombasa. Certain days of the week were set aside for playing. Men and women would come from their work, delighted to hear the band. And our parents rejoiced that their boys had skill to give this new pleasure.

When Bwana Mzuri was going home to England for good, he came to say good-bye, and that day the band played especially well. Bwana Mzuri was pleased with their zeal. He bade them farewell with words of advice, saying, 'Continue you in good deeds, and you will be blessed'.[1]

Bwana Mzuri's pleasure in hearing African boys playing European music was widely shared. Missionaries in the 1880s had few doubts of the civilizing and disciplining value of music. In Europe itself at this time the youth of the slums were being organized into Christian 'armies' and 'brigades', and marching to the sound of the fife and drum band. The Universities' Mission to Central Africa, which ran large freed slave villages and schools on Zanzibar, was supported in one 'large manufacturing town of the North of England' by a 'Children's

[1] James Juma Mbotela, *The Freeing of the Slaves in East Africa*, London, 1956, pp. 71-3.

Mission Army', with a boy Colonel and boy Majors presiding over it, and with Captains to collect contributions for the mission overseas. The U.M.C.A. journal, *Central Africa*, commented appreciatively on the singing of the Mission Army – 'whether it is the perpetual rhythm of the cotton mills, or what, these Lancashire people do know how to sing hymns and they do it well'.[1]

In Zanzibar itself the rhythm of hymns and of European band music was thought to be an excellent way of introducing the freed slave children to the necessities of industrial time. For the missionaries European music represented a world of order in contrast to the inexplicable monotonies and sudden passions of African drumming; musical ability was taken as a sign, a promise of potential for civilization. So in January 1883 a correspondent in *Central Africa* recorded the dances of freed slave children in Zanzibar with some alarm. 'It seems as if their savage instincts are only slumbering, and ready to wake again . . . they begin a wild frenzy of a dance, describing a hunt, or a fight; arms and legs begin to fly wildly about, the chorus is enlivened with wild screeches at irregular intervals.'[2] By May 1883, however, a more reassuring report was possible. 'The boys have very martial tastes and enjoy playing at soldiers. A kind friend has presented them with an excellent military drum and Mr Geldert thinks he could form a fife and drum band.'[3]

In these U.M.C.A. freed slave villages and schools on Zanzibar we can also see how the symbols of European naval power came to dominate the minds of the young just as they dominated the minds of Mbotela and his comrades in Freetown. The 'absoluteness' of this naval power was certainly impressed upon them. In January 1889 the Germans bombarded the mainland coastal towns opposite Zanzibar with terrible effect, and at once caused a stir among the freed slave schoolboys. The missionaries reported with dismay that the boys were making 'remarks of a most contemptuous nature' about the weakness of England as contrasted with Germany.[4] Later in the same year, however, the appearance in Zanzibar harbour of 'our new wonder, H.M.S. *Agammemnon*, the ironclad ship', gave a great boost to British prestige among the boys. They 'collected all the old boxes, boards, poles and an extraordinary collection of other odds-and-ends about

[1] 'Home Work', *Central Africa*, no. 52, pp. 60–1.
[2] 'Child Life in the Mission', *Central Africa*, no. 1, January 1883, p. 9.
[3] ibid., no. 5, May 1883, p. 79.
[4] 'The Position in Zanzibar', *Central Africa*, no. 76, April 1889, p. 62.

here, and constructed on an enormous scale what they played with as a supposed model of the iron ship! They gave receptions on board to the "Prince of Wales", "The Consul-General", "The Sultan", etc.'[1]

In 1890 some part of this fantasy came true, so thin was the dividing line between schoolboy pretence and colonial ceremonial. The Sultan of Zanzibar visited the mission. 'The Kiungani boys, with Mr Madan's help, had constructed a large ship in the yard where stands the printing office, and when the Sultan appeared, they fired a royal salute of twenty-one rockets. He was very delighted.' Once again a brass band provided the background music to this ironic anticipation of the devastating naval bombardment of the Sultan's palace six years later. 'The Sultan took his leave, the band from the *Boadicea* playing his national air . . . Our children were delighted with the band; they crowded round the musicians closer and closer till they were in danger of being stifled.'[2]

If there was still some ambiguity on this occasion between the power of the Sultan and that of the British, the naval bombardment of August 1896 made the realities very clear. The U.M.C.A. schoolboys watched as in forty minutes the bombardment broke a defiant Sultan's capacity to resist.

In such situations adjustments to absolute power were certainly made, whether at Freetown or on Zanzibar – or for that matter in the freed slave villages which the Catholics had established on the Tanganyikan mainland, and which were armed and drilled like little fortresses. These adjustments were accompanied and often expressed by an adoption of drill, the brass band, an imitation of the ceremonial side of European military, naval, and proconsular life. Most of the symbols of Beni were present. And there can be little doubt that the freed slave schoolboys with their imaginary receptions on board their model ship were fore-runners of the Mombasa Beni associations who paraded through the streets of the city before the First World War with floats depicting 'a man-of-war, with natives dressed as admirals and other officers sitting on the bridge, drinking whisky and sodas, and puffing cigarettes, going through a pantomime all the while of receiving reports from orderlies'.[3]

And yet, revealing though all this is of the inner significance of some major Beni themes, there is one very good reason for being cautious about explaining Beni solely in terms of adaptation to absolute power. That reason is quite simply that Beni did *not* arise in or out of the

---

[1] 'Our Boys at Play', *Central Africa*, no. 81, September 1889, p. 135.
[2] 'The Anniversary in Zanzibar', *Central Africa*, no. 95, November 1890, p. 173.
[3] Herman Norden, *White and Black in East Africa*, London, 1924, p. 48.

mission villages or schools. The Beni associations arose in the Swahili quarters of the coastal towns of Kenya and Tanganyika. The freed slaves had experienced so much that made the *themes* of Beni relevant to them. But they evidently did not possess other essential qualities, memories, traditions which were necessary for actually producing Beni itself. I shall argue below that these missing ingredients were a sufficient degree of autonomy from European control which allowed the brass band to be made use of rather than merely adopted; a continued self-confidence in communal values, which enabled young men to use the Beni mode to express the pride of their own groupings against others; and a continuing tradition of communal competition as expressed through dance, procession, and mimic combat, which enabled Beni to take a natural place as part of the sequence of Swahili festive life. Beni as it actually emerged was much more autonomous, more joyous, than Bettelheim's style of explanation would allow.

The freed slave communities could not – or at any rate did not – produce Beni as an expression of collective competitive prestige. The freed slave villages were allowed all too little self-confidence and they broke up before there was much chance of any natural growth. The young men produced by the mission freed slave schools often went on to impressive individual careers. But they did not form a community, even though their instructors had hopefully contrasted 'the isolation, mutual ignorance, distrust, fear and hopelessness of heathen degradation' with Christian boys who had 'a common home, a common language, a common training, a common cause, work and hope, a common religion with common means of communication, though now spread over hundreds of miles of country'.[1] It was not *this* network of communication which spread Beni throughout eastern Africa. The early mission school tended to produce an élitist individualism which was reflected in dance and music as well as in more important things.

A new dance form as an expression of prestige *did* emerge from the freed slave experience in the Mombasa hinterland. But it was not Beni. The new form was something called *dansi*, an emulation of European ballroom music and dancing rather than of the music and movements of the parade ground. *Dansi* was more individualistic, less integrated with the life and aspirations of the coastal community and more tied to the changing fashions of European dance than was Beni. The characteristic instruments of *dansi* were not trumpets and drums but the accordion, the mouth-organ, and the guitar.

[1] 'A Step Forward', *Central Africa*, no. 73, January 1889, pp. 4–5.

James Juma Mbotela, whose account of his father's experiences at Freretown I have quoted, has given the following explanation of the rise of *dansi*. According to him, it was developed by a special Freretown élite, the so-called Bombay Africans, who had been educated and trained in India and then brought to Freretown to assume leadership of the Christian community there as pastors, teachers, etc. 'On their arrival at Freretown they enjoyed a higher status than the rest. They teamed up with the Goans and started playing dance music. These dances killed native dances. People took to playing the accordion and later the guitar.'[1]

Dansi killed, or at any rate replaced, the brass-band enthusiasm as well. When pupils came to be educated at Freretown in the early twentieth century it was *dansi* which they encountered and which they accepted as the specifically Christian dance form. In this way, for example, Samson Kayamba, born of Christian parents in Kaloleni in 1902, began his long career as a patron of European-style music. When he attended Freretown, 'then the seat of education in the whole country' in the late 1910s, he 'saw the European dance. The music came from a solo playing of a piano accordion. This interested him so much that he bought his own and returned to Kaloleni in 1923. He does not know who brought this type of dance to Freretown. What he did know was that it was a European dance, hence a Christian one, which ought to be imitated by all Christians . . . Anybody who became a Christian was automatically excluded from being a *shenzi*; therefore it was unwise to go and participate in a native dance . . . Kayamba did not hesitate to start a dancing club which he called Weruni Dancing Club in 1924.'[2]

This club for performing *dansi* 'was almost one man's property – Kayamba's. The members regarded the new dance as "smart" indeed. It was an élitist type of an organization, for it was restricted to the small minority of Christian adherents.'[3] It was not until the 1940s that there was any interaction between Kayamba's *dansi* and the much more populous and populist Beni societies of the Swahili coast.

The emergence of Beni in Mombasa and Lamu

The *dansi* mode has its own complex history of diffusion in eastern Africa, and it will appear often in this book, sometimes co-existing or

[1] Interview with James Mbotela as recorded by George Mkangi, October 1968.
[2] Interview with Samson Kayamba as recorded by George Mkangi, October 1968.
[3] George Mkangi's commentary on his interviews, October 1968.

inter-acting with Beni, sometimes replacing it. But for the origins of Beni itself we need to leave the freed slave settlements and look elsewhere.

So far as the evidence stands at present, it seems that the first Beni associations were developed in Mombasa and Lamu in the late 1890s and that they were pioneered by young Swahili Moslems. Now, of course, the Swahili-speaking peoples of the Kenyan coast had had their own experience of the 'absolute power' of the Europeans. As early as 1875 Fort Jesus in Mombasa had suffered a three-hour bombardment by a British warship. In the 1880s reports travelled north about the devastating effect of the German bombardment of the Tanganyikan coastal towns. 'Cannon thundered like waves on a rock,' wrote the poet, Hemedi bin Abdallah El Buhiry, after one such bombardment, 'and houses were hit and fell down . . . The Europeans . . . came ashore with a crash of guns.'[1] In the early 1890s there were military operations on the mainland opposite Lamu. And all this came to a crisis in 1896, just before the emergence of Beni, with the bombardment of the Sultan's palace in Zanzibar, and with the final defeat of the Mazrui rebellion on the Kenyan coast.

The latest historian of the coast, Dr Ahmed Salim, tells us that by the mid-1890s it had become 'patently clear that a definite compromise had to be made between the traditional cultural way of life and the new order'. By 1900, he goes on to say, 'the shocks of military defeat . . . may be said to have died out' and to have been succeeded by 'a mood of reconciliation to European rule'.[2] It was certainly in this context of reconciliation, and following the shock of the Europeans coming ashore with the crash of guns, that the Beni associations emerged. Equally certainly Beni was danced by young men who were more ready than many of their elders to recognize the power of European culture as well as of European arms.

But, as Salim goes on to insist, in any compromise 'between the traditional cultural way of life and the new order' the Swahili people of the Kenyan coast were determined that 'western culture had to accommodate some of [their] own deeply-rooted values'. This was true of the young men who danced Beni. The dance *was* in some sense an adaptation to a new world dominated by European power. But the

[1] Hemedi bin Abdallah El Buhiry, *Utenzi Wa Vita Vya Wadachi Kutamalaki Mrima*, translated by J. W. T. Allen, Dar es Salaam, 1960, p. 49.
[2] Ahmed Idha Salim, 'The Swahili-speaking communities of the Kenya coast, 1895–1965', unpublished Ph.D. dissertation, University of London, 1968, pp. 297, 314.

Beni associations preserved and sprang out of some of the deeply rooted assumptions of Swahili urban life.

Competitive dance associations were, in fact, a long-established feature of the Kenyan coast – and dance associations, moreover, which possessed an elaborate hierarchy of ranks, which specialized in dances displaying military skills, and which were vehicles for musical and other innovations. Thus many features of Beni which struck outside observers as most obviously new and foreign were really inherited directly from coastal dance traditions.

Dance societies of this kind had long been important in the Swahili cities because they were competitive, and because they expressed their competition through elaborate dance and through song. For if two things characterized urban Swahili civilization more than anything else, and distinguished it from the 'tribal' cultures of the interior, they were, precisely, locational factionalism and an elaborate verbal and musical culture based on literacy. The Swahili townsman prided himself on being free from the bondage of tribe and on being master of an urbane style.

In towns like Lamu and Mombasa the location in which a man lived was more important in many ways than the family or lineage to which he belonged. In early nineteenth-century Lamu, for example, the town was divided into two halves – known as Zena and Suudi – which were the basis of both civil and military organization. Civic office was held by the aristocratic leaders of these two moieties in a system of rotation, and the army of Lamu was made up of the two regiments of Zena and Suudi.[1] By the 1890s the terminology of Lamu factionalism had changed. The two moieties were known as Mtambweni, the area at what is now the centre of the town, and Mkomani, the northern part of the city. These moieties were just as vigorously competitive as ever and each maintained its own *Chama*, or association of dancers under the patronage of the great families.[2]

Mombasa was not a republic like Lamu and its government did not depend on the rotation of faction leaders; moreover, in Mombasa the principle of duality was complicated by the additional balance between the two great federations of Swahili 'tribes'. Still, the existence of town moieties was important in pre-colonial Mombasa too. In the 1890s they were still known as *Gavana* and *Mji wa Kale* and their rivalry was still

[1] The fullest account of Swahili urban dualism is, A. H. J. Prins, *Didemic Lamu: Social Stratification and Spatial Structure in a Muslim Maritime Town*, Groningen, 1971.
[2] Interview with *Mzee* Salim Kheri, Lamu, 18 October 1972.

reflected in competitive dance. And this same factional rivalry was reproduced in the other Swahili towns and villages along the Swahili coast and on the Bajun islands north of Lamu.

The intense competition between the moieties sometimes led to fighting in the narrow streets of the cities. But modern scholars agree in regarding this factionalism as a basic integrative device for urban settlements which had constantly had to absorb new elements over the centuries. 'When a village is competitively divided into two sides,' writes Lienhardt, 'any small fragmentary group within the village is drawn to the support of one side or the other, and hence the opposition of the two halves produces solidarity within each of them in the place of a much greater number of oppositions between smaller groups.'[1] This sort of factionalism helped to create communities of commitment out of the very disparate elements of coastal society – a function which was certainly as necessary in the 1890s as at any earlier time. Clearly it was important that the rivalry of the factions should normally find expression in ways that were satisfying to the pride of the moieties but which were not destructive of the ultimate unity of the town. Moieties could gain prestige by being able to afford the more lavish feast or by having the wittiest poets. And they could gain prestige by having the best dancers. Thus the dance competition, during the course of which contestations of poetry and song took place, and which was accompanied by feasting, became a crucial expression of moiety solidarity.

The 'traditional' dance associations allowed many different elements within the moiety to achieve a sense of pride. There was the pride of the dancers and marchers themselves, the young men of 'free' Swahili descent. There was the more private pride of the well-born women members of the associations, who did not compete in dances in the open square or street, but provided elaborate music, dancing, and poetic recitation at the domestic celebrations of members of the association. There was the pride of the patrons, the great aristocratic families around whom the dancers grouped like a clientage, the plantation-owners who could provide food and drink for the lavish 'picnics' staged by the associations. There was the pride of slave women dancers, whose public performances were great attractions and sometimes ensured victory for one association over another. And there was the pride of the general population of the moiety for whom the dance associations filled something of the role now played by football teams.

These 'traditional' dance societies – or Beni itself for that matter – are

[1] Peter Lienhardt, *Swifa Ya Nguvumali, The Medicine Man*, London, 1968, p. 20.

very inadequately described *just* as dance societies. They were a way of recasting the network of relationships within a moiety or quarter; they were an expression of most of the existing values of Swahili urban society; and they were also mechanisms of innovation. 'If one or other rival side embraces an innovation,' writes Lienhardt, 'which proves to attract more people, the other has to copy it.'[1] During the nineteenth century the dance societies of the Kenya coast had reflected the movement of fashion. They had undergone an intensive Arabization and had experienced the spread of the influence of Zanzibar, with its strong Indian overtones. New instruments, new costumes, new weapons for display, new dance forms were constantly being incorporated. Nor did the dance associations borrow only from prestigious Oman or Zanzibar. Modes of dance and of display brought by slaves from the interior were picked up and made use of by the dance societies of the Swahili towns.[2]

In the early 1890s the dominant influence was still Arab. Skene has described the *Chama* dance, in which Swahili men adapted the Arab *Razha*, 'originally a war-dance practised by the Arabs . . . prior to starting out on a raid'. It was performed by 'the men standing in a row and jerking sticks in the same manner that Arabs jerk their swords, one of which may sometimes be seen in the hand of a Swahili dancer of the *Chama*'.[3] But even before the imposition of colonial rule, there is evidence that the dance associations were responsive also to contact with Europeans. Long before Beni developed, Baron Carl von der Decken recorded a significant episode during his visit in 1861 to the village of Magugu, north of Vanga, on the Kenyan coast. 'Towards evening the young people of the two towns did their best to honour us with a war game, a mock struggle in which one side called themselves Englishmen and the other Frenchmen, "since", it was said, "there are no worse enemies than these two".'[4]

As this episode indicates, there was no difficulty for the Swahili dance associations in adopting European forms. They had absorbed many musical styles and instruments – there was no reason why they

[1] Lienhardt, op. cit., p. 20.
[2] These paragraphs are based generally upon my interviews in Lamu in October 1972, to which more specific reference is given below. I should at this point, however, acknowledge the influence of James de Vere Allen, who is beginning to establish fashion sequences for Lamu.
[3] R. Skene, 'Arab and Swahili Dances and Ceremonies', *Journal of the Royal Anthropological Institute*, vol. XLVII, December 1917, p. 415.
[4] Otto Kersten (ed.). *Baron Carl Claus von der Decken's Reisen in Ost-Afrika : Band I*, Leipzig, 1869, p. 321. I owe this reference to Dr John Iliffe.

should not absorb European styles and instruments in turn. There was no reason why rifles should not replace Arab swords in a danced arms-drill; no reason why competitive factions should not cast themselves as French or German against English, or English against Scots. All this *could* be done with little essential modification of the dance associations themselves.

And this is precisely the picture which emerges from Mombasa and Lamu oral evidence on Beni. For all their subordination to colonial rule, the Swahili populations of these towns retained enough cultural autonomy to be able to take what they wanted from European music and the European military mode and to make use of it in the interests of communal prestige and of the festive life. It is significant for the self-image of the Beni dancers that oral tradition in Mombasa has nothing to say of the brass bands of British warships or the musical skills of the Freretown Christians. According to Mombasa Beni tradition, the idea of the brass band came from quite another source – from Zanzibar, where Islamic power and civilization fused with all sorts of innovating ideas at the court of the Sultan.

The founder of Beni in Mombasa is said to have been Khamis or Hamisi Mustafa, a resident of Mji wa Kale, the Old Town section of Mombasa city. Hamisi Mustafa was very much a member of Mombasa's Arab–Swahili 'establishment'. His mother, Mwana Uba, was a member of the important Omani family, the Shikeley. His half-brother, Bakari Mohamed bin Juma Mutwafy, who also took a leading role in early Beni, was a member of one of the leading Swahili families of Mombasa and became one of the town's richest men.[1] On Hamisi Mustafa's 'journeys to and fro Zanzibar', recalls his surviving brother, Mohamed Nassor, 'he became impressed by Sultan Said Khalifa's band. He was touched by the regimentation and the militaristic side of it. The Sultan's band used to play for the Royal House during big celebrations, and its resplendent colours were a sight many Zanzibaris as well as visitors like Mustafa could not fail to notice.'[2]

Said Khalifa was the last 'independent' Sultan of Zanzibar before the proclamation of the British protectorate over the island. His death in February 1890 had ended an era to which Mustafa and other citizens of Mombasa looked back with regret. And for him, and his successors, the brass band was an important symbol of prestige. Zanzibar had a complicated band history in the later nineteenth

[1] I owe this information on Hamisi Mustafa's family to Margaret Strobel.
[2] Interview with Mohamed Nassor, Mombasa, October 1968.

century. There was, to begin with, a 'band of Goanese and Portuguese minstrels kept by the Sultan. Later a band of Turkish musicians were sent out from Constantinople but as some trouble arose with these they were discharged and a band of natives formed.'[1] There is no indication in the oral tradition which of these bands impressed Hamisi Mustafa, but it will be seen that none of them symbolized the power of the new colonial invaders.

The story of Zanzibari inspiration for the creation of Beni in Mombasa is more than just a myth of origin designed to secure cultural autonomy – even though the British influence was soon so strongly felt that 'the whole concept of Beni came to be to imitate the regimentation of the Royal Navy'.[2] For one thing it *is* important to remember that Europe itself had drawn upon Constantinople for the making of its brass-band tradition. And for another thing there continued to be evidence of Zanzibari connections with Kenyan coastal Beni. In Malindi, for example, one of the two early Beni associations was called *Sultani* and flew the Zanzibar flag in its competitions with the *Kingi* association which flew the Union Jack.

At any rate, Hamisi Mustafa returned to Mombasa and some time in the late 1890s founded the *Kingi* Beni, or King Band, the first of the coastal Beni societies.[3] Hamisi himself became Field Marshal; his half-brother, Bakari Mohamed bin Juma Mutwafy, was patron of the new association; one of Hamisi's female relatives of the Shikeley family, Binti Salimu bin Rashid Shikeley, became leader of the women's detachment of *Kingi*.[4] 'It was mostly a flute band at the beginning,' we are told, because bugles were hard to obtain or to learn how to play. Hamisi, after all, was embarking on an ambitious enterprise; hitherto brass bands had been the monopoly of Sultans and King–Emperors.

---

[1] General Report, Censor's Office, 15 September to 31 October 1919, Secretariat 065, National Archives, Dar es Salaam.

[2] Interview with Mohamed Nassor, October 1968.

[3] A document in the Mombasa Municipal Archives suggests the date 1899 for the founding of *Kingi*. On 25 November 1932 the Bandmasters of all the Mombasa Beni societies, including Hamisi Mustafa, wrote to the Chairman of the Mombasa Municipal Board protesting against proposed restrictions on their associations. In this letter they said that Beni had begun in Mombasa 33 years earlier – i.e. in 1899. They also remarked that the principle of competitive *ngomas* had been known for 1000 years! Khamisi bin Mustafa, Sheikh Nasor bin Mohamed, Ali bin Mzee to Chairman, Municipal Board, Mombasa, 25 November 1932, file S/22, Municipal Archives, Mombasa. I owe this reference to Margaret Strobel.

[4] This information about the office held by members of Mustafa's family comes from an interview between Margaret Strobel and Fatma Saidi, on 1 June 1973, the gist of which Ms Strobel has kindly made available to me.

But soon this problem of instruction was solved. 'The first of these modern *ngomas* was established in Mombasa several years before the war', wrote a British administrative officer in 1919, 'at a time when the German native school of music, which maintained a capital brass band, produced the only native bandsmen outside of the military forces of the two neighbouring colonies. One of these German native bandsmen, named Mgandi, deserted and migrated to Mombasa where the youths of the town established the "Ngoma ya Kingi" and employed Mgandi to instruct some of their number in the notes of the bugle and cornet.' Soon *Kingi* possessed a big military drum, and cornets, and bugles in addition to its flutes. And Mgandi became the musical father of Beni, not only instructing the musicians of a whole series of different Beni societies, but also composing many of the early songs.[1]

Of course, when oral tradition speaks of Hamisi Mustafa as founder of *Kingi* a very different process is being described from Samson Kayamba's establishment of the Weruni Dancing Club in Kaloleni. Kayamba was virtually the proprietor of his club; Hamisi was certainly not the proprietor of *Kingi*. His role was to introduce the *idea* of the brass band and of the military parade to the younger members of already existing communal dance associations. The development of *Kingi* needed manpower and it needed patronage. In the oral accounts of the nature of *Kingi* and its rivals, we can see, indeed, how similar they were to the previous associations, despite their European veneer.

The whole concept of the Beni movement came to be an urge to imitate the regimentation of the Royal Navy. In each band small regiments were formed and each regiment imitated and copied the correct uniform as used by the Royal Navy. In both *Kingi* and *Scotchi* there existed *Marini* (Marine) corps. This group took to modelling wooden ships and flotillas for themselves. The different *Marini* corps in the two bands competed against each other in building these ships. Competitions were weekly between them . . . For such a competition each band leader wanted to present his followers to the people during *Gwarinde* – the march past – at their smartest. Consequently many debts were incurred in order to buy clothes, and the necessities to build 'ships' . . . The King of each respective band held this office by virtue of contributing more than others. The *Gwarinde* was free for the masses and practically no dividends returned to the band leader except popularity and, in the

[1] Political Officer, Tanga, to Secretary to the Administration, 10 September 1919, Secretariat 075–186, Secret Societies Natives, National Archives, Dar es Salaam.

long run, bankruptcy. The Queen played the same role as the King but in the Womens' Section. She was very influential indeed and wielded more power among women than anybody else.

At their parading competitions, both the King and the Queen would take the salute and then inspect a guard of honour. They would urge the regiments to display their *Vinyago* – ships, etc – and tow them around for the people to appreciate . . .

Just as Political Parties have Youth Wingers, so did the Beni organizations. The Youth Wing section of the *Kingi* Band was called the *Juja Crown* . . . as it happens nowadays that there are fights between opposing Youth Wingers, so did fights issue between the youth supporting the two bands. Admission to any of the bands was on a voluntary basis and not on a tribal basis. Nobody liked to be an 'island' among a majority of followers of a particular band . . . Before the introduction of Beni in Mombasa, the peoples' dances were *Chapa Uringe, Goma*, and *Tari la Ndia*. Flutes, drums, and swords were used for the different dances. They were all replaced by Beni.[1]

It can be seen then that the Beni mode replaced the Arab mode within the Mombasa dance society tradition, rather than a completely new tradition arising. The Beni mode itself was not only a matter of imitating the Europeans, but also drew upon the prestige of Zanzibar and even upon the *Vinyago* masking traditions of the despised slaves from Central Africa. In all these ways Beni was an accurate reflection of the complexities of coastal society and of its reactions to the whites.

In these circumstances Beni was bound to assume a competitive form. Coastal dance associations had always been sensitive to the possibility of dramatizing divisions and contestations in dance. Thus in 1824, at Pongwe town, Lieutenant Reitz saw a dance expressing the rivalry of the Mazrui family of Mombasa and the Sultan of Zanzibar;[2] in 1861 in Magugu village von der Decken saw a dance combat between the 'French' and the 'English' factions. Now in the 1890s there was a search for the right rival to balance *Kingi*. *Kingi* came to be thought of as representative of King Edward of England. In Malindi it was balanced by *Sultani*. In Mombasa it was first countered by the *Kilungu* band, which was founded by Sheikh Nasor, an Arab immigrant who

---

[1] Interview with Ali Khamisi and Mohamed Nassor, October 1968.
[2] John Gray, *The British in Mombasa, 1824-6*, London, 1957, p. 64.

broke away from *Kingi* to set up his own association.[1] Then a satisfying dichotomy was found.

The new rival to *Kingi* was named from the one observable division among the British of Mombasa – the division between English and Scots. Scotsmen had played a prominent part in the opening up of East Africa – Kirk, the British Consul on Zanzibar; Joseph Thomson, the explorer; Sir William Mackinnon, founder of the British East Africa Company; George Mackenzie, the Company's Administrator at Mombasa: all were Scots. So, too, had been a number of adventurous concession seekers before the establishment of the Company and a number of adventurous traders after it. After the British Government took over administration from Mackinnon's Company, Scots continued to form a noticeable proportion of Mombasa's European population. 'The Scotchmen of Mombasa' celebrated St Andrew's night annually, with the bag-pipes in attendance.[2]

The division between English and Scots in Mombasa may not have been so sharp as that ancient hostility had been in other colonial times and places. But it was good enough for the rivals of *Kingi*. By at least 1910 the great dance rivalry of Mombasa was the competition between *Kingi* and *Scotchi*.[3] Every weekend the trumpeters of *Kingi* confronted the bag-pipers of the *Scotchi* in a contestation that was as new as colonialism and as old as Swahili urban culture.[4]

This same picture of an essential continuity between Beni and previous coastal dance traditions emerges from the evidence for Lamu. The introducer of Beni into Lamu was Bwana Ali Mohamed Zeinala-bidin, remembered in the oral tradition as Bwana Zena. Bwana Zena was one of the most important of the 'big men' of Lamu. He was a

[1] I owe this information on Sheikh Nasor to Margaret Strobel's notes of her interview with Zubeda Salim, 31 May 1973. According to this informant *Kilungu* Beni later became *Sadla* Beni.

[2] *The Mombasa Times*, 2 December 1919.

[3] According to oral tradition collected by Margaret Strobel the founder of *Scotchi* was King Rastam, a Basheikh Arab. The association was then headed by Abdulrehman Namaan, and then by an African from Tanzania, Ali bin Mzee, who was Bandmaster of the *Scotchi* in 1932 when he signed the joint letter to the Municipal Board.

[4] It is interesting to note that a similar division into English and Scottish dance teams occurred among slaves in Jamaica in the 1780s. Elaborate competitive processions, with floats, took place; the competing teams were commanded by leaders who assumed British titles of rank; songs celebrating Scottish or English victories were sung; and Scottish planters on the island helped finance the slave dancers of the 'Blue' or Scottish team. See: Orlando Patterson, *The Sociology of Slavery*, London, 1967, pp. 239–41; Sylvia Wynter, 'Jonkonnu in Jamaica', *Jamaica Journal*, June 1970, p. 39. I owe this reference to Sandra Smith.

member of the Al-Bakari family, the most senior lineage of the core aristocracy of the town; he was an *Mzee Wa Mji*, or member of the traditional governing council of Lamu; he was an owner of large plantations; he was a patron of poets and a collector and translator of poetry. In short he lived at the very heart of the Lamu cultural tradition. In the 1890s Bwana Zena was chief patron of a dance association in the Mtambweni moiety of Lamu. His dance association affected the Arab mode of music and dress and was called *Nidhamu*, a word of Arabic derivation meaning 'a lovely thing'. The young men of *Nidhamu* danced the Arab sword dance; riddling poetry was recited in competition; great feasts were held and cattle slaughtered.

Around the year 1900 Bwana Zena gave a wedding feast for one of his children, at which the male and female dancers of *Nidhamu* performed. But Bwana Zena had also invited the *Kingi* band from Mombasa to come and dance – perhaps because *Nidhamu* had enjoyed a relationship of alliance with *Kingi*'s predecessors. The *Kingi* performance created a sensation, and Bwana Zena and his young men vowed that they too must have a brass band and a march past and all the splendours of the Beni mode. So a *Kingi* association was formed in Lamu, representing the Mtambweni moiety and under Bwana Zena's patronage. The old Arab mode of *Nidhamu* was abandoned; drums and bugles were ordered from John Gray of London; and soon Bwana Zena's association carried all before it.[1]

Before long, however, Mtambweni's rival moiety, Mkomani, took steps to meet the challenge. Towards the end of the nineteenth century there had been a single dance association in Mkomani under the patronage of another member of the Al-Bakari lineage, Sheikh Omar Nyekai. After his death the association had broken into two – the *Pumwani* and *Mubani* societies. Now faced with the popular success of *Kingi*, the Mkomani associations came together again under the leadership of Sheikh Omar's son, Sheikh Fadhil Omar Nyekai. There was no Scots settler population in Lamu. But Sheikh Fadhil discovered that in Mombasa the *Kingi* association was confronted by the *Scotchi*. He made contact with the Mombasa *Scotchi* and before long there were kilted pipers in the narrow streets of Lamu as well. Thereafter for decades the confrontation of the *Kingi* and the

[1] Interviews with Adam Ismail, 17 and 23 October 1972; with Abdalla Kadara, 18 October 1972; with *Mzee* Salim Kheri, 18 October 1972; with Ahmed. S. N. Nabahani, 24 October 1972.

Scotchi Beni associations was the main expression of moiety rivalry in Lamu.[1]

The 'traditional' features of the Beni associations in Lamu are very obvious. The new Beni associations were patronized by exactly the same families which had previously patronized the Arabized dances. *Kingi* remained under the patronage of Bwana Zena's family right into the 1930s and 1940s, and after his death the association was led first by his son Mohamed Zena and then by his son Abdalla. Mohamed Zena's reputation in Lamu oral tradition shows very clearly that he was at least as much a 'traditional' man as his father. Mohamed is remembered as the best male poet of his generation; the only man, in fact, to earn the title of *Shah*, or lord of poetry. Ahmed Nabahani, who is making a collection of Lamu poetry, tells a characteristic story about Mohamed Zena. A great wedding was taking place in Lamu, at which the men and women were to contest, through their chosen leaders, at riddling poetry. If the woman *Shah* were able to pose a poetic riddle which baffled the male representative, the men would have to provide a feast for the women. Mohamed Zena was the men's only hope – but he was away on a voyage across the Indian Ocean on a business expedition. The moment for the contest came; the chairs of the male and female poets were placed facing each other with a curtain in between. The men were in despair. Then came the sound of the conch shell heralding the return of Mohamed's dhow. The men rushed down to the sea front and carried Mohamed to the wedding, placing him in the chair of the *Shah*. Travel-stained and weary, he at once posed a poetic riddle which baffled and defeated the women's representative.[2]

The Beni songs which have come down to us are not very elegant specimens of Swahili verse, it is true, though they possess a vigour and simplicity which make them admirably suited for singing to a band. But Swahili poetry surrounded Beni in Lamu all the same. The women members of *Kingi* and *Scotchi* continued to attend the celebratory feasts of members of those societies, just as the women members of *Nidhamu* had done. At these feasts the women danced the *Changani* dance, and sang more elaborate songs, displaying the poetic gifts for which the women of Lamu were famous. Moreover, Mohamed Zena and others composed long formal poems celebrating the victories of their Beni dance societies, the vigour of their young men, their ability

[1] Interview with *Mzee* Salim Kheri, 18 October 1972.
[2] Interview with Ahmed Nabahani, Malindi, 24 October 1972.

to give great feasts and then to parade through the streets afterwards, carrying the heads of slaughtered cattle on poles as proof of their lavishness.[1]

So far as I know only one of these Lamu Beni poems has survived. But that one is very instructive. It was written by yet another member of the Al-Bakari lineage of Lamu, Muhammad bin Abubakar Al-Bakari. It describes a dance contest in Mkunumbi, the little mainland port opposite Lamu island. By 1913, in which year the *Utenzi Wa Mkunumbi* was written, the Beni mode had spread from Lamu to the mainland. The old competitive associations at Mkunumbi changed their names and took on Beni characteristics. The poem describes a competition between the followers of Shekuwe, who is called *Shekhe wa Harinauti*, and his great rival Ba Simba, who is able to call on the assistance of 'jamii ya Marini zijana za Mkomani', all the strong young men of the Mkomani *Marini*. There is no doubt that the *Harinauti* was a Beni association or that the *Marini* of Mkomani moiety were a detachment of the *Scotchi* society. In fact, as we shall see, these two names, *Harinauti* and *Marini*, eventually became by far the most widely spread Beni names. *Kingi* and *Scotchi* remained limited to the Kenyan coast but competitive dance societies called *Marini* and *Arinoti* spread through the whole of the Tanganyikan mainland.[2] The connection between this Tanganyikan development and the Mkunumbi associations remains one of the many unsolved problems of Beni history, but we can be sure that the *Utenzi wa Mkunumbi* is describing the confrontation of two Beni societies.

Yet what is strikingly noticeable in the poem is the totally Swahili character of the confrontation. We certainly do not have here men imprinted with the assumptions of an alien culture because of their adaptation to absolute power. The main form of competition between Shekuwe and Ba Simba is the slaughter of cattle, to be eaten by members of the associations at great feasts, and bought with funds

[1] Interview with Fatuma Athman, Malindi, 24 October 1972.

[2] The origin and meaning of the word *Harinauti* remain unknown. The journal *Swahili*, in notes to its version of the *Utenzi wa Mkunumbi*, defined the word as meaning 'a quarter of Mkunumbi'; Lyndon Harries's informant glossed the word as meaning merely 'association'; my own oral informants in Lamu in 1972 asserted that there was, or had been, a very influential woman in Mkunumbi named Harina Uti, after whom the dance society had been called. In view of the very wide diffusion of the name none of these interpretations seems convincing. In Tanganyika the word was variously interpreted. Before the 1914 war it was usually said to mean the unclean or perspiring ones, an opprobrious nick-name given by the cocky *Marini* and then defiantly taken up by their opponents. Later it was anachronistically said to derive from the word 'aeronautics'.

contributed by them. As the poet remarks, in no spirit of criticism, 'Simba took and slaughtered ten cows for sheer wilfulness and they covered the whole yard'. In fact an attempt was made by the 'absolute' local representative of British power to stop this wasteful display. 'The district commissioner, our knowledgeable magistrate . . . saw what was being done, it was a waste of property.' But he was answered by the Headman of Mkunumbi that 'since the beginning people compete in this way', and the rival leaders vowed that they would not allow British interference to stop their competition.

Nothing is so expressive of the atmosphere of pre-1914 Kenyan Beni as the confession of defeat which the poet puts into the mouth of the humiliated Shekuwe:

Slaves male and female
and young people at school
if they see me on the roadway
speak impertinently to me

All the villages of the mainland
and other towns there
together with the societies
have met to mention me disparagingly . . .

Bwana Simba has defeated me
in competing and singing
and when they make up their songs
they sing only to oppress us.

The praises of Sheikh Simba
have spread throughout the whole country
even to distant towns
the whole of the African mainland

Simba has got young men
ambitious, free-men
men of established reputation
that is why he could do these things.

Nobly-born Bwana Simba
his fame is great
[even] the feasts of the nobility
do not match these things.

His excellent renown
is known to those in Government
and the reason is [his] great wealth
which has gone into a bank.

From his dancers of the Mwasha dance
the rupees acquired
have filled a box to the full
from the beginning of these matters.

From his Chama dancers
the rupees completed
can buy him a slave
and yet some will remain in the bank

This man cannot fail
to increase his fame
so that it reaches the countries
of India and Europe.[1]

It was little wonder, after this glorification of Bwana Simba, neatly placed in the mouth of a defeated rival, that the poet could confidently remind 'all of the nobility' and 'the respectable free-women' that it was 'customary to make the *pukusa* gift' for so fine a poem, written 'to fulfill the respect that is yours'.

Our Sheikh Ba Simba
to him belongs the wearing of the turban
that the beauty of the dancing-leaps
may follow in procession . . .

And all the strong youths
the *Marini* from Mkomani
let them be in the reception-hall
making their *pukusa* gifts.

[1] Lyndon Harries (ed.), *Utenzi wa Mkunumbi*, East African Literature Bureau, 1967, pp. 54–6. According to Skene in his account of 'Arab and Swahili Dances and Ceremonies', the *Mwasha* dance was performed by Bajun women from the Witu area, who had taken it from the Somali. The dance 'tends to work the dancers up into a nervous state. It is often danced in competition with another dance faction'. Skene maintained that the *Mwasha* dance form for women had originated only around 1910. The *Chama* dance 'may be called a faction dance, owing to the element of competition which enters into it in regard to some other faction which has also organized a dance. It is danced by Swahili men . . . who do their best to make as fine and as big a show as possible in order to eclipse the other competing faction.' The *Chama* dance could be performed by men wearing 'Arab daggers and swords' but in Mkunumbi and elsewhere it was being modified by the influence of the Beni mode. Skene, op. cit., pp. 415–17.

Beni and 'modernization' on the Kenyan coast

It is salutary – and accurate – to stress the strongly 'traditional' and communal character of early Kenyan Beni as a contrast to the cultural uprooting of the freed slaves. But it would be foolish to take this too far. Clearly the British administrative officer was right who remarked that Beni was *both* 'a natural sequence of the old-fashioned coast *ngomas*' and a 'sign of the influences of Western civilization'.[1]

After all, in this very question of Western civilization the freed slaves posed a challenge to the Swahili free men. Those who had been slaves were now liberated. But more than that: those who had been the despised barbarians now spurned Swahili culture itself as a failed, backward civilization, exposed in its hollowness by the confrontation with Europe. The Christian converts regarded themselves as the destined heirs to the new power and the new culture.

There were, of course, a variety of ways of responding to this challenge. It was fully possible to regard British military power as merely the vulgar strength of the barbarian and to withdraw into 'traditional' Islamic coastal culture. Or it was possible to meet the challenge by a revived Islamic enthusiasm and a new thrust of Islamic energy into the interior. But one very powerful tendency of Swahili society over the centuries had been its readiness to assimilate innovations – often through the mechanism of changing fashions. Swahili urban society placed a great value on up-to-the-minute smartness; on fashionable dress and conduct. And fashion often, though not invariably, followed power. Lamu furniture and dress and dance followed Omani fashions in the later nineteenth century because of Omani power and success. In the 1890s many young men wished above all to follow Western fashions – to show that whatever was powerful in the way of life of their conquerors could be absorbed and mastered and displayed by themselves; to show that the Swahili coast, always in their view more civilized and more 'modern' than the societies of the interior, could now become even more so.

As it happened, this desire to mediate 'Western civilization' coincided with the wishes of the new Governor of Kenya, Arthur Hardinge. Hardinge had no intention of making the freed slave convert the mainstay of his administration. He admired Swahili culture, regarding it 'as the one civilized element which stands between us and

[1] Political Officer, Tanga, to Secretary, Administrator, Dar es Salaam, 10 September 1919, Sec. 075–186, National Archives, Dar es Salaam.

31

the utterly barbarous races of the interior'. It was his aim 'to enlist the rising generation of Arabs and Swahilis (of the better class) in the service of the Government . . . and so gradually create throughout the territory a body of men which could serve as a useful intermediary between the British ruler and the native population'.[1] For a few brief years, which were precisely those in which Beni developed, there seemed a real prospect that young Swahilis would have access to European secular education and to clerical, administrative, and judicial training.[2]

It is not perhaps irrelevant to notice how the brief British courtship of the Arabs and Swahili reduplicated many of the Beni themes. Arab officials whom the British wanted to bolster were allowed naval gun salutes and the right to inspect military guards of honour. Prize Day at the Mombasa Arab School was celebrated in the following manner: 'After tea had been served, during which time the Swahili Band was playing selections, the proceedings were opened by the singing of "Hearts of Oak" by the entire school, the accompaniment being played by two cornet players from the band.'[3] It was hardly surprising that the young men of the Beni associations took such activities as inspecting the 'guard' of their societies, or firing rocket salutes from model battleships, or even of playing the cornet, as perfectly serious indications of prestige.

More importantly, though, we can see how the young men who danced Beni and sang its songs responded to this prospect of sharing in the new skills and the new power. They sang that they were 'favoured by God. To be able to read and speak the language of Europe the gates of Heaven are opened for us.' They called themselves 'children of the coast, which stretches from Europe to Africa'; the 'people of paradise', in whom was combined all the prestige of the coast and of those who came from the sea.[4]

Nor was this mere wish-fulfilment. In Mombasa between the late 1890s and the First World War there were 'practically no up-country natives in the societies'.[5] They were restricted to young Swahili free

---

[1] Hardinge is quoted to this effect in, G. H. Mungeam, *British Rule in Kenya, 1895–1912*, Oxford, 1966, p. 26.

[2] For Hardinge's policy see, A. I. Salim, 'The Swahili-speaking communities of the Kenyan Coast, 1895–1965', pp. 142–67.

[3] 'Mombasa Arab School Annual Prize Day', *The Mombasa Times*, 3 November 1916, p. 5.

[4] H. E. Lambert, 'The Beni Dance Songs', *Swahili*, vol. 33, no. 1, 1962/3, pp. 18–21.

[5] Acting D. C., Mombasa, to Acting P. C. Mombasa, 1 December 1919, Coast Province, 52/1319, National Archives, Nairobi.

men, a class whom the administration somewhat fitfully regarded as possible collaborators. Writing as late as August 1919, the District Commissioner of Mombasa remarked that membership in Beni was restricted to those with 'sufficient cash or clothes to conform to the orders given re "uniforms" . . . There are groups of officers . . . elected by the members and subscriptions paid for working expenses only. The certain degree of obedience and discipline and the *esprit de corps* which is engendered are of value, and personally I regard these societies with favour and am in close touch with them all, having found them, on more than one occasion, of use in administration work.'[1]

Even in Lamu, much less touched by development and change than Mombasa, where one might have expected Beni to be much more superficially fashionable, there was a connection between Beni and 'improvement'. The most remarkable example is the career of Bwana Zena's second son, Abdalla, who inherited the patronage of the *Kingi* Beni after the death of his brother Mohamed. If Mohamed is recalled as the master-poet and Indian ocean trader, a figure of traditional Lamu, Abdalla is remembered in a very different fashion. Abdalla served in the Zanzibar Rifles, the 7th King's African Rifles and the 6th King's African Rifles. He saw action in German East Africa and in the Somaliland campaign of 1920. Remarkably, he was one of the very few Africans to achieve officer's rank, at a time when that distinction was more or less restricted to the Sudanese. He held the title of *Mulazim Awal*, or 'Native Lieutenant', with the right to wear the 'Sam Browne' belt and gilt ceremonial sword. Abdalla's portrait in uniform is still to be seen on display in Lamu and it may be imagined what a boost it gave to the military aspect of *Kingi*, already intensified by the experience of the war, when Abdalla Zena returned with his experience of drill and command and with the full right to wear those symbols of rank which hitherto Beni had counterfeited. It is said in Lamu that Abdalla became adviser to *Kingi* in Malindi and Mombasa and some informants erroneously regard him as the founder of the whole *Kingi* tradition.

After his return to civilian life, Abdalla continued to play the role of modernizer. He acted as contractor for all of Lamu's most significant public works – the building of the sea-front wall, the making of the market-place, and the surfacing of the alleys of the town. In short, Abdalla combined the prestige of the Al-Bakari lineage and inheritance from Bwana Zena with such achievements in the new colonial world,

[1] D. C., Mombasa, to P. C., Mombasa, 12 August 1919, C.P. 52/1319, N.A., Nairobi.

that it is not surprising that his medals and his dress sword are still reverently preserved among *Kingi* relics, along with the 'Dulcetta' drums from John Gray of London.[1]

The rise of Beni on the Tanganyikan Coast

Beni in Mombasa and Lamu before the First World War reached a greater elaboration and was taken more seriously than perhaps ever again. 'About nine years ago,' recalled a British administrative officer in 1919, 'I saw a detachment of the *Scotchi*, about 50 strong, all dressed in well-fitting uniforms with kilt, and carrying wooden dummy rifles, march down the Main Street of the native quarter [of Mombasa] with a bugle band at their head. Hundreds of townspeople turned out to watch the fun and the performance became a regular weekly diversion, with such variations as the reception of the Governor, or Sultan, represented by an immaculately uniformed person who on occasion arrived at the *ngoma* parade in a carriage and pair, with suite and outriders on bicycles.'[2] 'Before the war,' remembered another official, 'when money was more plentiful, huge floats were dragged through the streets, and the effect was like the carnivals at Nice or at New Orleans. There were bee-hive towers and many snakes, but the favourite float was a man-of-war.'[3] The Beni societies became so central a part of Mombasa festive life that they were given a prominent role in the town's officially organized victory celebrations in 1919, and *The Mombasa Times*, delighted by Mombasa's capacity to be joyful, agreed that 'the Swahili bands added much to the pleasurable occasion'.[4]

The Beni societies of the Tanganyikan coast did not reach anything like this degree of elaboration; were not so securely set in the long context of urbane Swahili culture; and were not officially countenanced

[1] Abdalla's dress sword, sash, and medals are in the possession of his nephew, Adam Ismail, whom I interviewed in Lamu on 17 and 23 October 1972. I have been able to reconstruct his military career and rank from the inscriptions on his medals. Adam is perhaps naturally inclined to stress Abdalla's influence. Some other informants denied that he was ever the sole and dominant patron of *Kingi* in the way that his father and elder brother had been. But their information, in turn, was coloured by the fact of a large-scale break from *Kingi*, which is described below, and I am satisfied that Abdalla Zena is to be regarded as a major figure in Lamu Beni history.

[2] P.O. Tanga, to Secretary, Administration, 10 September 1919, Sec. 075–186, N.A., Dar es Salaam.

[3] Herman Norden, *White and Black in East Africa*, London, 1924, p. 48.

[4] *The Mombasa Times*, Wednesday, 22 July 1919.

to the same degree. Yet Beni in Lamu, and Malindi, and Mombasa exercised hardly any influence on dance modes inland from the coast, while Tanganyikan Beni diffused throughout the whole of German East Africa before 1914. If Mombasa was by a narrow margin of time the progenitor of the Beni mode, it was from Tanga and Dar es Salaam that Beni began its extraordinary penetration of East Africa.

Beni sprang up in Tanga and Pangani not long after the formation of *Kingi* in Mombasa, and from Tanga and Pangani the mode soon spread to Dar es Salaam. There was, of course, a great deal that was common between this early development of Beni in Tanganyika and the Kenyan developments described above. In Tanganyika as in Kenya competitive dance societies had long been a feature of Swahili life. In Tanga and Pangani at the end of the nineteenth century the most prominent dance societies were the *Dar-i-Sudi* and the *Dar-i-Gubi*, 'who were friendly competitors'.[1] On the Mrima coast, around Dar es Salaam, 'there were many dance competitions', as Swahili informants told the German scholar, Carl Velten, in the 1890s. 'For they used to say, "Let us make a single society as between such-and-such a district and another district". They would choose their head-man and one councillor and a committee and a messenger . . . In these competitions there were dances; all night long, for six or seven days they would just dance. They spent a lot of money, because if people of one society slaughtered two goats, the others would slaughter four. On the last day of the dancing they would make a feast . . . and unless this was done the relevant district was disgraced.'[2]

Moreover, the Tanganyikan coast suffered even more drastic demonstrations of European naval and military power. 'The Germans had won bloody victories at . . . Tanga and Pangani', writes the latest historian of the coastal war, 'and declared themselves masters of these now utterly devastated towns.'[3]

And finally, the Germans made even more of the brass-band ethos than did the British. The German ethnographer, Karl Weule, stated the terms of the cultural equation after his visit to German East Africa in 1906. 'Where there are Germans there is music . . . The Negro *has* to dance. As the German . . . feels irresistibly impelled to sing, so the

[1] A.P.O., Dar es Salaam, to D.P.O., Dar es Salaam, 8 October 1919, Sec. 075-186, N.A. Dar es Salaam.

[2] Lyndon Harries (ed.), *Swahili Prose Texts*, Oxford, 1965, pp. 197–8.

[3] Robert D. Jackson, 'Resistance to the German Invasion of the Tanganyikan Coast, 1888–1889', in R. I. Rotberg and A. A. Mazrui (eds.), *Protest and Power in Black Africa*, New York, 1970, p. 68.

35

African misses no opportunity of assembling for an *ngoma*.' Weule also described the rise of the brass bands.

> Dar es Salaam enjoys the advantages of two bands – that of the sailors from the cruisers, and that of the *askari*. Both are under official patronage . . . At Tanga . . . the Boys' Band of that town is a purely private enterprise. Tanga is a scholastic centre *par excellence*, hundreds of native children being instructed in the elements of European knowledge and initiated into the mysteries of the German tongue . . . The more intelligent, in whom their teachers discover any musical gift are admitted to the famous Boys' Band. This is just now in excellent training. When the passengers from the *Admiral* presented themselves in the evening on the square in front of the club, the band turned out to welcome them and the playing was really remarkably good.[1]

From Weule and other writers one can also glean the kind of evidence which would make the theory of adjustment to absolute power tempting in the case of German East Africa. We read of African soldiers in German employ delightedly showing off their drill and playing up the prestige of their uniforms; we read of African peoples in southern Tanganyika performing dances representing the German defeat of the Maji Maji warriors; we read of the Beni societies themselves, when they emerge, establishing an elaborate hierarchy of German ranks – the Kaiser, the Bismarck, the Hindenberg, and so on.

Yet once again Beni in Tanganyika did not grow straight out of German military victory or even out of the skills of the Tanga Boys' Band. In Tanganyika, as in Kenya, Beni grew out of the pre-existing dance association tradition and was an indication of the adaptability of Swahili culture. An early stage of the process, similar in many ways to the situation described in *Utenzi wa Mkunumbi*, was recounted in 1902 by Velten's Swahili informants. According to them, the older dance competitions had ceased to be performed with any frequency on the Mrima coast by the first years of the twentieth century. What took their place, and in 1902 was being performed 'every day, whether there be a wedding or just for joy', was 'the dance called *banji*'.

> In the dance called *banji* the people make a society of two camps for dance-competitions. One camp is called *goboreni* and the other is called *seneda*. They build a hut and buy lengths of calico and sew a sail . . . and they put it up with pieces of wood. In the middle of

[1] Karl Weule, *Native Life in East Africa*, translated by Alice Werner, London, 1909, pp. 62, 412.

the canopy they put a flag. When they have fastened the hut . . . they place stools and the men and women are invited. For calling them the *mrungura* proclamation drum is beaten at every house, and the people are told, 'Today there is a *banji* dance'. And they have their elder and their one chief-counsellor and a messenger, and similarly the women have a woman elder, a woman chief-counsellor, and a woman messenger appointed. And the counsellors and elders give money, and when the money is being given the *banji* drums are played. A person stands on a chair and the one who wants to rule sits on a chair. The one standing says, 'Let God rule the elder.' All the people respond, 'So be it.' The one standing on the chair says, 'So-and-so has come to our place, he wants the dances, and he has brought such-and-such money, he is taking the office of an elder, do you want him?' All the people reply, 'We want him.' When he has acceded he receives a name: 'This is Chief so-and-so.' . . . Then the *banji* dance is performed either all night or for three or four hours. And this sport sometimes includes a day when they go to the outskirts of the town and cook a meal, the people of the town are invited by the society. They sometimes stay all day in the outlying district, eating and dancing, returning to the camp with rejoicing in the evening . . . It is customary in the camps that if something unusual happens in the town, or someone who is a member of a camp does something shameful, to reproach him in song during the dance of the shameful thing he has done.[1]

This account describes the situation in the villages of the Mrima coast. Fully urban Beni developed first in Tanga. The process was unsympathetically described by a British administrator, writing soon after the British conquest of German East Africa.

> In Tanga and Pangani some years ago, amongst many *ngoma*, there were two named respectively the *Dar-i-Sudi* and the *Dar-i-Gubi*, who were friendly competitors . . . As usual the contact of European civilisation affected the rising generation. The obtrusive simulation of a superior race by the specious elegants of the youth was not an effect that was lacking. The brass instruments of the military band appealed to them and eventually the younger section of the *Dar-i-Sudi ngoma* formed 'The Marine Band', which constituted itself on military lines with ranks ranging from Kaiser down to Gefreite and Soldat . . . After the institution of the Marine Band it was not long before the *Dar-i-Gubi ngoma* produced a similar offshoot under the name of the 'Arnoti Band' . . . The young bloods

---

[1] *Swahili Prose Texts*, pp. 200–1.

joined. Anything in the nature of *Kishenzi* was eschewed . . . European apparel and, with the higher ranks, grotesque pretensions to military uniform, were *en règle* at ceremonial meetings. The various ranks were recognized according to degree. The old songs, dances and figures were eliminated and their peculiar ideas of a modern European musical club substituted. Considerable punctiliousness in their attention to etiquette is exhibited.[1]

Before long this rivalry between *Marini* and *Arinoti* sprang up also in Dar es Salaam, Kilwa, Lindi, and other coastal settlements, so that by 1914 the Tanganyikan coast had a network of allied *Marini* and *Arinoti* bands, very similar to the Kenyan coastal network of *Kingi* and *Scotchi*.

The spread of Beni to the Tanganyikan interior

Up to this point the Tanganyikan data have merely confirmed the pattern of the Kenyan evidence. Even the names *Marini* and *Arinoti* are present, as we have seen, in the *Utenzi wa Mkunumbi*. But in fact there were some very important differences between Kenyan and Tanganyikan Swahili society which led, among many other larger effects, to a very different development of Beni.

In the first place there was a difference in the cultural atmosphere of Tanga and Dar es Salaam as contrasted with Lamu and Mombasa. Dar es Salaam was in no sense an old Swahili city. It was the creation of the Omani Sultans of Zanzibar and had passed through many vicissitudes since its founding in the 1860s. It was hardly possible to say in the early twentieth century, even though at that time the population of the town was growing rapidly, that there was any significant *long-standing* Swahili settlement. The Sudanese and Ngoni mercenaries of the Germans and the Manyema ex-slaves came to be thought of as the oldest permanent African populations of the city; so far as I can determine there never developed in Dar es Salaam the kind of dualism which characterized Mombasa and Lamu and I have come across no reference to competition between rival moieties. The Swahili-speaking population of Dar es Salaam, moreover, was not a wealthy one, nor accustomed to elaborate and expensive festivals. Nor was there any literary tradition to match that of Lamu or Mombasa.

All this meant that Beni could not fit into the life of Dar es Salaam

[1] A.P.O., Dar es Salaam, to D.P.O., Dar es Salaam, 8 October 1919, Sec. 075–186, N.A., Dar es Salaam.

in the same sort of way that it fitted into the life of late nineteenth-century Lamu or Mombasa. The *Marini* and *Arinoti*, whatever other distinctions were represented by their competition, did not represent town moieties; their processions were not as lavish; nor were there striking links with a high Swahili poetic culture.[1]

Tanga, of course, was a much older settlement than Dar es Salaam. Here there was a much longer tradition of Swahili urbanity; here, too, there was a division within the town between 'the two groups of Mkokwani and Chumbageni'. But Tanga had had a turbulent history in the nineteenth century; its Swahili population had been far outnumbered by immigrants from the hinterland; it had suffered severe economic decline; and its inhabitants had for a period almost abandoned the town after its conquest by the Germans. In 1890, when Baumann visited Tanga, it had less than 3000 inhabitants, and he noted that 'few of the local people own houses of stone as most of them were destroyed in the bombardment of Tanga in 1888'. He also noted that 'while Europeans mostly call all these people simply Swahilis . . . he who is not content with merely a superficial observation will soon see what a variety of different elements are cloaked by what seems outwardly to be the same mantle'. Particularly in the Mkokwani part of the town very many of the inhabitants of Tanga were of recent Digo origin.[2]

In Tanga, as in Dar, there was not much prospect of the Beni societies spending lavishly or celebrating their success in classical Swahili verse. And what is particularly interesting is that although in Tanga the division between *Marini* and *Arinoti* could have corresponded to the rivalry between the moieties of Mkokwani and Chumageni, the sources are agreed that it did not do so.

In Mombasa, as we have seen, membership of all the rival Beni societies was virtually restricted before 1914 to free born Swahili. Neither in Tanga nor in Dar es Salaam was this the case, and it seems that it had not been the case with the predecessor organizations either. 'The Dar-i-Sudi was select in the admission of its members,' wrote the British administrator already cited, 'in that it was composed of Swahili *khassa*. The Dar-i-Gubi, on the other hand, appears to have been much less restrictive in its membership, and it is suggested that the name is a

---

[1] For an account of the founding and development of Dar es Salaam, see J. E. G. Sutton, (ed.) *Dar-es-Salaam, City, Port and Region*, special issue of *Tanzania Notes and Records*, no. 71, Dar es Salaam, 1970.

[2] Oscar Baumann, *Usambara and its Neighbouring Regions*, translated by M. A. Godfredsen, unpublished manuscript, Dar es Salaam, p. 4.

corruption of the word Delagoa Bay, implying foreigners who were not coast *Wangwana* [freemen] . . . Their bastard off-spring followed the parent bodies in that the Marine at first limited entrance to pure "coasters" while Arinoti was not so select.'[1] Another Political Officer asserted that *Arinoti* had broken away from the *Marini* in Tanga, and that they were 'a more or less nondescript body thereafter known as the *Hari Not* or Harinoti, i.e. "the perspiring or unclean ones", or otherwise "Masaidizi wa Maadui". The bitterest rivalry exists between the Marini and the Harinoti.'[2] And a third administrator recorded that the *Marini* of Tanga 'turned away the rougher men who formed Arinoti Ben, which means the Unclean Ones'.[3]

It seems that something is going on here that is different from the competition between *Kingi* and *Scotchi*. In Lamu, admittedly, the two moieties of Mtambweni and Mkomani were thought of as being occupied by the more recently settled as against the longer established residents of the town, but both Lamu Beni societies were under the patronage of the senior aristocratic lineage; both consisted of Swahili free men; both participated fully in the urbane culture. In Tanga, where Swahili urban culture was much less secure, the *Marini* at first claimed a monopoly upon it. But even this did not last for very long. Soon the *Marini* became the society of the élite, the educated, the smart – no matter what their origin. By 1914 Christian clerks from up-country and Ngoni *askaris* shared the leadership of *Marini* with young Swahili of good family. *Arinoti* remained essentially the society of the unskilled labour migrant, 'the unclean ones', even though it had its own quota of literate men with bureaucratic skills. This division between the 'posh' Beni society and the 'vulgar' one, which later on developed in Lamu itself, was present from the start in the Tanganyikan towns.

All this had two important consequences. It meant that it was fairly easy for 'modernizers' who came to work on the coast to gain admittance to the Beni societies: even *Marini* was not exclusively an extension of the old Swahili patronage connections. And it meant that the *Marini–Arinoti* competition was exportable to the interior in a way that the *Kingi–Scotchi* competition was not. A classical division into

[1] A.P.O., Dar es Salaam, to D.P.O., Dar es Salaam, 8 October 1919, Sec. 075–186, N.A., Dar es Salaam.

[2] A.P.O., Makalama, to P.O., Kondoa Irangi, 10 November 1919, Sec. 075–186, N.A., Dar es Salaam.

[3] Assistant Resident, Lilongwe, memo., 10 March 1921, S 2/11/21, National Archives, Zomba. I am indebted to Jaap Van Velsen for this reference.

urban moieties, with a resident aristocracy, was necessary to sustain the rivalry of *Kingi* and *Scotchi*. Such a division in fact existed in a few up-country Tanganyikan towns, such as Ujiji. But it did not exist in most. The rivalry between *Marini* and *Arinoti* could be sustained by any consciousness of a distinction between an élite and the vulgar and in this form it spread easily to the interior towns. Moreover, the elaboration and sophistication of Mombasa and Lamu Beni was rather intimidating. Visitors to these cities stood gaping in the streets as they saw the floats go by: it was difficult to imagine that it was possible to reproduce this splendour in an up-country settlement. The less elaborate Tanganyikan Beni was easier to reproduce.

Even in Tanganyika, of course, the spread of Beni to inland *rural* districts was a good way in the future. Before the 1914 war when branches of *Marini* and *Arinoti* began to spring up all over Tanganyika it was in the towns and administrative centres that they developed. For here lies the second large difference between Kenyan and Tanganyikan Swahili society. In many ways Swahili culture on the Tanganyikan coast was much less self-confident, much more secular, much more permeable than in Kenya. At the same time, though, it was in some ways more influential.

The outreach of Swahili culture and language into the Tanganyikan interior had begun before colonial rule. As Wilfred Whiteley writes, 'It is important to note that it was predominantly in what is now Tanzania that the most effective expansion of the [Swahili] language took place. The main trade routes went from places along the coast, like Bagamoyo, Saadani, Mboamaji, and Kilwa through Ugogo to Tabora, or south-westwards, skirting Uhehe, to the gap between Lakes Nyasa and Tanganyika. From Tabora caravans went west to the lake at Ujiji, north-west to Karagwe and Uganda, or north to Lake Victoria . . . On the other hand there was little expansion at this period from the Mombasa area towards Nairobi, because of the threat from Masai raiders, and the route into Uganda went round the west of Lake Victoria from Tabora.'[1]

It was because of this deep penetration of Swahili language and culture, and the existence of trading centres like Ujiji and Tabora, that a further difference between the Kenyan and Tanganyikan situations developed during the early colonial period. Hardinge had dreamed of using the Kenyan Swahilis as allies in administration but it was never more than a dream – and by 1914 it was plain that the Swahili youth of

[1] Wilfred Whiteley, *Swahili. The Rise of a National Language*, London, 1969, pp. 52–3.

Mombasa and Lamu had no future as allies of the British governors. The first modernizing aspirations of Mombasa Beni had to give way slowly to the realities of a Kenya in which the emphasis had shifted to Nairobi and the White Highlands.[1] But in Tanganyika, once the conquest of the coast was complete, the situation was very different. As John Iliffe has written:

> A literary sub-culture had existed on the Tanganyikan coast for centuries before the German invasion and . . . after the first resistance of 1888–9 sections of coastal society came to terms with European power. The coast became the base for German operations. The first government schools were opened there and the coastal peoples gained an educational lead over all but a very few other societies in Tanganyika. As the Germans pushed inland, the coastal peoples followed them as servants, traders, and administrative subordinates, swelling the Swahili-speaking trading colonies already established in the interior.[2]

Many young men were able to appear in the interior of Tanganyika with the combined prestige of Islamic Swahili culture and of familiarity with the western world. These young men took Beni with them. 'Wherever trading and administrative centres were populous enough,' it was reported, 'a branch of the Marine generally started. Frequently the Arnoti followed the lead of the Marine . . . Branches of both these Bands are found in all the large centres from Bukoba to Lindi.'[3] Clerks and police carried Beni to the towns; *askaris* carried it to the military camps of up-country Tanganyika, for the Germans continued to rely heavily on Swahili troops at a time when the British in Kenya were replacing the Swahili with up-country levies.[4] In any case, *Marini* was quite prepared to accept as members those clerks and police and *askaris* who were not coast Moslems, though the language of *Marini*, and of *Arinoti* for that matter, remained very definitely Swahili.

In this way a network of Beni societies was built up in the Tanganyikan interior. The links between them, moreover, were more formal

---

[1] Dr Salim writes: 'Hardinge's vision of a cadre of Arab and Swahili officers, being trained and employed beyond the confines of the coastal strip was never fulfilled . . . Even on the coast, events were leading to a significant subordination of their position.' Op. cit. p. 167.

[2] John Iliffe, *Tanganyika Under German Rule, 1905–12*, Cambridge, 1969, p. 187.

[3] A.P.O., Dar es Salaam, to D.P.O., Dar es Salaam, 8 October 1919, Sec. 075–186, N.A., Dar es Salaam.

[4] Salim, op. cit., p. 174.

than the ties of loose alliance which bound the Lamu *Kingi* to the *Kingi* societies of Malindi and Mombasa. In Tanganyika the up-country Beni societies were very definitely thought of as branches of the parent associations on the coast. The key members were minor government servants who had no permanent roots in the towns to which they were posted and who were often moved from one posting to another. Wherever they moved they fitted easily into the familiar competition of *Marini* and *Arinoti*, and they were able to conduct a bureaucratic correspondence between the Beni branches and the headquarters, or among the branches themselves.

Sometimes, of course, the *Marini–Arinoti* competition fitted so well into the realities of a large urban centre that it came to be dominated by local men rather than by these migrants. This was the case in Ujiji, where pre-existing tensions between the free men who moved into the town from the surrounding countryside, and the ex-slaves who had formed the original proletariat, now found its expression in Beni competition. It may also have been the case in Tabora. And everywhere some of the local youth attached themselves to *Marini* or to *Arinoti*. But the dominance of the parent associations on the coast was nearly always plain. It extended to the fostering of Beni musical styles by bands of 'wandering minstrels on tour', who travelled from Tanga or Dar es Salaam along the line of rail to Tabora and on to Ujiji teaching 'the *ngomas* at each place the latest tunes'. These musicians 'were paid wages and were found in everything during their stay at each place, the expenses being found by the King and members of the local *ngoma*'. When these 'wandering minstrels' were of *Arinoti* origin they taught songs and tunes composed by the famous Mgandi, graduate of the Tanga Boys' Band, instructor of the first *Kingi* musicians in Mombasa, and now chief composer of *Arinoti*.[1]

Mgandi's tunes were very much in the European military band tradition, and some of them were later adopted by the bands of the German and British armies. Their diffusion into the Tanganyikan interior was obviously in some senses a minor aspect of colonial cultural aggression. At the same time Mgandi and the other musician instructors made Africans independent of European mentors. Beni

---

[1] P.O., Tanga, to Secretary, Administration, 10 September 1919, Sec. 075–186, N.A., Dar es Salaam. One of the unsolved problems of Beni history is the relationship of Tanganyikan societies to those in Zanzibar. There is some evidence to suggest that the dance associations of Ujiji and Tabora at any rate remained strongly influenced by competitive developments in Zanzibar. I have been unable to discover enough about dance history on the island, however, to allow me to disentangle these complex interactions.

was performed in the up-country towns in an atmosphere of merriment. To 'the dancers themselves', wrote a sympathetic observer, and to 'the hundreds of people who enjoy looking on . . . their *ngoma* is equivalent to the Europeans' club, theatre, and dance' all rolled into one.[1]

Moreover, there was an aspect of Beni which caused some Europeans alarm. Very many years later Clyde Mitchell found that a successor to Beni – the *Kalela* – was a 'tribal' dance, even though it was performed in European clothes and in the locations of the Copperbelt. Beni before 1914 was nowhere tribal. In Kenya, Beni was the expression of competitiveness within non-tribal Swahili society. In Tanganyika, Beni was the expression of competition between two levels of those young men who had moved out of or away from a 'tribal' context. Europeans, realizing that their own advantage lay in superior communication, looked with some dismay at the rise of the Beni network, in which 'control is exercised from headquarters over the branches in widely separated parts of the country, comprising a membership drawn from a number of different tribes'.[2] However much the Beni dancers might 'mimic' the whites, this was a degree of co-ordination which the Europeans had certainly not intended or expected them to be able to achieve.[3]

[1] P.O., Tanga, to Secretary, Administration, 10 September 1919, Sec. 075–186, N.A., Dar es Salaam.

[2] Report from Officer i/c Censorship, 16 April 1920, Sec. 075–186, N.A., Dar es Salaam.

[3] 'There is no doubt that they form an encouragement to a certain class of native to keep in touch with their friends in different parts of the country,' wrote the Assistant Political Officer, Dar es Salaam, in 1919. 'They should in all probability evolve into a more formal social club and possibly with political importance . . . The general question of the *Chama* . . is a matter worthy of investigation.' Sec. 075–186, N.A., Dar es Salaam.

2 Beni and the Great War for Civilization, 1914–19[1]

The War and Beni in Lamu and Mombasa

The First World War was the most awe-inspiring, destructive, and capricious demonstration of European 'absolute power' that eastern Africa ever experienced. The scale of the forces involved, the massiveness of the fire-power, the extent of devastation and disease, the number of African lives lost – all these dwarfed the original campaigns of colonial conquest, and even the suppression of the Maji Maji rising. The fact that the operations were not directed against Africans but against other Europeans merely increased the sense of helplessness of hundreds of thousands of people. The Europeans were not even directly concerned to hurt Africans – and yet their crops were ravaged, their chiefs treated as 'traitors' to one or other European power, their young men conscripted to act as carriers in campaigns from which most of them did not return. Famine, epidemic, upheaval of populations – all these were produced almost casually, as side-effects of European power.

Yet the impact of the war was very uneven. It was felt terribly in some parts of Tanganyika; less terribly in others; hardly at all in Lamu; little more so in Mombasa. And even in Tanganyika this terrible time for most Africans was a time of adventure and even of triumph for a few Africans. All these differing effects can be discerned in the history of Beni.

In Lamu the war had the least impact of all. Abdalla Zena, the African officer, was very atypical of Lamu involvement in the 'Great War for civilization'.[1] At one time most of the Kenya colony's armed forces had been coastal Swahili; but that situation had long since passed away. 'The war had little effect on Lamu,' wrote a District Officer; 'the people were not called on as porters for the Carrier Corps to the same extent as up-country tribes.'[2] Dr Salim notes the 'high

[1] Two of Abdalla Zena's medals are inscribed with the legend 'The Great War for Civilization'.

[2] J. H. Clive, 'A Brief History of Tanaland', now in the manuscript collection of James Allen, Curator of the Lamu Museum.

45

degree of passivity towards the war and reluctance to serve in it' which characterized coastal society generally and which was particularly striking on the northern coast.[1]

In Lamu the war left its mark mainly in rumours and in the stationing of men of the King's African Rifles in the town. Lamu oral tradition remembers these soldiers as arrogant but impressive – and two splinter Beni societies broke off from *Kingi* in these years in order to express more precisely the reaction of Lamu's youth to the presence of the soldiers. These were *Keya* (K.A.R.) and *Chura*, associations which stressed the military aspects of Beni more than *Kingi* and which were much less connected with the classic patronage structure. But with Abdalla's return from the war, possessor in reality of the symbols of military authority, these splinter groups returned to *Kingi* and for some years everything was very much the same as it had been before.[2]

Even this minimal response to the war is of some interest, however. The formation of *Keya* and *Chura* show the way in which Beni acted as a means of *defining* the essence of a sequence of alien intruders into Lamu. Some years later another Lamu breakaway group, the *Sadla*, did the same thing for the white settlers who were becoming so obviously a force in Kenyan politics. The *Sadla* paraded in bush hat and khaki clothes and its members behaved with the informal and rough vigour which they thought to characterize settler life. These reactions were neither quite mimicry nor quite mockery, though there were elements of both.

In some ways they were similar to the way in which some up-country societies defined the essential characteristics of aliens through the contrasting medium of spirit possession. Thus at the same time as *Keya* and *Chura* emerged in Lamu, the Acholi and Lango peoples were also experiencing the impact of the King's African Rifles, who were recruiting in their country. In their case they did not define the military by means of Beni societies. But a new type of spirit possession came into existence known as *Jok Marin*, which represented 'Armyness', and the possessed people behaved in what was taken to be a characteristically 'Army' way and wore characteristically 'Army' clothes. It is interesting to note how the Acholi and Lango picked up the word *Marin*, just as the Tanga Beni dancers picked up the word *Marini*, to represent the essence of 'Armyness', but the connection is less superficial than that. In their very different ways, Beni masquerad-

---

[1] A. I. Salim, 'The Swahili-speaking communities of the Kenya Coast, 1895–1965', p. 364. [2] Interview with *Mzee* Salim Kheri, 18 October 1972.

ing and Central Luo spirit possession were both directed towards the same ends of definition and comprehension.[1]

The war affected Mombasa considerably more than it did Lamu, though even then indirectly. Mombasa's development as a modern port with a large and very mixed population was accelerated. The harbour was busy with warships, troopships, and supplies. Naturally enough, Mombasa Beni societies responded by emphasizing even more the naval and military aspects of their activities. 'During the campaign', wrote a British Intelligence Officer in 1919, 'the symbols worn were usually identical with those worn in the Army and Navy and the wearers were addressed according to the grade or rank they wore.'[2] The *Scotchi* adopted an aggressively loyal marching song,[3] and the Beni societies reached a peak of respectability with their enthusiastic participation in the victory celebrations.

A second effect of the war was an exportation of *Scotchi* to other places, as some of its members found themselves carried far afield by the war. After the British capture of Dar es Salaam a number of Mombasa Swahili were employed by them as 'shore boys'. The result was described in 1919 by the Assistant Political Officer of the town. 'During the war the "Scotch Band" was inaugurated in Dar es Salaam. It is a follower of the Scotch Band in Mombasa . . . It is the only one in Dar es Salaam with a Club House.'[4] In the same sort of way *Scotchi* reached the locations of Nairobi.

But these effects of the war were as impermanent as the brief existence of *Keya* in Lamu. The Dar es Salaam *Scotchi* soon withered

[1] Okot p'Bitek, *Religion of the Central Luo*, East African Literature Bureau, 1971, pp. 114-16.

Another more recent manifestation of *Jok* described by Bitek shows very clearly how the metaphor of the dance was associated with European-ness and throws some light on the history of *dansi* even if not on the history of Beni. This manifestation is called *Jok Rumba*, after the dance. 'Because it requires modern articles for the possession dance, the *jok* is one of the most expensive ones to be possessed with. The patient must wear a suit, and if a woman, a good frock, and provide either a gramophone and records, or a small band; and, of course, a number of cases of bottled beer.' *Jok Rumba*, writes Bitek, 'personifies the vast social changes brought about by European . . . activities'. p. 115.

[2] Intelligence Officer, K.A.R., to Chief Secretary, Nairobi, 4 October 1919, Coast Province, 52/1319, National Archives, Nairobi.

[3] The marching song was cited in official correspondence as:

> King George Shuja sana, Sote Wapendeza
> Leo imba, na kesho imba,
> Twaimba hai! Tawampie kwele
> Furahini sana, Mabibi na Mabwana.

[4] A.P.O., Dar es Salaam, to D.P.O., Dar es Salaam, 8 October 1919, Sec. 075-186, N.A., Dar es Salaam.

away. 'It is a weak organization, makes a pretence at wearing the kilt, has no branches or affiliation.' In 1919 it had only some 35 members and although it tried to take advantage of the political situation by claiming to be a 'British' society while *Arinoti* and *Marini* were 'German', it did not take root in Tanganyika. Even the military emphasis in Mombasa Beni itself rapidly faded away. 'The attraction of military titles and dress is diminishing,' it was reported from Mombasa in December 1919, 'and now the aim is to produce a sensational "Kinyago" every week. A few weeks ago there was an elephant made of canvas and bamboos some 40 feet long which moved by bearers inside. Last week it was a box made to resemble an aeroplane working by a pulley on a rope between two posts.'[1] Mombasa was easily able to return to carnival; the war left no traumatic memories there.

In the longer term, however, the war was a watershed for Mombasa Beni. Carnival continued, but with two major differences. One was that money was less plentiful in the years after the war, so that people looked back to the pre-war days as the time when Mombasa Beni really rivalled 'the carnivals at Nice or New Orleans'. The other was that Mombasa became increasingly cosmopolitan and the Beni societies, which in origin had been restricted to the Swahili, began to adjust to the new character of the town.

The war and Beni in Nairobi

The most important effect of the war on Beni history in Kenya was the introduction of the Beni mode to Nairobi and to the Kamba rural area. Nairobi was a town different from Lamu or Mombasa, Tanga or Dar es Salaam. Whatever the variations among those towns in terms of the quality of their Swahili cultural tradition or their pre-colonial historicity, Nairobi was distinct from them all in being entirely a colonial creation. In Nairobi Beni could have no pre-colonial roots.

Beni began in Nairobi in the last years of the war. This fact is significant in itself. One of the African quarters of Nairobi was called 'Mombasa village' and there were numbers of Swahili from the coasts, resident in the town. By 1919 the Swahili of Mombasa village had created a branch of *Scotchi*. But the documentary evidence is emphatic that it was not the Mombasa influence which brought Beni to Mombasa. Even the war could not bridge the gulf between Mombasa and Nairobi.

---

[1] Acting D.C., Mombasa to Acting P.C., Mombasa, 1 December 1919, C.P. 52/1319, N.A., Nairobi.

All the documentary evidence – and I have no oral evidence for Nairobi Beni – insists that the mode was introduced to the town from Tanganyika and by prisoners of war.

The Governor of Kenya, summarizing reports from his administrative officers, thought that Beni was 'primarily Nyamwezi in origin'.[1] The Swahili scholar, H. E. Lambert, who collected Beni songs in Nairobi at the end of 1918, tells us that the dance spread from German East Africa into Kenya during the war and that 'by the Armistice of November, 1918, had reached a considerable number of townships in Kenya'. It was carried, he thought, by *askaris* of the King's African Rifles, returning from the campaign in Tanganyika, and especially by 'prisoners and internees in Prisoner of War Camps' in Kenya.[2] The Assistant District Commissioner, Fort Hall, reported that 'this dance was introduced by prisoners from late G.E.A., the object of it being to assist them to forget the war and their position as prisoners'.[3]

Beni in Nairobi, as observed by Lambert in 1918, certainly bore every trace of this Tanganyikan origin. 'The songs were almost always in Swahili of the southern type'; the *Marini* and the *Arinoti* were the two dominant societies; and all the songs cited in Lambert's article were sung by followers of one or other of these two associations and were replete with references to Tanga, Mahenge, Tabora, Masasi, and other Tanganyikan settlements.[4]

What appears to have happened was that the *Marini–Arinoti* competition was introduced by soldiers and prisoners of war from the Tanganyikan campaign. *Arinoti* was then taken up by the inhabitants of 'Pangani village', another of the Nairobi African quarters, and was sustained by a formal link between this Nairobi branch and the *Arinoti* of Tanga. Then when the prisoners of war were repatriated the competition between *Marini* and *Arinoti* was replaced by a confrontation between the *Arinoti* of Pangani village and the *Scotchi* of Mombasa village.

Some vivid accounts of this Nairobi Beni are on record. Lambert gives us a description of the dance itself:

> The form of dance practised was very simple, the dancers forming an arc which moved very slowly round a circle, shifting

[1] Report on Beni by the Governor of Kenya to the Governor of Nyasaland, 14 September 1921, S 2/11/21, National Archives, Zomba. I owe this reference to the kindness of Dr Van Velsen.

[2] H. E. Lambert, 'The Beni Dance Songs', *Swahili*, Vol. 33, no. 1, 1962-3, p. 18.

[3] A.D.C., Fort Hall to Senior Commissioner, Nyeri, 16 June 1921, Provincial Commissioner, Central Province, File 6/4/3, N.A., Nairobi.   [4] Lambert, op. cit., p. 18.

their feet an inch or so at a time to the rhythm of the song. There was a master of ceremonies who moved here and there inside the circle and often led the singing. He kept order and exhorted the dancers to sing with vigour . . . The songs were cast in verse form . . . Their subject matter was generally topical, and often . . . good-natured ridicule of one of the other sections or praise of their own.[1]

Summarizing the reports of his officials, the Governor of Kenya thus described the organization of Nairobi Beni:

> Organization in the Nairobi Villages. A Governor was the supreme official. There was also a Queen, a Judge, a General, and numerous other ranks. There was a scout and police organization for the maintenance of order at dances and for the execution of orders issued by superior officials. Cases of general importance such as the removal of a high official, had to be referred to Tanga for sanction. Any case of dispute between the *Wascotti* . . . and the *Ardnots* was referred to an impartial judge who belonged to neither society. Petty offences such as an absence from a meeting or a dance, neglecting to dress smartly for a dance and so-on, rendered the offender liable to small fines. In Nairobi money collected in this way was banked with an Arab, Salim bin Abdulla of Pangani village, and used to defray expenses of repairs to drums, purchase of drums, decorations, refreshments, etc. Profession of the Mohammedan faith is not the necessary condition, though many members are Mohammedans . . . All tribes may be admitted . . . A list in writing is kept of all local members.[2]

The capacity of African prisoners of war to influence the social life of Nairobi in this way is an indication that even in this situation the Beni mode represented rather a display of self-respect than a submission to absolute power. Some sort of cultural initiative was being taken. As Lambert tells us: 'The melody and some of the tunes were extremely attractive to European as well as African ears; a few were subsequently incorporated into the repertoire of the famous regimental band of the battalion of the King's African Rifles then stationed in Nairobi.'[3]

The influence of Beni was also felt in some Kenyan rural areas at this time. The Assistant District Commissioner, Fort Hall, reported a 'dance of recent origin' among the Kikuyu of the district, which was

[1] Lambert, op. cit., p. 18.
[2] Report on Beni by the Governor of Kenya to the Governor of Nyasaland, 14 September 1921, S 2/11/21, N.A., Zomba.
[3] Lambert, p. 18.

known as 'Beni or *Drumma* . . . because of the noise of the drum to which it is danced'.[1] Lambert saw Beni danced after the war in Kitui, in Kamba country, and the Governor of Kenya reported in 1921 that 'during my tour at Kitui the Beni dance was revived, some of the old songs sung and new ones made and the dance was held over Saturday–Sunday'.[2]

What happened to this up-country Beni in Kenya remains at present unknown. In 1921 the Governor was confident that Beni was dying out; in Kamba country it 'was merely an imitation' and dances there represented no more than 'spasmodic attempts to get the society going'. '*Ardnot* activities in Mombasa–Pangani villages', it was claimed, 'died out about February 1920 when two of its leading members – Swedi Friday and Ali-bin Shakwe – left the district for work elsewhere.'[3] After 1921 an official silence falls.

And yet, some doubts remain. There is oral evidence that Beni was still danced in Nairobi in the 1950s.[4] Henry Anyumba has remarked on the interaction of Beni with other dances during 'the last thirty or so years in Machakos district'.[5] It looks as if this bit of Beni history still remains to be written.

Beni and the African members of the German forces in Tanganyika

Meanwhile the members of the Beni societies in German East Africa, together with almost all other Africans in that territory, were experiencing the full shock of the war. It was a time of very confused impressions. European power was displayed in the most terrifying way – but at the same time it was shown that the African *askaris* of the German army were more than a match for white troops. The fighting summoned up extremes of loyalty to the Germans on the part of some of their African soldiers and clerks – but at the same time these men had to reconcile themselves to the vulnerability of the apparently invincible Germany.

---

[1] A.D.C., Fort Hall, to Senior Commissioner, Nyeri, 16 June 1921, PC/CP/6/4/3 N.A., Nairobi.

[2] Report on Beni by the Governor of Kenya, 14 September 1921, S 2/11/21, N.A., Zomba.

[3] ibid.

[4] One of the patrons of Beni when it spread to Faza island in the 1950s was Omar Mohamed, then a hotelier in Nairobi. He remembers that at that time Beni was played by the Sudanese who lived in Kibra location, especially during *Idd*, when their band used to go around collecting money. Interview with Omar Mohamed, Faza, 20 October 1972.

[5] H. O. Anyumba, 'Historical influences on African music', *Hadith 3*, Nairobi, 1971, p. 199.

Thousands of other Africans, who felt no loyalty to the Germans at all, were nevertheless caught up in the war as carriers for the German columns and had to learn to adapt themselves to the world of the German empire on the march. Thousands more, some of whom had expressed their deep hostility to German rule by betraying German troop movements to the British, nevertheless found themselves pressed into service as carriers on the British side. Very many of the men who found themselves in these various predicaments used the Beni mode to express either pride or acceptance of dislocation and defeat, either bewilderment or a tenacious will to survive.

The first effect of the war was to shift the balance of influence within the existing Beni societies. Before the war *askaris* had been prominent in Beni but the dominant figures had been the clerks; despite the emphasis on drill, the parades had been reviewed by Kings and Governors, rather than by military officers. Now the military theme became completely dominant as the Germans ceased to be represented in Tanganyika by any formal civil régime and German power came to reside only in the columns on the march. By the time the in-coming British began to describe Beni in Tanganyika it had assumed an almost exclusively military appearance. 'The war naturally gave an impetus to the military side of the show,' reported one British officer. 'The "Band" is sometimes referred to as the "such-and-such regiment".'[1] 'Military ranks were introduced since the war in lieu of pre-war civil ranks,' wrote another official.[2] The British Political Officer in Lindi, who was alarmed by the subversive potentialities of Beni, described the societies as 'military in form, all ranks from General to Private existing . . . even "Nursing Sisters" are represented; badges of rank are worn and the junior ranks salute the senior.'[3] An Administrative Officer in Ufipa, who encountered Beni in that rural area in May 1919, described it as 'a Masque, representing a German column in the field'.[4]

In Lamu and Mombasa it might be possible for Beni to return to carnival very rapidly after the war. In Tanganyika the military theme remained the essence of Beni for years after the war was over. This was partly because very many people had first seen Beni in military guise, as they encountered it during the fighting. It was also because

[1] A.P.O., Dar es Salaam, to D.P.O., Dar es Salaam, 8 October 1919, Sec. 075-186, N.A., Dar es Salaam.

[2] ibid., P.O., Tanga, to Sec., Admin., 10 September 1919.

[3] ibid., P.O., Lindi, to Sec. Admin., 28 February 1919.

[4] Monthly Report, Namanyere, July 1919.

Beni remained important to the *askaris*, whose fighting performance in the war so astounded the British and enabled the long German resistance to continue.

It seems that when the war began the *askaris* already recruited to the German forces were members of both *Marini* and *Arinoti*. But as the campaign continued a new polarization began to take place. The *Marini* came to be thought of as the association particularly appropriate to the original professional *askaris*, so many of whom were Swahilis or Moslems of other kinds. The *Arinoti* came to be thought of as the association for more recently recruited troops, or for carriers, who were mainly drawn from up-country. The Beni songs which have come down from that period clearly show the rivalry and mutual insult of the two groups. 'We Marini are coastal people! Savages from up-country, Ah! you are not able!', sang the *Marini*. Or again; 'We Marini are favoured by God. To be able to read and speak the language of Europe the gates of Heaven are opened for us.' Or again: 'We Marini are the people of Paradise; we long to go to our home on the coast. These Arinoti are people of Hell.' In reply the *Arinoti* songs turned these insults to their own advantage, boasting of their up-country origin, of their strength as porters, accusing the *Marini* of effeminacy and threatening to scatter them as easily as if they were women.[1]

But in addition to these songs of mutual insult, which maintained the competitive nature of Beni within the German forces, some of the Beni songs of the war period strike a different note. It seems plain that with all its horrors the war gave both *Marini* and *Arinoti* something to be proud of.

Even before the war the African *askari* was a highly privileged man. 'He has his boy to wait on him,' wrote Weule in 1905, 'even to take his gun from his hand the moment the word has been given to "dismiss" . . . The respect commanded in Africa . . . by anything in the shape of a uniform secures him the best of everything wherever he goes.'[2] But one thing the pre-war *askari* did not have. He did not have confidence that he could perform against Europeans in a European war.

Once the war began the Tanganyikan *askaris* rapidly achieved that confidence. They first achieved it at Tanga where the British and their Indian troops were decisively defeated when they attempted a landing

---

[1] The first of these songs is given in, Anon, 'The Beni Society of Tanganyika Territory', *Primitive Man*, vol. XI, nos 1 and 2, January and April 1938. The others are given by H. E. Lambert, op. cit., pp. 19-20.   [2] Karl Weule, op. cit., p. 386.

in November 1914. Tanga had been the place of origin of the *Marini* and now the defeats of the British were celebrated in *Marini* song. In 1918, for example, a British officer heard *Marini* members singing the song, 'Askari yetu shaua kabisa' – Our soldiers are exceedingly brave – as they paraded in Kilosa. This song turned out to be one of the longest lived and most widely diffused of all Beni compositions. Another version of it was recorded in Ufipa some years after the war, and I have heard it sung myself in Mbala, Zambia, in 1972. As sung in 1918 it contained 'words to the effect that the African lion had proved too much for the British animal of the same species. This song . . . was composed by a German in celebration of the destruction of the "Pegasus" and was first sung at Tanga by the "Marine Band".'[1] Even in 1972, when the song had lost any reference to the defeat of the British, it still contained the assertion that the Beni lion would 'reach the heart of Europe.'[2]

In south-western Tanganyika after the war, where the Beni societies were regarded as 'Germanophil' by British administrators,[3] a number of Beni songs were collected by an African Christian for the information of his church. One of the *Marini* songs he interpreted as a proud boasting of the achievements of the German *askaris*.

> 'I shall go with them far away
> Bring cannons for a terrible war
> Let's return to the coast, we brave soldiers,
> We have beaten the Mitamba savages.'

'The word Mitamba,' he noted, 'is used in derision of the swaggering gait of the English soldiers.'[4]

But these triumphs could not be monopolized by the *Marini* alone. After all, what had happened at Tanga and elsewhere was a temporary discomfiture of those who commanded the sea by those who commanded the land, and members of *Arinoti* rationalized things in this way as they looked back on the war. The *Arinoti* had been mocked as the people of the inland, but now they proudly claimed the title.

[1] Minute by E. R. to Secretary, Administration, 24 July 1919, Sec. 075-186, N.A., Dar es Salaam.

[2] Interview with Charles Sinyangwe, Chisanza, Mbala, 12-13 September 1972.

[3] Monthly Report, Namanyere, July 1919.

[4] Anon, 'The Beni Society of Tanganyika Territory', *Primitive Man*, vol. XI, nos 1 and 2. If this interpretation of the word Mitamba is correct, we can count a song collected by Lambert in Nairobi in 1918 among these celebrations of British humiliation: 'You Mitamba, we shall confront one another; your power will end and you be lost to each other; you will be scattered abroad like wild beasts.'

'Arinoti was the name of a place where the land soldiers won a victory over their enemies,' says one old member of *Arinoti* in Dar es Salaam. 'Marini meant the navy.'[1] 'All my informants,' writes Mr Chijumba, who carried out research on Beni in Dar es Salaam in 1968, 'told me that *Marini* represented or rather symbolized sea-power while *Arinoti* symbolized the infantry (land soldiers).'[2]

One of Mr Chijumba's informants, old Thabit bin Ismaili, whose father was King of *Arinoti* in Dar es Salaam after the First World War, expanded on this theme. *Marini*, he said, was 'mostly associated with Europeans, Indians, Arabs and other races who were found joining the navy in great numbers. To the Africans all soldiers of races other than African were regarded as sea soldiers since they came here from their countries by sea. Later *Marini* came to represent the wealthy people irrespective of race.' *Arinoti*, on the other hand, 'represented the infantry (*askari wa nchi kavu*) who included the porters and were more numerous than the European soldiers. Later it came to be associated with poor people, not only Africans . . . He guessed that the word *Arinoti* could be the name of a famous African soldier who commanded the infantry.'[3]

Plainly *Mzee* Thabit has been influenced in these memories by the revaluation of the relationship between the coast and the interior which has come with the triumph of nationalism. But it seems plain, too, that the First World War itself represented a radical revaluation for many people of the nature of the power that came from the sea.

These were some of the deeper meanings behind the dancing *askaris* and porters whom the European participants in the East African campaign described – sometimes with admiration for an *askari* who danced in the battle-line to rally his men; sometimes with unreflective mockery; sometimes in uneasy astonishment that the suffering and death in East Africa could be responded to by a dance.[4]

---

[1] Interview with *Mzee* Rashid Hindo, Dar es Salaam, 16, 19, 27 September and 1 October 1968.

[2] B. J. Chijumba, 'The Beni Dance – Research Project', October 1968.

[3] Interview with *Mzee* Thabit bin Ismaili, Dar es Salaam, Magomeni, Dar es Salaam, 15, 25, and 30 September, 2 October 1968. *Mzee* Thabit is in origin a Matumbi from Kilwa district. He was himself a member of *Arinoti* and 'still loves the idea'. He cited a song text to show how *Marini* was identified with the Europeans: 'Marini, products of the coast, from Europe up to Africa. Who does not know Marini, with their first-class empire?' The translation is Mr Chijumba's.

[4] A German account of Beni in the field is A. R. Lutteroth, *Tunakwenda*, Hamburg, 1938, in which an *Arinoti* performance is described. The dance was performed in October 1917 by the 23rd Field Regiment south of Mahenge.

Yet, however much a member of *Marini* or *Arinoti* might remember his service under German command with pride, in the end he had to come to terms with Germany's defeat. The evidence suggests that for many members of Beni this did not present much difficulty. In so far as Beni *was* an accommodation to power, then British power was likely to be accepted just as German power had been. In so far as Beni was an expression of the desire to work within the colonial administrative structure and to be accepted as an ally by the colonialists there was clearly nothing to be gained by clinging to a damaging past. There were many rapid changes of heart. The *Marini* may have sung of British defeat during the war, but the Assistant Political Officer, Mkalama, could report in 1919 that the local *Marini* 'used to play the British National Anthem on every occasion when I appeared outside the Boma. I stopped this and they now give me what they call the General Salute . . . They fly the Union Jack and the flag of Islam.'[1] 'Since our occupation of the Territory,' noted the Governor's summary of all Beni evidence in 1921, 'German titles have been prohibited in the "Marini" and the English equivalents adopted.'[2] Even the reports that in some places Beni groups continued in 1919 to regard themselves as German in competition with other Beni groups who were 'British' was less evidence of any persistent loyalty to Germany than evidence of the long-standing practice of casting dance competition in terms of current dominant European rivalries.

At the same time, however, it is plain that some leading members of the Beni societies deeply resented the British victory. Some of them had been captured by the British and interned in prison camps. Many of them had lost the status they had enjoyed under the Germans, and were now employed at lower rank, if at all. To such men, it seems, Beni became even more important than it had been before. Before it had been a sort of complement to their prestige; now it became a substitute for more material influence and success.

The clearest case of this is that of a remarkable man, Saleh bin Mkwawa. Saleh was the son of the great Hehe chief, Mkwawa, who had compelled German respect through his long resistance to them. Saleh himself had been brought up by the German missionaries. 'He was a native teacher at the Benedictine Mission at Mihawana from

[1] A.P.O., Makalama, to D.P.O., Kondoa Irangi, 30 October 1919, Sec. 075-186, N.A., Dar es Salaam.
[2] Governor of Tanganyika to Governor of Nyasaland, 10 June 1921, Sec. 075-186, N.A., Dar es Salaam.

March 1909 to August 1912. From 1912 and during the war [he] was a native Government Official, *Akida*, in the Dodoma district.' Saleh combined both 'traditional' and 'modern' sources of prestige. He was a man whom even the British military administration conceded to 'have somewhat remarkable intelligence and also power of organization and control over his tribe'. In October 1917 this formidable man 'was made prisoner by the British forces at Kilimatinde and . . . was prisoner of war in Nairobi'.[1]

After his release from detention Saleh returned to Iringa, in the heart of Hehe country, where he had to rest satisfied with an appointment as 'hut counter' for the new administration. But despite this lowly occupation, Saleh remained 'the leading spirit' in *Marini* throughout eastern Africa. With little else to occupy his talents for organization and command, Saleh began to co-ordinate *Marini* activity. He wrote under the title of S. M. Friedrich Aug. Konig von Sachsen to his friend Thomas Plantan, who held the title of M. Konig von Hindenberg in the Dar es Salaam *Marini*, asking Plantan 'to send him certain particulars regarding the songs, customs, and scale of subscriptions in vogue, and to obtain similar information from Mohamed Zuberi of Lindi, in order that the customs of the Marrine band may be standardized everywhere'.[2] He wrote to Saleh bin Omar, head of *Marini* in Tanga, to protest against the translation of Omar's old title, Kaiser, into the English title, King. 'The name of King is not yours, but you are Emperor. The meaning of Emperor is a Possessor or Sultan, who is superior to various Sultans or Kings . . . Do not call yourself King but Emperor. Do understand, then inform all Marine all over the world that Kaiser is Emperor, Kaiserin is Empress, Konig is King, Konigen is Queen. Think much . . . Reflect much. Understand much. I do not like you to be called King; your respect is great.'[3]

So far as *Marini* was concerned Saleh bin Mkwawa himself enjoyed great respect. Other branches of the association reported to him on the results of their encounters with *Arinoti*.[4] He enjoyed powers of

[1] Report from office of Censor, 15 April 1920, 22 July 1920, Sec. 075-186; Censor's General Report, September/October 1919, Sec. 065, N.A., Dar es Salaam.

[2] Censor's General Report, September/October 1919, Sec. 065, N.A., Dar es Salaam.

[3] Saleh bin Sultan Mkwawa to Saleh bin Omar, 10 June 1919, Sec. 075-186, N.A., Dar es Salaam. This letter was intercepted by the Censor's office and translated by them from Swahili.

[4] The Censor's General Report for September/October 1919 recorded that the *Marini* branch in Tanga had sent word to Saleh of their victories over both the *Arinoti* and the *Yanga* bands.

appointment to and suspension from office, which he exercised over branches of *Marini* as far afield as Kismayu.[1] The British regarded him as the chief co-ordinator of *Marini* activity everywhere in East Africa.

It seems clear that Saleh used Beni to remind himself and others of the old days in which he had enjoyed authority, and also that he used it to make up for his lack of authority in the present. He began a long report to Mohamed Zuberi of Lindi with a passage in German: 'The following lines I have written in our late lamented language. The above writing in the German language is enough to remind us!'[2] In February 1920, 'on the anniversary of his release from imprisonment, an *ngoma* was held by the *Marini* band in his honour. He appears to have arrived on the scene in prison garments with a guard of two *askaris* with rifles. He was then released and the *Ehrentanz* (Honour Dance) was performed.'[3]

The men with whom Saleh bin Mkwawa corresponded shared his regrets for the passing of the German system. Mohamed Zuberi, known within *Marini* by the title of S. M. Kaiser Wilhelm II, was 'a former German agent'. Thomas Plantan, the Hindenberg of the Dar es Salaam *Marini*, was the son of the senior African non-commissioned officer in the German forces, *Effendi* Plantan, who had died early in the war. Thomas himself had been a signaller in the *Schutztruppe*; had served at Tanga and been promoted to Corporal for his part in the fighting; had later acted as scout for the German commander, von Lettow-Vorbeck, both men being injured during the same engagement at the Umba River. In short, Thomas had played as central a role in the fighting as was possible for a young African. Still alive in 1967, and Chairman of the Ex-Askaris Association, Thomas Plantan voiced in a newspaper interview his pride in the Tanga victory and his regret at German defeat. Tanga was 'for me personally a very proud day', he declared. 'We had great respect for the Germans because the Germans also had respect for us. They treated us as brothers not as inferiors. Discipline was harsh, but we'had respect. They were very good soldiers.' Tanga had been a triumph of good soldiery and self-respect: 'Many of the British troops were killed as they came ashore. I think we surprised them.'[4]

[1] Report from office of Censor, 15 April 1920, Sec. 075-186, N.A., Dar es Salaam.

[2] Saleh bin Mkwawa to Mohamed Zuberi, 13 July 1920, Sec. 075-186, N.A., Dar es Salaam.

[3] Report from office of Censor, 15 April 1920, Sec. 075-186, N.A., Dar es Salaam.

[4] Interview with Thomas Plantan, *Sunday News Magazine*, Dar es Salaam, 31 December 1967.

Saleh bin Mkwawa and Thomas Plantan were still surprising the British in 1919. It was hard to understand why men of their ability should be so concerned with the Beni associations. A political motive seemed plausible since 'the fact that most of these societies appear to be organized by educated natives, who held posts of some little local importance under the Germans, coupled with an adherence to the German system of organization and discipline, would render them a valuable aid to any person who might be entrusted with the work of anti-British propaganda among native tribes'.[1] 'Saleh and other leaders,' the Censor concluded, 'should be put under observation.'[2]

It is to this observation that we owe the preservation of a text second only to the *Utenzi wa Mkunumbi* as a document from within the Beni mode of thought. This is Saleh bin Mkwawa's long report of a 'war-game' between the Iringa *Marini* and the Iringa *Arinoti* in June 1920. The report was intercepted by the Censor, who had it translated into English, leaving 'untranslated the German words and phrases which Saleh so freely uses . . . in order to give some idea of the close imitation of the German military organization which Saleh appears to be endeavouring to attain in the Marine Band.'[3]

In fact the 'war-game' described by Saleh was the product of both Swahili competitive tradition and German military practice. On the one hand it was a continuation of the mock-battles fought in the towns of the coast throughout the nineteenth century. On the other hand it was a continuation of the mimic combats which the Germans had staged as training exercises. A description of one such German 'war-game' is available. It took place in 1902 and involved the garrisons of Bagamoyo and Dar es Salaam, which were made up overwhelmingly of African *askaris*. The two garrisons engaged in a 'battle' which ended when the Dar es Salaam garrison captured Bagamoyo. Then both sides assembled; the Governor of German East Africa addressed them; and they marched together into Dar es Salaam, the Governor at their head, and all singing lustily.[4] It was this atmosphere which Saleh was seeking to recreate.

In the month of June of this year 'one thousand nine hundred and twenty' [runs the Censor's translation of his report], there was the

---

[1] Censor's General Report, September/October 1919, Sec. 065, N.A., Dar es Salaam.

[2] Report from office of Censor, 15 April 1920, Sec. 075-186, N.A., Dar es Salaam.

[3] Report from office of Censor, 22 July 1920, Sec. 075-186, N.A., Dar es Salaam.

[4] This war-game is reported in *Deutsch-Ostafrikanische Zeitung*, 8 February 1902. I owe this reference to Dr John Iliffe.

Kingdom of the Regiment Arinecke von Zeiger. They sent a letter, wishing Manöver; fighting or war of dance. The great Kingdom of the Marrine accepted . . . I, the Emperor of M.B.G., signed the agreement for Manöver and for the conditions of the Government which should be defeated in the Manöver and asks for peace. I gave much time to the arrangements . . . I gave orders to General v. Langmann to be Kriegsminister and General von Manteufel to be Befelshaber of this Manöver. On the 12th June, evening, the Army of Marrine convenanted with their Majestät, Friedrich August, and gave him a promise that they would fight without retreating until the Arnicke were tied with ropes, and their King put in iron fetters on his hands.

On the night of the same day General Langemann and his Major and Lieutenant were captured by the enemy because they were in Kriegsminister Feldquarter, they were giving out plans for weapons and ammunition. This General and the 2 Offizieren managed to run away and come back to their Army. On that night the Compagnie of Obersleutnant Heinrich, which was posted on the south, came back with a song of victory: they brought with them these prisoners: 3 Generalen, 1 Leutnant, 59 Unteroffizieren u Mannschaften u Medical beamte 63 in die Hande der Marrine Siege ab-gefallen.

On the 13th June . . . Feldwebel Hussein bin Isa with his 3 askaris . . . captured the King of R.A.v.Z, his name Saleh bin Fundi . . . coming out of his quarters . . . At once he (the Feldwebel) ordered his 3 askaris, who went with Hurrah and captured the King . . . they put fire to the quarters of this King, put him in fetters and took him to the Feldquarters of Oberbefehlshaber of M.B.G. . . .

The Army came back, and left Arnecke who were in the hills and who concealed themselves in caves . . . By order of the Ober-befehlshaber of M.B.G. all prisoners were tied with ropes by their necks and kept in the middle of the glorious Marrine Army du Corps, and started for the Town. When they came near the Town they sent a letter to me, their Emperor, they wrote the following:

'Se Mäjestat König von Sachsen und Emperor M.B.G.

By your glorious preparations, and by the devotion of the Marrine toward you, I and my Army du Corps, are coming back with very many prisoners and Se Mäjestat King R. Arionoti von Zeiger. Hurrah may God glorify you, our Se Mäjestat . . .'

Happiness increased when the company of women appeared – the great daughter – Society of the Marrine – Bibi Konigin in the front, Prinzessinen, and other Bibis, walking with great pride and shouts of happiness in their mouths . . . The prisoners were taken around the town in order to show people . . .

At 4.30 the chiefs of the Kimarrine were assembled, the Reichstag was filled with them and all wore uniform and the prisoners were brought in . . . The General wrote their names and their father's names, their tribe and any marks on their faces, arms and legs. Then they were shut up until Se Mäjestat of R.A.v.S. agreed to the conditions of surrender and put his signature on the Peace Treaty . . . Their King read the conditions of Peace and signed it in Arabic and in KiSwahili . . . The Offizieren and the troops agree as follows, they say: We admit that we were defeated by the M.B.G., we admit that we were taken prisoners, nor were we defeated because the Marrine were many and we were few. We were weak and we were defeated and captured.

It must have been pleasant for Saleh bin Mkwawa to transpose his own experiences in this way, and to record how he kept the *Arinoti* prisoners of war shut up until their King had agreed to 'give up his Krone and flag, the records of his Kingdom, his Court, his counsellors of war, his drums and trumpets' and agreed 'not to be called King again but President'.[1]

This strange document reveals some of the processes by which the son of the proud Hehe chief, Mkwawa, had come to identify himself with the German conquerors. 'The Wahehe of all tribes would, one would imagine,' wrote the Censor, 'have little cause to love the Germans.'[2] It is a question which every reader will determine for himself how far we are back again here to the submission to absolute power; how far the document represents what the Censor called 'a mere childish imitation of reality'; or how far it shows Saleh's 'remarkable intelligence' at work in devising outlets for his 'power of organization and control over his tribe'.

The state of Beni in the Tanganyikan towns in 1919

The suspicious scrutiny which preserved Saleh's letter has also provided us with by far the fullest set of reports on Beni that exist for any period or place. The Censor was by no means alone in thinking that Beni should be watched. In February 1919 the Political Officer, Lindi, pointed out that the Beni 'organization exists at all ports from Mozambique to Mombasa, and also at the principal centres up-country'; alleged that African soldiers and policemen in Lindi paid

[1] Saleh bin Mkwawa to Mohamed Zuberi, 13 July 1920, Sec. 075–186, N.A., Dar es Salaam.
[2] Report from Office of Censor, 22 July 1920, Sec. 075–186, N.A., Dar es Salaam.

improper respect to civilian members of Beni, saluting them and even accepting punishment at their orders; and asserted that 'this society is undeniably subversive of military and police discipline and . . . lends itself to all kinds of abuses and extortion, while it might grow to have considerable political importance'. He asked that all other administrative officers be required to investigate Beni in their areas.[1] The resulting inquiries give a full and vivid, if somewhat slanted, account of Tanganyikan urban Beni in 1919.

The evidence thus assembled fully documents the impact of the war on Tanganyikan Beni; the dominance of the military theme; the existence of a group of leaders who regretted the passing of German power. But it also reveals an attempt to reconstruct the old patterns of 'civilian' Beni; an attempt to establish a satisfactory relationship with the new colonial power; and an attempt to bring into Beni the chief African agents of that power.

Saleh bin Mkwawa was not the only man who was trying to re-establish the old correspondence between Beni branches and to standardize Beni practices. During the war the old urban network of Beni had broken down; many administrative centres were abandoned; some towns had been in German hands; others in the hands of the British or the Belgians. During the war the skeletal structure of Beni was provided by army camps rather than by towns or *bomas*. By 1919 the army camps had been abandoned in their turn and the task was to rebuild the old urban communications system. However important ex-soldiers might still be in Beni, command was back in the hands of the clerks. Something of the bureaucratic flavour of this revived correspondence comes out of letters intercepted by the Censor. 'A demi-official notice from General Brigadier K. Zibe Kidasi, Government Press, Dar es Salaam, to Konig Mzee Sehemu, Tanga,' for example, was 'in formal terms and headed: Kommando der Arnot Regt. [It] inquires whether a rubber stamp for the Regiment is required as the writer can obtain one.'[2]

The British investigators were suspicious of the implications of the re-organization because they believed that its main intention was to centralize control of the whole wide-ranging network of the Beni societies in the hands of a few individuals. It seems more likely that communication rather than centralization was the main aim. The idea

---

[1] Political Officer, Lindi, to Secretary, Admin., 28 February 1919, Sec. 075–186, N.A., Dar es Salaam.

[2] Censor's General Report, September/October 1919, Sec. 065, N.A., Dar es Salaam.

was to restore the Beni societies to their pre-war role as mutual aid associations for the new élite. 'Common funds are used in order to entertain members of the same society when away from their homes,' it was reported, 'and also to give temporary assistance in case of need.'[1] 'In the majority of *ngoma* associations,' ran another report, 'funds are raised by monthly subscription from each member . . . the head of a particular *ngoma* sometimes advances money from surplus balances in urgent cases to those visitors who may have been admitted to that *ngoma* on the introduction of their chief of a similar *ngoma* elsewhere.'[2] 'If a member of *Arinoti* or *Marini* wanted to visit some other places,' recalls *Mzee* Thabit bin Ismaili in confirmation of these reports, 'he went to his King where he got an identification to take with him so that he could be received by the members of the same group in that place. No one who was a member of a Beni dancing group could starve.'[3]

The Beni societies also had a strong mutual aid character within each urban centre. The Political Officer of Mkalama, a small administrative centre in northern Tanganyika, gave the fullest account of this, stressing that 'these two societies do not yet affect . . . anything of a political or seditious or Pan-Ethiopian nature and their objects . . . appear to be merely the establishment and furtherance of social intercourse.'

The duties of the King are to superintend generally the running of the Society and its *ngomas*. He is also called upon to entertain or to arrange entertainment for any members of the societies of other towns who may come to Mkalama . . . He also provides for or arranges for the provision of clothes and food to visitors and needy members . . . The duties of the Bismarck are to provide for the sick and needy and if unable to do so himself to report their wants to the General who then makes arrangements for a general collection for that purpose . . . The General attends generally to the needs of all members of the Society and visits each member once a day to satisfy himself of their health and whereabouts and to arrange to supply their wants. He manages the *ngoma* and is responsible for the proper conduct of all members who attend it . . . The duties of the Queen and her subordinates are with regard to the female members of the

[1] Report from office of Censor, 16 April 1920, Sec. 075–186, N.A., Dar es Salaam.
[2] P.O. Tanga, to Secretary, Administration, 10 September 1919, Sec. 075–186, N.A., Dar es Salaam.
[3] Interview with *Mzee* Thabit bin Ismaili, Dar es Salaam, 15, 25, and 30 September and 2 October 1968.

Society similar to those of the King and his assistants. The Bwana Fetha collects the fees, subscriptions and presents of the members and keeps an account thereof . . . rendering a monthly return to the King, Bismarck and the General and other chief members. The Bwana Shauri adjusts matters of dispute and punishes misbehaviour and crimes, such as failing to obey rules, to salute a superior, to attend an *ngoma* when ordered and so on . . . On the death of a member a shroud and funeral feast is provided by the Society out of its funds. Letters of introduction and cash for the journey . . . are given to travelling members.[1]

In places like Mkalama the Beni societies were not so much reflecting pre-existing communal identities as *creating* community contexts. No doubt it was for this reason, rather than the personal desire to compensate for lost influence which motivated Saleh bin Mkwawa, that so many members of the administrative élite continued to support Beni so strongly. The evidence shows that already in 1919 the *Marini–Arinoti* division was regaining its pre-war significance as a sorting out of 'posh' and 'vulgar' modernizers. In Mkalama itself the chief officers of *Marini* were described as a 'Political Clerk. A quiet, intelligent, sober and hard-working man,' and as the 'son of the Liwali of Mkalama'. *Marini* in Mkalama put on quite a show. 'The dress at *ngomas* for males is white trousers with black piping, white tunic, and tarbush, also with black piping, a stick, badges of rank in gilt or silver, medals, a red cross for the doctor and so on. The women wear flowers or a single string of silver beads . . . Iron crosses are also freely worn.' But *Arinoti* was 'much less desirable than the *Marini* from the point of view of law and order, since its members are drawn from the riff-raff of the town'.[2]

The same distinctions were reported from elsewhere. At Kondoa Irangi 'the Political Native Staff are nearly all members of the *Marini*', and the Political Officer expressed himself as 'impressed and disquieted by the enthusiasm displayed among the higher ranks for the interests of their Societies, to which they seem prepared to make almost any sacrifice'. 'A most intelligent member of my native staff,' whom he had tried to dissuade from participation, in fact continued to hold office as General.[3] Once again oral memory substantiates these reports.

[1] A.P.O., Mkalama to D.P.O., Kondoa Irangi, 30 October 1919, Sec. 075–186, N.A., Dar es Salaam.
[2] ibid.
[3] P.O., Kondoa Irangi, to Secretary, Administration, 10 November 1919, Sec. 075–186, Dar es Salaam.

'*Marini* was joined by wealthy people or daughters and sons of wealthy families,' recalls Urban Tamba. 'Its members could afford to buy good uniforms, and slaughter more cows, goats or chickens at ceremonies than the *Arinoti* could.'[1]

Looking back on urban Beni of this period, oral informants remain impressed by precisely those aspects of it which most struck British observers – the influence of the military mode, and the supra-tribal character of the societies. Urban Tamba speaks of 'the military discipline taught to the Beni dancers'. *Mzee* Rashid Hindo speaks of the impact of the war in another sense. 'The Beni dance was detribalized because those who began it were men who had been detribalized. When Africans were recruited in the European forces they fought not as tribal people but as Colonial subjects under the same master . . . How could something originating from detribalized people afford to be tribal?' *Mzee* Hindo stresses 'the sense of oneness among the members of the dancing group'.[2] *Mzee* Thabit bin Ismaili recalls thinking of Beni as 'the greatest influence of unification I had ever seen . . . The Beni dance was the first organization that transcended tribalism. It was a very powerful influence on the African way of life.'[3] It was only much later that these men came to regret the division between *Marini* and *Arinoti*, between the 'rich' and the 'poor', between the coast and the country, and to regard Beni 'as the greatest dividing force' after all.

The war and the expansion of Beni to the Tanganyikan rural areas

So far I have been describing the impact of the war on the sort of people who had been Beni members even before it began. I have described how the dominant influence within the Beni societies shifted from clerks to soldiers and then back again, and how new soldiers and new clerks were absorbed into the urban Beni network. But the wartime expansion of Beni went very much further than this sort of assimilation.

During the fighting in Tanganyika the German columns moved away from all established lines of communication. They needed thousands of porters to carry equipment and food – and to carry the loot which the *askaris* were allowed to sieze during raids on enemy

[1] Interview with Urban Tamba, Dar es Salaam, 14, 17, and 28 September 1968.
[2] Interview with *Mzee* Rashid Hindo, Kariako, Dar es Salaam, 16, 19, 27 September and 1 October 1968.
[3] Interview with *Mzee* Thabit Ismaili, Magomeni, Dar es Salaam, 15, 25, 30 September and 1 October 1968.

villages and bases. The pursuing Allied forces – very much more numerous and more encumbered with equipment than the German columns – needed very many more porters. Some of these they brought into Tanganyika from their colonial possessions which encircled the territory. But hundreds of thousands of Tanganyikan Africans were recruited as porters, road and railway builders, and so on.

These men, drawn into the war on both sides and usually much against their will, made use of Beni. They used it to claim status – because during that period of upheaval it was very important for a man to be able to think of himself as in some way a soldier, a man in uniform, rather than merely a carrier.[1] They also used it to comment on the chaos which the war had created. Many of the Beni songs recorded in this period – usually, so it seems, *Arinoti* songs – are concerned with social dislocation rather than with boasting over victories or extolling the superior culture of the coast.

One such song comments on the tragic evil of women camp followers:

> Our sister, Nganga's daughter,
> wanders about listlessly,
> She made ready to go to Masasi
> and killed her husband to get the chance.

Or again:

> Tatu's mother, pray be quiet!
> Saidi wants you no more.
> You go with Goans and Banyans.
> You are summoned to headquarters at Tabora to be syringed.[2]

A third song 'is a remembrance of the troubled days of the Great War because many native women were rendered pregnant when caught by the soldiers':

> Listen my loved ones! Sister.
> She cried on marrying in Zanzibar. Listen, men of Mkanda.
> I first conceived because of a soldier in the 7th K.A.R.
> That soldier came and deflowered me in Zanzibar.[3]

[1] Geoffrey Hodges in his unpublished study of the Carrier Corps, emphasizes that status 'was always important among African participants. Various non-combatants were uniformed, disciplined, and drilled as soldiers . . . Gun-porters, medical personnel, and some transport drivers were uniformed and disciplined . . . If possible a man liked to think of himself as an *Askari* rather than as a Carrier, and the wearing of uniform was felt to confer that status.' G. Hodges, 'The Carrier Corps. A study of the demands for Military Labour in the East African Campaign'.

[2] H. E. Lambert, 'The Beni Dance Songs', *Swahili*, vol. 33, no. 1, 1962/3, pp. 19–20.

[3] Anon, 'The Beni Society of Tanganyika Territory', *Primitive Man*, vol. XI, nos 1 and 2, January and April 1938, p. 77.

At the end of the war these reluctant participants – or those of them that survived – had their own grievances of status and of poverty. They were bundled out of service as quickly as they had been caught up in it. The Dar es Salaam Annual Report for 1919 recorded in reference to the early months of the year that 'although great care was taken during the dispersal of the military native organizations that none, except those with right, should remain in this district, yet many hundreds managed in various ways to avoid return to their districts of origin'. These people wished 'to remain in town to spend their military pay' but some 4000 of them were 'forced out of the town either to their own district or to the country to cultivate'.[1] In Lindi it was reported that 'large numbers of the natives found themselves suddenly without the easily obtained work and food of the military days and doubtless the period of transition from military work to their pre-war occupations as tillers of the land was a fruitful time for crime to be above the normal'.[2] A Beni song documents the humiliation and insecurity of men suddenly stripped of uniforms and wages:

> Our clothes have been taken from us;
> give us sacks.
> Sisters, stop laughing!
> It's the way of the world.[3]

These men, returning from 'military work' to 'their own district or to the country to cultivate', were effective ambassadors of Beni. The Political Officer at Lindi, who was worried about the implications of Beni in February 1919, was worried at the same time about the consequences of the sudden unemployment of carriers. He connected the two things together, remarking that he was 'inclined to believe that the Carrier Police were mainly responsible for [Beni's] spread; it has certainly grown enormously during the war . . . It may therefore happen that the society will die a natural death as its chief supporters disappear.'[4]

Exactly the opposite occurred. Beni in the towns was not of course dependent on the 'carrier class' and continued to flourish once they had returned to the rural areas. But the carriers and other demobilized

[1] Annual Report, Dar es Salaam, 1919, Sec. 1733/1, N.A., Dar es Salaam.
[2] Annual Report, Lindi, 1919, Sec. 1733/1, N.A., Dar es Salaam.
[3] H. E. Lambert, op. cit., p. 20.
[4] P.O., Lindi, to Secretary, Dar es Salaam, 28 February 1919, Sec. 075–186, N.A., Dar es Salaam.

men took Beni with them when they went home to the country. It was soon being reported that 'the *ngoma* has spread like wild fire all over' and the timing of this diffusion coincided perfectly with the demobilization process. Carriers and others were being forced out of Dar es Salaam and Lindi and other centres in the first months of 1919. In rural south-western Tanganyika 'the *ngoma* known as "Beni" made its appearance . . . in May and June' 1919 'and spread very rapidly'.[1] At the same time Beni reached Unyamwezi and Ugogo, where it reportedly gave some trouble to the British administrators who were endeavouring to 'settle' those districts after the war.

In this initial period of Beni diffusion to the rural areas a great effort was made to reproduce its essential features. Later, as we shall see, rural Beni changed a very great deal and was modified to fit each environment. But immediately after the war the men who danced Beni intended it to strike a novel, foreign note. 'The demobilized African soldiers loved to be admired,' says *Mzee* Rashid Hindo about the post-war boom in *Arinoti* membership, 'and so they thought the Beni dance was something new that could not only keep them together after they had been demobilized but could also show their countrymen what they had learned when they were in the forces.'[2]

The fullest account we possess of this form of Beni is an anonymous description written in Swahili by an African Christian in Ufipa district, south-western Tanganyika. I quote from the English translation eventually made by an equally anonymous missionary and published in the journal of the Catholic Anthropological Conference.[3]

> Beni is an organized society. Persons wishing to play Beni must first agree to enter the society and have their names inscribed in it. Every inscribed member must agree to follow the laws of the *ngoma* and to obey all orders given by the heads thereof. Members must also agree to co-operate in helping members in trouble, whatsoever the trouble may be. Thus if a person is taken for a crime, he must be helped in paying any fine imposed . . . The society is a disciplined one. Officers are respected just as European army officers are . . .

[1] Monthly report, Namanyere, July 1919.

[2] Interview with *Mzee* Rashid Hindo, Kariako, Dar es Salaam, 15, 25, 30 September, 2 October 1968.

[3] Anon; 'The Beni society of Tanganyika Territory', *Primitive Man*, vol. XI, nos 1 and 2, January and April 1938. No date is assigned to the original Swahili account, which is merely said to be in the 'archives of the vicariate'. Every detail of the report, however, dates it to the immediate post-war period.

When the chief of the Beni orders his players to go to a village to play or dance, the order is obeyed, even if they must stay there for many days. If the head of the Beni intends to assist at the dance, he sends a letter to that effect, and immediately on receipt a house and some food are prepared for him. On arrival he is met outside the place of entertainment. A flag must be flying to welcome him. The high officials on meeting him shake hands with him and the soldiers form a guard of honour . . .

There are more members of the *Alinoti* than of the *Marini* . . . The *Marini* seem to consider themselves superior to the *Alinoti*. The *Alinoti* is also called *Lukusanya*, that is, the *ngoma* open to all, even to those who have no nice clothes. Certainly *Alinoti* does not make pretensions to élite membership. Even a man who wears only skin clothing can enter it. *Marini*, on the contrary, keeps aloof from poorly dressed people. The members of *Marini* all dress well, the women especially so. The wealthy members wear a head dress, Arabic dress, and a cloth for the head. *Marini* members love to show themselves off, and they pride themselves on their cleverness at Manoevres . . .

Although the two branches laugh at each other, nevertheless on certain occasions they meet and exercise together to see which is the better . . . The dance starts with all standing to attention. Then the dancers turn slightly and the circle starts in motion . . . The two singers begin singing and the others respond. At times the two singers sing alone while the others stand to attention just like soldiers. The dancers have each a stick in the right hand, and the left hand is up-raised showing the last three fingers. The women make head movements and flaunt themselves to their utmost . . .

[Another competitive activity is *Manova*, the war game.] The Kaiser on a given day orders his soldiers out in the bush or open country for drill. The soldiers separate themselves into two divisions, the second division being the 'enemy'. The Kaiser takes command of the first division and stands at the right; the Major takes command of the second division and stands at the left. Both divisions then set off in marching order and walk for about two hours. They then have a 'battle'. Meanwhile the women remain at home to prepare the food. The 'battle' starts, and when an enemy is captured a rope is tied around his loins and he becomes a prisoner. Captured high officials are not tied with a rope but are guarded by soldiers . . . The battle continues until a line is captured . . . Then a trumpet is sounded as the signal to stop the battle and to come together . . .

> The victors with grass tied around their loins and placed on their heads, walk behind their prisoners, and sing as they go along . . .

> The Beni players go around to different villages to play. If a member of Beni dies the others go to play in his honour. The cloth in which the body is wrapped is paid for by the society . . . If a member marries, the players go and dance in his or her honour.

Clearly at this date, at least in Ufipa, rural Beni was recognizably the same as Beni in Iringa or even as Beni in Mombasa, even if there were no parades with floats and no riddling poetry. But it was likely to be difficult to maintain this degree of elaboration away from the urban network of communication and correspondence.

Beni as a commemoration of the defeat of the Germans

The Beni societies of Ufipa were regarded as 'Germanophil' by the British; they continued to use German titles, sang songs commemorating British defeats, and mocked prisoners taken in *Manova* with songs of derision about the 'Mitamba', which the anonymous African recorder interpreted as a reference to the swaggering British soldiers. But rural Beni in Tanganyika sometimes had quite different connotations. Sometimes the Beni mode was quite explicitly used to express joy at the downfall of the Germans.

The clearest example of this comes from the hinterland of Kilwa and Lindi, an area which still remembered with bitterness the German suppression of the Maji Maji rising. Some revenge for this was taken when African inhabitants of the area informed the British of German troop dispositions, thereby precipitating the battle of Mahiwa which more or less forced the German evacuation of southern Tanganyika. 'Mahiwa is a river in Lindi in whose valley the fiercest battles between the Germans and the British were fought in southern Tanganyika,' says *Mzee* Thabit bin Ismaili, himself a Matumbi from Kilwa district. According to *Mzee* Thabit and other informants, many members of *Arinoti* and *Marini* broke away from them to form a new and specifically southern society. This new society was strong in Kilwa, Lindi, and Mikindani districts, and was brought by migrants from there to Dar es Salaam. It was called *Ngondomaiba* which means, according to all informants, 'there is a battle, or war, at Mahiwa', and it was danced 'in commemoration' of the German defeat.[1]

[1] Interview with *Mzee* Thabit Ismaili, September 1968.

The war and the diffusion of Beni into Central Africa

The same sort of processes which spread Beni to Nairobi and to the rural areas of Tanganyika spread it still further afield. It spread during the war itself. African *askaris* and porters serving with both the German and the British armies introduced Beni to the peoples of northern Mozambique. African prisoners of war carried Beni to Kismayu in British Somaliland. And then, with the great demobilization and with the return of the armies from German East Africa, Beni was carried into all the territories bordering Tanganyika by *askaris* and by demobilized soldiers and porters.

Everywhere it went Beni was associated with the war. As it spread into the northern province of Northern Rhodesia in early 1919 it was danced especially by those who had been away fighting in the war, men like Charles Sinyangwe of Chisanza village, Mbala, who had seen action at the battle of Karonga. Though still a young man, Sinyangwe was permanently marked by his military experience. Even today he wears a khaki bush hat, and carries a metal swagger-stick, and is teased by the younger men for 'marching' everywhere instead of walking. 'When we returned from the war we found Beni,' Sinyangwe says. 'In the war there was no Beni, there was only fighting.' But he soon became a 'Captain' in his village Beni team and sang the Swahili songs which had been picked up from Tanganyikan Beni with a soldierly gusto.[1]

According to a report made to the government of Nyasaland in July 1921, Beni in the Congo was danced only by 'old soldiers and their children' as a mark of pride in their distinguishing experience.[2] In Nyasaland itself the Beni associations of the early 1920s continued to bear ample evidence of their origin in the experience of the war. Dancers 'wore appropriate badges of rank fashioned out of lead' in order to indicate whether they were major-generals, colonels, captains, non-commissioned officers, or privates. 'Those who had fictitious commissioned rank wore helmets and had whistles on lanyards, and some wore Sam Browne belts.'[3]

At the same time it is plain that Beni was not limited to ex-soldiers or ex-porters. Its uses and forms were too varied for that. Even at this early stage in its Central African history Beni was taking on many

---

[1] Interview with Charles Sinyangwe, 12-13 September 1972.
[2] Report by Captain Fairbairn, July 1921, S 2/11/21, N.A., Zomba.
[3] Clyde Mitchell, *The Kalela Dance*, pp. 10-11.

forms. In some places a real attempt was made in the immediate post-war years to keep up the ceremony associated with Tanganyikan Beni. Clyde Mitchell's informant, who described early Beni dances in the garrison town of Zomba, waxed ecstatic over their elegance and refinement. 'This was a clean dance because everyone wore good clothes. People who were dirty were not allowed to dance. Whenever they were called they brought their drums with them and they wore garments like the King. When they reached the courtyard . . . they appeared splendid. Also the women were very clean. They danced slowly and gently, the women on the one side and the men on the other; at daybreak they looked as clean as if they had not been dancing at all.'[1] But from the beginning Charles Sinyangwe and his fellow Beni dancers in Mbala had 'only a cloth and a shirt'.[2]

In some places there were efforts to maintain the full competitive apparatus of *Marini* and *Arinoti* but in many others those names died out or were never introduced so that the dance and the group that danced it was known simply as Beni. In some places in Central Africa the Beni dancers were able to obtain real bugles and trumpets. In other places the lack of these important instruments – which had been a *sine qua non* for Tanganyikan urban Beni – led to the development of ingenious substitutes, such as 'calabashes . . . making a sound extraordinarily like real trumpets'.[3] Indeed, the spread of Beni and its various mutations gave rise to a new zone of indigenous instrumentation which is described by the musicologist, Gerhard Kubik, as the '*kazoo* zone', which includes the Tonga, the Nyanja, the Henga, the Kissi, and the Nyakyusa peoples, and in which *kazoo* bands with drums 'attempt to imitate the sound of European military music'.[4]

Scholars have responded to this early Central African Beni with interpretations as varied as Beni manifestations themselves. Clyde Mitchell asserts that:

It is abundantly clear that these early dances were a sort of pantomime of the social structure of the local European community . . . The Governor and the militia presented to the Africans a formal social structure, the striking feature of which was a rigidly fixed

[1] Clyde Mitchell, *The Kalela Dance*, p. 10.

[2] Interview with Charles Sinyangwe, 12–13 September 1972.

[3] A. M. Jones, 'African Music: the *Mganda* Dance', *African Studies*, vol. 4, no. 4, December 1945.

[4] Gerhard Kubik, 'Recording and Study in Northern Mozambique', *Journal of the African Music Society*, Johannesburg, vol. 3, no. 3, 1964, footnote, p. 80. This *Kazoo* zone was strictly speaking the province of the *Mganda* dance rather than of Beni proper.

hierarchy and a set of distinctive uniforms which advertised the social position of each person. The pantomime of the social structure in the *mbeni* therefore represented the social structure *as the African saw it*. It should be appreciated that, in the twenties, Africans were not admitted by the local European population in Zomba as equals and had no opportunity of appreciating the social pattern in the local community except through military rank, and through the clear evidence of uniforms and public ceremonies. The appeal of the *mbeni* dance, therefore, seems to have been the vicarious participation of the Africans in social relationships from which they were normally excluded. This attempt to cross insurmountable barriers, as it were, in fantasy, is a feature particularly of nativistic movements such as the cargo cult, but there is a distinct difference in that there is no evidence that *mbeni* dancers ever believed that by reproducing the external characteristics of the culture to which they aspired they would automatically achieve their wishes. Their participation in the 'European' social structure was vicarious: the aspiration was satisfied in fantasy only.[1]

A. M. Jones, on the other hand, in his discussion of the musical effects achieved by the *kazoo* and drum bands, describes the resulting music as 'thoroughly African' and as revealing 'what the African will do when he takes over something he has seen and makes it really his own'. In the only musicological analysis which has been made of the Beni mode, Jones shows how 'this wonderfully clever imitation is achieved by reproducing a European sounding rhythm by the employment of African technique, which is fundamentally different in conception . . . We have four different rhythmic patterns intertwining, each having main beats which cross with the others. The intertwining of rhythms is to the African what the intertwining of harmony is to the European. Each drum and the song are in strict relation to each other, and yet, as it were, mutually independent, going on their own ways and preserving an individual freedom. The freedom of the individual is absolutely inherent in the very notion of African life and more particularly of African dancing and African music. Africans do not take kindly to any regimentation in dancing which would compel everyone to do the same thing at the same time. The freedom of the individual to act on his own inspiration is to the African a fundamental concept which exists side by side with his bondage to solidarity.' To Jones, then, the Beni societies and their derivates were not a reproduction of European social or musical forms but a transformation of them,

[1] Mitchell, op. cit., pp. 11-12.

replacing European ideas of disciplined uniformity with an African idea of 'solidarity' and penetrating the European idea of regimentation with the gay individuality of each member of a Beni 'regiment'.[1]

Again, while Mitchell finds no evidence that Beni was ever a medium for 'the expression of hostility towards a ruling group through satire', Bruce Fetter makes the contrary point in his brief description of early Beni in Elisabethville. 'The *mbeni* dance, brought in 1918 by Malawians who had served in the East Africa campaign, introduced new elements into the function and organization of the dance associations. The satirical attitude towards Europeans was an effective means of protesting against unpleasant conditions. The associations, which now called themselves *Les Belges*, so annoyed Belgian officials that they threatened to jail men involved in Mbeni activities.'[2]

I have not had the opportunity to carry out oral fieldwork in Zaire or in Malawi and only a very little in Zambia. Nor have I been able to work in the National Archives in Zomba, while the Zambian National Archives appear to be silent on the subject of Beni until the dance associations were involved in the 1935 Copperbelt strike. I cannot fill in these bare outlines of the spread of Beni to Central Africa, nor do I know enough about each particular situation to be able to endorse or dispute the interpretations advanced. I hope, though, that the very full information which it is possible to present on Beni history in eastern Africa will by comparison and contrast illuminate Beni history in Central Africa.

On this basis, and this basis only, it appears that Clyde Mitchell has overstated the importance of military hierarchy as the only way open for Africans to understand European society. The military emphasis in Beni in 1919 was the product of the immediate historical situation; Beni societies in eastern Africa had employed civilian symbols of authority before, and Beni societies in Central Africa were to do so later. Moreover, he overstates the extent to which Beni in 1918 and 1919 was a 'fantasy' participation in social relationships from which Africans were in reality excluded, and underestimates the extent to which achievement of high rank in Beni, and the exercise of Beni patronage, gave very real and tangible status in the society to which Africans actually belonged.

[1] A. M. Jones, 'African Music: the *Mganda* Dance', *African Studies*, vol. 4, no. 4, December 1945.

[2] Bruce Fetter, 'Elisabethville: Secondary Center for the Dispersion of Kalela', African Studies Association, Los Angeles, 19 October 1968, p. 3.

On the same sort of lines, although Tanganyikan oral history certainly does remember 'songs expressing their hatred for the Europeans or their fear of European power',[1] it seems that the satirical element in Beni was directed more against other Africans than against the whites. 'They dearly love to give performances,' noted the Assistant Political Officer in Dar es Salaam, in October 1919, 'in which parodies of incidents in, or phases of European life in its contact with the native are depicted in the form of light comedy, with the laugh against the ignorant or inexperienced blackman.'[2] Once again the point seems to have been to emphasize that the Beni leaders were at the top of their own particular section of 'modern' society. Even in Tanganyika, where European power had been so terribly displayed and might have been thought to have monopolized all attention, the Beni societies were much less consciously concerned with the whites and much more consciously concerned with African urban society as such than at first sight seems possible. Fundamentally Beni societies were not panto-mimes of white power nor protest movements against it. They were above all concerned with the survival, success, and reputation of their members, acting as welfare societies, as sources of prestige, as suppliers of skills.

And this last point perhaps necessitates some modification of Jones's fascinating analysis. A Beni procession or dance certainly did allow for more expression of individuality than a European parade, just as the African *askaris* whom Karl Weule saw in 1905 loved to do their drill, which they regarded as a kind of dance. But it is clear in the oral historiography that Beni participants themselves felt that they were participating in something which called for and taught a new discipline. The man who became so famous a leader of the Lamu *Scotchi* that he is universally addressed today as *Kingi* rather than by his real name, remembers that he was chosen not because of his agility as a dancer, or his skill as a singer, but because he was 'strong enough to stand still at attention for hours'.[3] One of the *Arinoti* informants in Dar es Salaam speaks of 'the military discipline taught to the Beni dancers'.[4]

---

[1] Interview with Urban Tamba, Magomeni, Dar es Salaam, 14, 17 and 28 September 1968.

[2] A.P.O., Dar es Salaam, to D.P.O., Dar es Salaam, 8 October 1919, Sec. 075-186, N.A., Dar es Salaam.

[3] Interview with Kingi Rajub Abdalla, Lamu, 17 October 1972.

[4] Interview with Urban Tamba, Magomeni, Dar es Salaam, 14, 17, and 28 September 1968.

It seems that at least a little regimentation was sought by the Beni 'regiments'.

The evidence on Beni during and just after the First World War in eastern and central Africa alike reveals above all the extraordinary resilience of Africans under colonialism. When we read of 'light comedies' being put on to illustrate black–white relations such a brief time after the ravages of the war, we may well deplore the lack of a developed political consciousness thereby displayed, or feel that urban Africans had been culturally and intellectually emasculated under colonialism. But we can hardly deny admiration for the survival capacity of these young men of the towns.

Just as Edward Thompson describes how the English workers taught themselves to survive and cohere by making use of improbable and even constricting forms and ideas, so in Beni we can see these young men, for good and ill, making 'really their own' certain themes and structures of the colonialists and using them towards survival and coherence. They did this with a certain gaiety, in the midst and the aftermath of the war, and made Beni so much their own that Europeans were very disconcerted by it. It was an achievement celebrated in Beni oral tradition – 'Actually,' says *Mzee* Hindo, 'it was in origin a colonial dance – but the colonialists themselves later hated and tried to abolish it.'[1]

[1] Interview with *Mzee* Rashid Hindo, Kariakoo, Dar es Salaam, 16, 19, 27 September, 1 October 1968.

3 Beni in the Towns of Eastern Africa between the Wars

Beni in Lamu, 1919–39

By 1919 there were very big differences between Beni in its place of origin and Beni in its widest rural outreach. In Lamu in 1919 Beni was still an affair of wealthy and aristocratic patrons, of lavish processions and feasts, of formalized moiety competition. In many rural areas of East and Central Africa at the same period it had been reduced to the essentials of a military drum beat, a circle of dancers, songs in Swahili, and the use of military titles. Yet one general tendency affected Beni almost everywhere in the years after 1919. Almost everywhere Beni passed out of the control of the men who dominated it in 1919 – whether they represented an élite of aristocratic plantation owners, or a newer élite of clerks, or a rural élite of returned ex-service men. This process took place for two reasons. On the one hand there was an élite withdrawal from Beni as its demands in time and money came to seem disproportionate to its rewards in terms of prestige or skills. On the other hand Beni was taken over and utilized by other elements in eastern African societies, sometimes quite consciously in defiance of the élite which had previously dominated it.

At first sight it is certainly hard to see this sort of change taking place in Lamu. Official reports show that in the 1950s Beni processions were still being staged in Lamu on a lavish scale; the *Scotchi* and *Kingi* still marched as they had done for more than half a century; elaborate floats of warships and planes were still being constructed; cattle were still being competitively killed for feasts. It is tempting to conclude that Beni in Lamu had not changed because Lamu itself remained unchanged. It is often said that Lamu remains a museum of Swahili maritime culture, and one might think that it remained also a museum of Swahili competitive dance.

Lamu only seems unchanging, though, because it has not changed along the lines of most of the rest of Kenya. It remains a pre-industrial city but a pre-industrial city in which very significant social and economic changes have taken place. These have been reflected in Lamu

Beni history; and as a matter of fact Beni can be used as a sort of 'decoder' of wider social change in Lamu.

The only clue to this which the official reports offer is a shift of names. In 1919 the crucial dance competitions in Lamu were between *Scotchi* and *Kingi*. In the 1950s the crucial competitions were between *Scotchi* and *Kambaa*. Now, the emergence of *Kambaa* does not seem to amount to much or to demand much explanation. Beni on the coast was nothing if not the mirror of fashion and fashions in carnival changed rapidly. We might expect a constant change of names and styles within the Lamu Beni sequence.

Yet this is precisely what did *not* happen. There has been a remarkable consistency within Lamu Beni. *Scotchi* remained the main association for the moiety of Mkomani for over fifty years. If there was a craze, as there certainly was, for cowboy styles, or a craze to come to terms with the rising power of the United States of America, these enthusiasms did not lead to breakaways from *Scotchi*, or to the formation of rival Cowboy and American associations. What happened instead was that *Scotchi* absorbed these new fashions by including detachments bearing their names in the *Scotchi* procession. A *Scotchi* parade of the 1950s, described for me by the man who marched in front of it as 'King', reveals several layers of such innovation, as if the procession were a sort of archaeological deposit of carnival. Immediately after the 'King' himself came several leading members of the association dressed as Princes and Peers of the Realm; then came the Scotch as such, dressed in kilts, and sporrans, and bonnets; then came a squad of young and boisterous men dressed as cowboys; then came the 'Americans', with bright shirts hanging out of their trousers; then came the band; and after the band came the women.[1]

Kingi was certainly just as ready to innovate as its old rival. Its surviving protagonists boast proudly of the many novelties it introduced – it was the first society to possess Indian silk processional umbrellas, the first to have pressure-lamps for night parades. The seventeen different 'companies' of *Kingi* allowed for many different variations of style and costume.[2] Thus the rise of *Kambaa* requires some additional explanation.

Lamu oral tradition explains it in a dramatic way, which can serve as a sort of parable of Lamu social change. According to *Mzee* Salim Kheri, the acknowledged custodian of *Kambaa* tradition, the new

[1] Interview with *Kingi* Rajub Abdalla, Lamu, 17 October 1972.
[2] Interview with Adam Ismail, Lamu, 23 October 1972.

association came into existence in the late 1920s or early 1930s. In the 1920s *Kingi* was still dominated by those who lived in Mtambweni, once the southern half of Lamu but now the town centre, because extensive southern 'suburbs' had grown up. In these southern suburbs, known collectively as Langoni, lived an active population of seamen and merchants – captains of dhows, sailors, fishermen. For a time these men accepted the lead of the patrons of *Kingi*. Mohamed Zena was himself a merchant who travelled widely by dhow, and no doubt when he was carried shoulder high to the wedding contest of poetry the sailors followed on behind. But after his death troubles arose.

The most important Beni contests were staged at a time when the dhows were in port. The seamen felt themselves to be a main strength of *Kingi*. Some of the young men of Langoni began to describe their 'company' of *Kingi* as 'The Royal Kings'. According to *Mzee* Salim Kheri, this gave rise to much mirth among the young bloods of Mtambweni, who regarded the sailors, many of whom were Bajuni from the islands, as not really Swahili and as deficient in both culture and wealth. The idea that they should call themselves 'The Royal Kings' or claim a dominant role in *Kingi* seemed absurd. So the young wits of Mtambweni found a more appropriate name for the sailor dancers – *Kambaa Mbovu*, a rotten length of palm rope, full of weak strands.

As the oral tradition has it, this insult led to the breakaway of the young men of Langoni. They defiantly adopted the name of *Kambaa*. Equally defiantly, and in breach of all Beni tradition in Lamu, they adopted as their leader and patron a certain Sabirina, a man of no family, a fish-seller in the very market-place that Abdalla Zena had built. Sabirina, so the Swahili of good family remember, was 'very big, very tough, and very black', a man who could hardly have been more different from the Zena family.[1] The idea that such a man could lead a Beni society seemed laughable. The young wits of Mtambweni sang verses mocking Sabirina's lack of education, his ignorance of 'Arab' manners, his poverty.

The founding songs of *Kambaa* were songs which defied these jeers and which proclaimed quite a new idea of the sources of strength for a dance association. As *Mzee* Kheri, now blind and very old, recited them for me, the passion which he still brought to them made it plain that these songs were more than the customary exchange of competitive abuse.

[1] Interview with Ahmed Nabahani, Malindi, 24 October 1972.

'You call us *Kambaa Mbovu*', runs one of the songs. 'Take note that we are really as strong as the June monsoon. You will want to make peace with us later on, but we shall never allow the scars to grow over the wounds.' 'We are not a rotten rope,' claims another song, 'but a strong chain neck-lace. Anyone with eyes to see can notice how far we stretch out in our procession.' 'Our president may not be an Arab or rich or live in a stone house. But one can white-wash a rough house and make it fine, and our president shall be made great by our united support.' Jointly, the many poor men who founded *Kambaa* could raise the money to pay for elaborate processions and lavish feasts and in this way they could demonstrate to the old-style patrons that they were not dependent on them.[1]

Mzee Salim Kheri certainly sees the rise of *Kambaa* as a protest against privilege. The leaders of *Kingi*, he asserts, tried to stifle the new association by complaining to the colonial administration that common men like Sabirina could not be trusted to control their followers, and by asking that no permit be given to *Kambaa* to hold processions. For their part, the surviving protagonists of *Kingi* still stress the lack of skills of *Kambaa*. *Kingi* processions, they say, were marvels of taste and wealth; *Kambaa* processions were 'mere queues'.[2]

Of course this was not a clear-cut 'class' confrontation. The leaders of *Kambaa* were captives of the very aristocratic assumptions they were challenging. They did not dispute that it was prestigious to stage lavish spectacles and to hold great feasts; to kill many cattle and to bestow gifts upon many women – they merely claimed that they were perfectly able to do all these things. Moreover, Sabirina appreciated the value of prestigious connections and was shrewd enough to be able to exploit the rivalries among the big families of Lamu. After a time he offered the presidency of *Kambaa* to a young Arab, Sherif Ahmed Alwiy of the Shatriy family. The young man was generous and popular; he had the prestige of being a *Sherif*; but his family had come to Lamu from Oman and 'in some social contexts . . . [did] . . . not count'.[3] Sherif Ahmed Alwiy had been a member of *Kingi* but now he was flattered to act as a patron of a Beni society in competition with the Al-Bakari lineage.

Still, the image of *Kambaa* as the association of the populous 'vulgar'

[1] Interview with *Mzee* Salim Kheri, Lamu, 18 October 1972. I cite here not the exact transliterations of the *Kambaa* songs which he sang with such passion, but the paraphrases of their meaning which he supplied during the interview.

[2] Interview with Adam Ismail, Lamu, 23 October 1972.

[3] A. H. J. Prins, *Didemic Lamu*, Groningen, 1971, p. 9.

and of *Kingi* as the association of the 'posh' is quite clearly retained to this day. Moreover, something of the same sort was happening in the northern moiety of Lamu, Mkomani. I was not given the same sort of dramatic personal details of a quarrel between the élite and the 'vulgar' in this case, but it seems clear that *Scotchi* changed its character during the 1930s. After the death of its founding patron, Sheikh Omar Nyekai, no other aristocratic patron had come forward to dominate the association. *Scotchi* came to depend on the subscriptions of its members, just like *Kambaa*. In the eyes of the continuing supporters of *Kingi*, which to the very end was associated with the Zena family, *Scotchi* became just another 'queue', full of 'tailors, donkey riders, and shamba men', just as *Kambaa* was full of 'sailors and dhowmen'.[1]

The transformation of *Scotchi* shows that there was a retreat of the 'posh' as well as a revolt of the 'vulgar' and that the two combined to 'proletarianize' Lamu Beni. And we have only to turn to the archival evidence to understand why an aristocratic retreat was taking place. The 'proletarianization' of Lamu Beni coincided with the period of greatest economic crisis for the town's aristocracy. It is true that Lamu's economic problems had already begun by the time Beni was founded in the town, because the attack on the slave system and the upheavals involved in the colonial conquest of the coast had already undermined what had been a very prosperous plantation agriculture. But the 1920s were a decade of economic disaster. In 1924 the British administration finally rejected the claims which had been submitted by the big families of Lamu for the restoration of their mainland plantations. Dr Salim, in his study of the Kenyan coast, remarks that all 'subsequent reports on the coast and its people speak of seemingly unrelenting depression, stagnation, apathy, and poverty'. The very few wealthy families of the past were ill-equipped to make a successful transition to modern agriculture. Their wealth had been in slaves, cash, and lands; the slaves were gone, much of the land had been taken from them and what remained was steadily sold to raise more cash, and the cash was steadily drained away to meet the expenses of an aristocratic way of life. The cost of concubinage, kin obligations, weddings, circumcision feasts, funerals – and the cost of dance societies – was becoming crippling. 'By the early twenties,'[2] writes Salim, 'the old commercial prosperity of Lamu town had to a great extent van-

---

[1] This characterization is Mr A. S. M. Nabahani's.

[2] A. I. Salim, 'The Swahili-speaking Communities of the Kenya Coast, 1895–1965', pp. 127–279.

ished, its inhabitants largely reduced to living on their savings as their plantations became derelict.' The economic crisis touched all sections of the town. Many younger men left for Mombasa or other centres of economic growth. Between 1914 and 1923 the population of Lamu fell by nearly half. The older men and the members of the Lamu great families did not leave. But in such a situation they had to give up something.

Expenditure on Beni seems to have been one of the things which the Lamu big families increasingly gave up. This sort of expenditure was in any case under relentless attack both by Islamic reformers and by the British administration. In 1924 the District Commissioner, Malindi, blamed dance competitions for the poverty of the coast. '*Ngomas* are their curse,' he wrote, 'and they will spend their savings of a hard year's toil on the useless *ngoma* competitions . . . The improvidence of the Bajuns will show itself in the consumption in one evening of the entire reserve of village food supply in wanton entertainment with no other idea than that of making a more imposing display than its rivals of the next village can accomplish.'[1]

The critique was extended to Lamu in 1925. 'The usual Arab "fitina" and intrigue continues . . . When it comes to a question of paying taxes the plea of poverty is invariably put forward in the most audacious manner, yet these same people – young Arabs – manage to squander very considerable sums of money during the year over vain rivalries between the bands, *ngomas*, and such like amusements, a fact to which the Liwali has more than once drawn my attention. It is of course an undoubted fact that the prosperity of Lamu has steadily declined since the abolition of slavery and that poverty is widespread; but surely it is time that the younger generation which has grown up since slavery was abolished should be expected to make an effort to improve their condition.'[2]

There had once been a time, as the *Utenzi wa Mkunumbi* records, when Arab and Swahili dignitaries could reply to such criticisms, 'without fearing', that 'since the beginning people compete in this way'. But in the late 1920s and 1930s Beni was more vulnerable. The modernizing alliance with the British which the founders of Beni had anticipated had come to nothing. Aristocratic patronage for Beni fell away. The more plebeian members, who were taking over *Kambaa* and *Scotchi*, gained command at the most difficult time, when money was

[1] Annual Report, Malindi, 1924.
[2] ibid., Lamu, 1925.

very short. In 1933 the Lamu Annual Report recorded a low point in Beni history. 'A noticeable feature, possible not a matter of regret, has been the decrease of *ngomas* and band meetings. In the past much money was squandered on these amusements, and not a little friction occurred between members of rival *ngomas*, more particularly the female element. On the other hand,' the report concluded with one of those irritating changes of opinion which was the result of frequent changes among colonial officials, 'they were not unduly vicious past-times, and served to keep the people from being too depressed by present day conditions in Lamu.'[1]

By the 1950s, when Prins carried out his fieldwork in Lamu, there were many signs of economic recovery and Beni activity had strikingly revived. But Prins found that the aristocratic families had 'largely withdrawn from public dyadic opposition and rivalry . . . as for instance in the processions of the two *beni* or *ngoma* (as the dyads are called nowadays)'. It was the general membership of Beni rather than aristocratic patrons who spent the money which restored the societies to their former magnificence.[2]

Beni in Mombasa, 1919–39

The history of Beni in Mombasa between the wars was very different from its history in Lamu. By 1919 it had already been determined that Mombasa would become a modern port city. The economic depression of the 1920s and 1930s, which drained Lamu of men, did not prevent the African work force in Mombasa from growing. But it meant that the city grew without adequate housing or other facilities for its African labour force. Mombasa was in some ways a half-way point between a town like Lamu and the industrial towns of Central Africa. Like Lamu, Mombasa retained an Arab–Swahili population and was thought of as a centre of Swahili culture; like the towns of the Copperbelt it attracted workers from all over eastern Africa in such numbers that they came to form the majority of the inhabitants of the town. Beni in Mombasa also occupied a mid-way position. It remained in some ways like Beni in Lamu, and it became in other ways like Beni in the industrial towns of Katanga and the Copperbelt.

Lamu had its tensions – between the moieties, between the sailors and the young bloods of Mtambweni, between the 'posh' and the 'vulgar'. But Mombasa had more numerous and more serious tensions.

[1] Annual Report, Lamu, 1933.　　　[2] Prins, op. cit., p. 57.

There was tension between Arab and Swahili;[1] there was tension among different elements of Swahili as they argued about how best to react to the changing character of the city; there was a tension between the longer established families of Mombasa and the Swahili migrants who came from Lamu and other depressed areas seeking for work. There was tension between Swahili speakers and the migrant labourers from up-country, who lodged in Swahili houses and competed with Swahili for jobs. And there was the over-arching tension between African workers of all kinds and their European employers. Mombasa was a town of riots, and stoppages, and strikes. To all this Beni had to adapt.[2]

The Mombasa of 1919 comes vividly, though with prejudice, out of a report made in June of that year by the District Commissioner. He described a town in which the older Swahili areas were becoming decrepit and from which many Swahili were moving into newer settlements around the edges of the town. These newer settlements contained many good houses, large and high, with many rooms, but were already becoming very overcrowded as Swahili landlords rented rooms to migrant workers. There were no exclusively Swahili residential areas. In the old town there had been an influx of what the Commissioner called 'very poor Indians', and everywhere there were up-country migrants looking for accommodation. 'These people at present live everywhere, on the back quarters of Indian dukas, on verandahs . . . or as lodgers in Swahili houses . . . Serious over-crowding results.'

'It is difficult to write of the social conditions of such a heterogenous population as is found in Mombasa District today,' complained the Commissioner. 'Every year sees a greater influx of natives foreign to the coast . . . The immediate result is an augmented demoralization of the whole population. The high cost of living has only in the case of particular classes of labour been compensated for by an adequate increase of wage. The tendency to indulge in more and more expensive tastes was rapidly creating an abnormally high standard of living. This has now been complicated by the unprecedented increase in the cost of all commodities. The coastal native has little sense of proportion and he, finding himself accustomed to an expensive scale of living, sees

[1] For this see, Hyder Kindy, *Life and Politics in Mombasa*, Nairobi, 1972. Unfortunately the book does not contain references to Beni but it is a mine of information about the Mombasa football competitions which were closely linked with dance societies.

[2] I base this paragraph particularly on a seminar presentation by Professor Donald Savage, 'Labour and Politics in Mombasa', Dar es Salaam, January 1968.

the attainment of this becoming rapidly more difficult and expects to receive a proportionately higher wage, failing to realize that he in return offers no better service than he did years ago.'[1]

The Swahili of Mombasa were increasingly under pressure from newcomers and it was increasingly difficult for them to define their superiority in terms of a notably higher standard of living. One might have expected Beni to be used aggressively as a way of defining and asserting 'Swahili-ness'; as a means of claiming a monopoly of access to new sources of power and prestige. Indeed, Beni in Mombasa did remain particularly associated with the Swahili right to the end of its history. In 1919, when the Beni associations joined in the peace cele-brations, they were firmly described in the press as 'the Swahili bands'; and there were opportunities for the same sort of affirmation in 1924 and 1928, when the visits of the Duke of Gloucester and of the Prince of Wales provoked great displays of carnival ingenuity. In the Christian areas of the Mombasa hinterland the Beni associations of Mombasa were thought of right into the 1940s as exclusively Islamic.[2] And Professor Mohamed Abdul Aziz has told me that he remembers the Beni societies of Mombasa in the 1940s and 1950s as still expressing the clan and quarter rivalries of the town's Swahili population; still performed with great elaboration, with floats of battleships, with pipe-standards imported from Scotland, and with resulting bankruptcy for the more lavish patrons of the carnival.[3]

But just as the apparent similarity of Lamu Beni processions in the 1950s to those of the first period of Lamu Beni is deceptive, so also in Mombasa the fact that after fifty years floats representing warships manned by officers in full dress were still being drawn through the streets masked some large changes. It was not possible for Beni in Mombasa to be simply an expression of the continued dominance of the Swahili over the city's festive life, partly because the Swahili themselves were so divided in opinion over Beni, and partly because non-Swahili came to play an important role in the associations.

Two divisions of Swahili opinion about Beni appear in the Mombasa evidence. The first is a difference of generation; the second is a differ-ence of philosophy. Generational rivalries are always present in Beni, as young and vigorous men, who can dance better and who feel that

[1] Mombasa District, Annual Report, June 1919, file CP/52/1289, N.A., Nairobi.

[2] This opinion was expressed by George Mkangi's Christian informants in 1968.

[3] I have been fortunate enough to have a number of conversations with Professor Abdul Aziz. His fullest exposition of the theme of Kenyan Swahili culture in the modern period was a seminar on 12 February 1968 in Dar es Salaam.

they better understand the latest fashion, become restive with the leadership of older men, and as older men come to repent the extravagances of their youth and to criticize similar extravagances in others. It was no accident that one of the breakaway Beni associations was named *Yanga*. *Yanga* had branches in both Lamu and Mombasa, but it seems from the evidence that generational tension was particularly acute in Mombasa.

This is certainly the opinion of Dr Ahmed Salim. 'Dramatic changes in the town appeared after the war,' he writes. 'Manners, modes of dress, and appreciation of material things changed perceptibly . . . the taste for European luxuries – clothes, shoes, the gramophone, the cinema – gained ground . . . It was inevitable that comparative liberation from the old patriarchal controls and modernism which loosened these controls, would be bewailed by the older generation. The passing generation seems to have been alarmed by the new modes of entertainment taken up by the young ones in the increasingly urbanized town of Mombasa – the cinema, lottery, dancing, and alcoholic beverages.'[1]

Logically Beni could be distinguished from other forms of modern entertainment. It did not necessarily involve the consumption of alcohol and it did not involve the immorality of European-style partnered dancing. When it was reported in 1923 that 'imitation of the European has developed' pre-existing clubs 'into night clubs at which dances are held attended by women' and at which 'guests able to do so provide their own whisky, and ex-mission girls, Seychelles, Swahili, and other prostitutes attend', and when this was attributed to the decline of parental authority, it might have been argued that Beni should be encouraged as an acceptable alternative to this kind of entertainment.[2] It might have been argued, as it is today in Lamu by the middle-aged men who once danced Beni and who dislike the new enthusiasms of youth, that Beni was communal as opposed to the selfish individualism of 'the European style of dancing'; that Beni contests involved members of all ages, not merely the young; that Beni called for organizational skills which were creditable to the community.[3] Perhaps this was indeed argued by those men of substance who went on supporting Beni in Mombasa. But the evidence suggests that once

[1] Ahmed Salim, op. cit., pp. 318–19.

[2] Regional Commissioner, Mombasa, 17 September 1923, CP/56/1548, National Archives, Nairobi. The Mombasa Annual Report for 1930 recorded 'a growing popularity . . . for the European style of dancing', and accused the youth of the town of squandering its time and energy at 'cafes and *ngomas*', DC/MSA/3/3, N.A., Nairobi.

[3] These views were generally expressed in Lamu in 1972.

the elders identified lavish expense on 'modern' entertainments as the chief offence of the young, Beni was condemned along with all the rest.

This condemnation of Beni was supported also by more philosophical arguments than the high tempers of the debate between old and young. As the development of Mombasa as a modern port threatened the Swahili and Islamic dominance of the town; as mission-educated Kikuyu took over more and more of the clerical jobs in the port; so Moslem intellectuals began to debate the reasons for this decline and the best ways to recover from it.

One tendency in Mombasa Islamic thought was represented by the Mohamedan Reform League, which urged the Mombasa Municipal Board to suppress competitive *ngomas*. Dr Salim has stressed the importance of the leading spokesman of the 'Reformers', Sheikh Al-Amin bin Ali bin Abdallah bin Nafi Al-Mazrui, a scholar well acquainted with the Islamic Reform movement in the Middle East. In his weekly, *Al Islah*, ('Reform'), he argued for a modernization which was rooted in the fundamental principles of Islam. He admired Japan, which had modernized within the terms of its own culture. He urged a programme of education for both boys and girls financed and controlled by the Islamic community itself. But he was 'distinctly conservative' in his opposition to the 'adoption of foreign modes of dress and entertainment'.

In Lamu at this time the most important Islamic teacher was Habib Salih, founder of the Mosque College, who was much more 'distinctly conservative' than Al-Mazrui in almost every way and who stood essentially for a repudiation of any sort of modernization. Habib Saleh did not desire an Islamic technology – but nor did he condemn Beni dancers in kilts. The annual *maulidi* festival which had developed under his patronage in fact provided the Lamu Beni associations with their greatest opportunity for competitive display.[1] But Al-Mazrui, the Reformer, chose Beni as a key example of false modernization. In *Al Islah* for 7 March 1932 he attacked Beni, using the alternative Mombasa name for it, *Gwaride*. Dr Salim paraphrases and translates the passage:

> The coastal Muslims, instead of demanding or acquiring the kernel of knowledge had been satisfied with the shell – the aping of the external culture of the West. 'We have preoccupied ourselves with foot-ball and *Gwaride* at a time when others are preoccupied

[1] A brilliant account of Habib Salih's career is, Peter Lienhardt, 'The Mosque College of Lamu and its Social Background', *Tanganyika Notes and Records*, no. 53, 1959, pp. 228–42. All my Lamu informants agreed that the Mosque College had supported Beni.

with education and work . . . We are engrossed in entertainment we consider civilization whilst those who are wise laugh at us, and politicians cheer us in order to distract us and prevent us from giving them trouble in future'.[1]

The attack on Beni by the Mohamedan Reform League put the dance associations into deep trouble. There had been growing European criticism of the bands – *The Mombasa Times* complaining in January 1931 that 'the noise created by the pipes would make any Scotsman envious' and asserting that it was 'high time something was done to prevent professional native bandsmen from creating such a lot of noise in the middle of the night . . . The police should do something.'[2] When this criticism was backed by Al-Mazrui the Mombasa Municipal Board felt free to act. On 31 May 1932 an executive order was made limiting the number of bandsmen to fifteen; prohibiting any procession outside 'Native Locations' or within 100 yards of motor roads; and even prohibiting any change in uniforms without police permission.[3] The bandmasters of *Kingi*, *Kilungu*, and *Scotchi* joined together to protest this order, asserting the loyalty with which they had celebrated victory in 1919, the reception they had given to the Duke and Duchess of York, their regular celebration of Empire Day, and blaming their problems on 'a political association in Mombasa which is opposing *ngomas* very strongly'.[4] But the tide was running against them and, in 1934, permanent by-laws were adopted which imposed strict controls on *ngomas*.[5]

The opposition of the elders, of Europeans, and of the Mohamedan Reform League, together with the openly expressed mockery of more frankly secular 'modernizers', affected the morale of Mombasa Beni. When I raised the objection in Lamu that Beni was 'too colonially minded' the ex-members of the associations reacted with sheer incredulity that anyone could think of Beni in that way. When I raised the objection that Beni was a waste of money which should have been spent on education and development, these Lamu veterans answered

[1] Salim, op. cit., p. 333.

[2] *The Mombasa Times*, 17 January 1931.

[3] Superintendent of Police, Mombasa to Hamisi Mustafa, *Kingi*, Ali bin Mzee, *Scotchi*, Sherif Nasur bin Mohamed, *Kilungu*, Hamis bin ??????, *Tanganyika* Band, 31 May 1932, file 5/22, Municipal Archives, Mombasa.

[4] Mustafa, Ali bin Mzee, Nasur bin Mohamed to Chairman, Municipal Board, 25 November 1932, 5/22, Municipal Archives, Mombasa.

[5] 'Native Dances, Processions and Strolling Musicians', By-laws, 1934, 5/22, Municipal Archives, Mombasa. These by-laws are still in force in Mombasa.

robustly, 'Yes, we must have schools for education; hospitals for health; mosques for prayer – and we must give money for all these. But we must have something to keep us happy as well.'[1] But when George Mkangi talked with ex-Beni members in Mombasa in 1968 it was a very different story. 'The Beni movement has retarded people's progress very much,' said the brother of the founder of *Kingi*. 'It has caused much loss. People used to sell their farms and houses to get money to make carvings, "submarines", and so forth. Beni was of no value whatsoever.'[2]

Thus Beni between the wars was not an expression of undivided Swahili commitment to continue the tradition of competitive carnival. Nor could it remain exclusively Swahili. It is true that the different groups who came to Mombasa to work formed their own clubs and danced their characteristic *ngomas*. The Mijikenda peoples of the coastal hinterland founded and supported in Mombasa 'The Original Dancing Club'; migrant workers from Tanganyika danced *Bati* and *Tanganyika Beni*, 'whose membership was restricted to people whose origin was Tanganyika'.[3]

But the migrants lived so mixed up with the Swahili, and Mombasa Beni was so striking a sight and so obvious a source of prestige, that it was not surprising that many up-country men managed to penetrate the Mombasa Beni associations. George Mkangi interviewed one of them, Juma Msabaa, a migrant from Uganda who has lived in Mombasa since he first came there in 1932. Msabaa first joined 'The Original Dancing Club' with its mainly Mijikenda membership. Then, 'when *Sadla* Beni was formed by Rastamu in 1938, Msabaa joined it. This was a break-away youth movement from the two prominent bands, *Kingi* and *Scotchi*. Since it was mainly composed of young people, *Sadla* always won during competitions. Msabaa became a lieutenant in this *Gwaride*. *Sadla* is a corruption of Settler. This Beni called itself after the Settlers and sometimes its uncouth behaviour was like that of the Settlers. They imitated the rough type of living of the Settler community of Kenya, and fashioned their uniforms according to the Khaki shirts and trousers and wide hats, just like those worn by the Settlers.'[4]

It was perhaps appropriate that a Beni association formed in

[1] Interview with Ali Musa, Lamu, 18 October 1972.
[2] Interview with Mohamed Nassor, Mombasa, October 1968.
[3] Interview with Juma Msabaa, October 1968.
[4] Mkangi's summary of Msabaa's testimony, October 1968.

89

acknowledgement of the power of the White Highlands should take in up-country members. But up-country migrants had been joining Beni, or at least taking part in Beni processions, for many years before the founding of *Sadla*. When Herman Norden saw a Beni procession in Mombasa in the early 1920s, he was struck both by its carnival element and by the variety of people who participated in it. 'A man covered from head to foot in deer skins walked on stilts twenty feet tall, and a white-clad albino free-lanced in and out of the procession walking with whichever band he fancied, for the bands were many.'[1] According to Norden, Swahili, Kikuyu, Kamba, Nandi, Luo, Luyia, Baganda, Giriama, and Tirkana could all be identified among the marchers.

Thus in Mombasa during the 1920s and the 1930s Beni came to be criticized by many members of the Swahili élite and it came to be used by many members of the migrant work-force in the town. More-over, the continuing price increases made the sheer cost of carnival prohibitive and men with good salaries became increasingly reluctant to 'waste' them on Beni. By the end of the 1930s, so George Mkangi believes, the old leadership which had sought above all for popularity and prestige and which had been prepared to spend money in order to gain followers had given way to a new leadership which was much more interested in profit than in prestige. In the 1940s the Beni societies came to see themselves essentially as performers, available for hire, and they began to change their musical styles to meet the demands of their customers. They began to look outside Mombasa for 'bookings' and 'engagements'. As I shall seek to show later, this led to a new rural expansion of the Beni mode which illustrated how much life it still had in it. But in terms of the old communitarian values which had once dominated Beni in Mombasa it was a sad decline.

Beni in the towns of Tanganyika, 1919 to 1939: the treason of the clerks

Tanganyikan Beni had from the beginning admitted many up-country men into its ranks. It had never been as lavish as Beni in Mombasa and Lamu. But the withdrawal of a controlling élite was just as noticeable in the Tanganyikan towns. In 1919, it will be remembered, *Arinoti* and *Marini* were active in every urban and administrative centre in the territory. Leading members of the African administrative and police staff were busily engaged in building up the old urban Beni network, and spending a good deal of time and money in the process. They were

[1] Herman Norden, *White and Black in East Africa*, London, 1924, pp. 47–9.

allied with prominent African traders and with influential ex-soldiers. Ten years later very few of these men were still connected or concerned with Beni.

There were many reasons for this. One was the attitude adopted by the British administration. In Mombasa, Beni was regarded as a more or less amusing tradition. But in Tanganyika the British were suspicious of Beni because of its origin under the Germans, the activity within it of men still 'loyal' to the Germans, and its remarkable territory-wide diffusion and communication. In one or two places the opportunity arose to ban Beni altogether, as was done in Kilosa where Beni rivalries led to a serious fight in the old town.[1] In other places urban Beni associations were prohibited from performing in the neighbouring rural areas, as in Bukoba district where Beni was believed to be an Islamic dance which must be excluded from the Christian country-side.[2]

But in most of Tanganyika the policy was rather to discourage than to disallow. 'It would be unwise, I think,' wrote the Governor of Tanganyika in June 1921, 'to proceed to open suppression under present conditions, but non-recognition, lack of encouragement, and unostentatious slights should go far to contribute to its decay.'[3] The Governor put this policy into immediate effect. When he visited Dodoma region, 'his visit had one curious effect. After seeing thousands of Wagogo in their tribal dance he would not visit the Beni *ngoma* in the town. This was such a shock to the self-esteem of the *Arnote* and *Marine* corner-boys that we had no Beni *ngomas* since.'[4] As the Governor reported, his snubs had 'been observed, and enthusiasm for the societies, once high, appears to be less ardent than it was two years ago'.[5]

Beni performances were also discouraged by the new apparatus of control of all publicly held dances and the demand that fees be paid for licences to hold them. 'During the year licence fees for public *ngomas* were charged for the first time,' noted the Iringa Annual Report for 1920-1, 'and as a result they are now seldom held, and the two

---

[1] District Commissioner, Kilosa, to P.C., Dar es Salaam, 2 December 1948, Kilosa district, file 13/9, Ethnography General, National Archives, Dar es Salaam.

[2] Annual Report, Bukoba, 1920-1, Sec. 1733/11/4, N.A., Dar es Salaam.

[3] Governor of Tanganyika to Governor of Nyasaland, 10 June 1921, Sec. 075-186, N.A., Dar es Salaam.

[4] Annual Report, Dodoma, 1920-1, Sec. 1733/5, N.A., Dar es Salaam.

[5] Governor of Tanganyika to Governor of Nyasaland, 10 June 1921, Sec. 075-186, N.A., Dar es Salaam.

ngoma associations, "Arinoti" and "Marinyi", though by no means extinct, are not so often heard of.'[1]

I have seen no official evidence to suggest that African employees of the government were actually prohibited from membership in Beni. Oral tradition is emphatic that this was so, however. 'The Europeans looked on Beni with disfavour,' says *Mzee* Thabit bin Ismaili, 'because the songs were sometimes directed against them. Thus they forbade African leaders, e.g. Liwalis, Akidas, Jumbes, and government clerks to join either of the groups. They even instructed them to investigate about the Beni dance. They feared the Beni dance.'[2] 'The European administrators did not like Beni,' says *Mzee* Hindo. 'The sense of oneness among the members of the dancing associations threatened the Europeans and they chose to abolish it. They first barred all Africans serving in their government from joining a dancing society, and then in some places a very high fee was charged if Africans wanted to have a Beni dance.'[3]

The British are remembered as having been especially sensitive about policemen or *askaris* being involved in Beni; about any possible confusion between Beni ranks and uniforms and army and police ranks. 'There was one incident,' recalls Dar es Salaam oral tradition, 'when a Beni dance was organized and the two groups, Arinoti and Marini, put on the actual military uniforms of the demobilized African soldiers. When the English District Commissioner heard of this he was very angry and sent policemen armed with guns to order the dancers to take the uniforms off. They disobeyed and force was used to drive them away. From then onwards the European hated the dance because he could not tolerate Africans using military uniforms in their associations.'[4]

The character of Tanganyikan urban Beni changed radically. The clerks, and police, and *askaris* who had been its mainstay and who had handled the bureaucratic correspondence of the branches, withdrew. Their withdrawal coincided with the development of other sorts of openings for their energies and other sorts of assertions of their prestige. In March 1922 the Tanganyika Territory African Civil Service Association was founded in Tanga, partly as a welfare association, partly as a trade union. As TACSA spread so it took up much of the

---

[1] Annual Report, Iringa, 1920–1, Sec. 1733/19, N.A., Dar es Salaam.
[2] Interview with *Mzee* Thabit bin Ismaili, 15, 25, 30 September 1968.
[3] Interview with *Mzee* Rashid Hindo, 16, 19, 27 September, 1 October 1968.
[4] Interview with *Mzee* Hindo.

same energy and met some of the same needs previously catered for by Beni.

Moreover, men like Saleh bin Mkwawa who resented their demotion when British rule replaced German began fairly rapidly to make reassuring progress within the new administrative structure. 'Because so many aspects of the administration in Tanganyika were conducted in Swahili,' writes John Iliffe, 'there was considerable continuity of subordinate staff despite the war – the staff list of the provincial administration in Tanga in 1924, for example, is surprisingly similar to that of 1912. As the 1920s progressed, these German-trained civil servants began to regain political influence . . . English-educated Africans were beginning to lose the near monopoly of high status which they had enjoyed in the early 1920s.' There was no longer any need for ex-*Akidas* to console themselves by laying on guards of honour made up of *Marini* members![1]

The young civil servant no longer needed Beni as a welfare society nor as compensation for lack of influence. No more did he need Beni as a 'modern' leisure-time activity. There were now more varied possibilities. One good example of the atmosphere of the 1930s is the early career of Elias Kisenge, later a prominent member of TANU. 'In 1938 he joined the Provincial Commissioner's office at Arusha as a clerk. At Arusha he became the Secretary of the Tanganyika Territory African Civil Service Association, Secretary of the Football Association, part-time-librarian of the Gymkhana Club, English teacher for the servants of the Arusha Europeans . . . and Secretary of the Christian Youth Organization.'[2]

And so the situation arose which is described in a survey of Tanga made in the early 1930s. Tanga had been the place of origin of Tanganyikan Beni; in the 1930s its clerical staff was still exclusively African; and Tanga was still a great centre for African education. But Beni no longer commanded the attention of these men.

'The Beni is a modern *ngoma*,' commented the survey. 'It is a hybrid affair; a mixture of the old Arab pageant, the tribal *ngoma* and semi-military evolutions welded together by music supplied by cornets and drums of European type. The dresses worn are often inspired by military and naval uniforms or by the films, while the

---

[1] John Iliffe, 'The Role of the African Association in the Formation and Realization of Territorial Consciousness in Tanzania', U.E.A.S.S.S.C. paper, January 1968, p. 5.

[2] E. B. Amos, 'The Life of Elias Kisenge', Student Research Paper, Dar es Salaam, July 1968, p. 2.

names of the *ngoma* – Young Rich Men, Settlers, etc – indicate their inter-tribal nature and the amount they have borrowed from Western civilization . . . Formerly members were given help in times of sickness or bereavement. The pageantry, which in days of prosperity was the chief feature of the *ngoma*, has now disappeared and shortage of money has reduced the affair to a bedraggled march past in which the riff raff of the town take part.

'It has frequently been suggested that the Beni *ngoma* might be used to control the urban population as a substitute for the lost tribal organization, but it is difficult to imagine this taking place under present conditions. It is disapproved of by the better class native, who considers that it is a direct incentive to drink, and will rarely attend it in any other capacity than that of a casual on-looker. In times of prosperity competitions are organized between the different *ngomas*, the main object of which is to see who can make the greatest expenditure on feasting, and financial distress . . . results.

'If the Beni is to have any beneficial influence it will need thorough re-organization under a very much stronger body of natives than those at present acting in an official capacity. But in my opinion it is moribund, and its place is being taken by the dance-hall run on European lines. The detribalized native with social aspirations dances the fox-trot or the waltz in preference to performing the Beni *ngoma* in the public streets, and he uses his club or one of the dance halls rented for the purpose.'[1]

As this quotation makes clear, it was not only the African civil servant who had deserted Beni by the 1930s. One might have thought that if the British made it impossible for civil servants to hold office in Beni then leadership would surely pass to other successful Africans – to trade, teachers, or clerks in private employment. But this did not happen. Successful and influential Africans outside government employment also moved out of Beni and into new forms of association. If the founding of the Tanganyika Territory African Civil Servants Association can be taken as symbolic of the flight of the civil servants from Beni, the formation of the Tanganyika African Association in 1929 can be used to mark this more general movement away from *Arinoti* and *Marini*.

Among the founder members of the African Association were men who had earlier taken a leading role in the Beni associations but who were now exploring different kinds of combination. One such founding

---

[1] E. C. Baker, *Report on Social and Economic Conditions in the Tanga Province*, Dar es Salaam, 1934, p. 99.

member was Zibe Kidasi, a clerk. In 1919 and 1920 Kidasi had held the rank of Brigadier-General of *Arinoti* in Dar es Salaam; he had supplied rubber stamps and advice on bureaucratic procedures to other *Arinoti* branches; and he had used his authority to suspend branches who did not honour the association's law of hospitality to visitors.[1] Another founding member, and the first Vice-President of the African Association, was Ramadhani Ali, a Zaramo trader. Ramadhani Ali had been 'King' of the Dar es Salaam *Marini*.[2] The Secretary of the first executive committee of the T.A.A. in 1929 was Kleist Sykes Plantan, ward of the famous *Effendi* Plantan, and a leading representative of professional *askari* families who formed one of Dar es Salaam's original African groupings. Kleist Sykes had served as orderly to Von Lettow Vorbeck during the war; had been held in a prisoner-of-war camp; and had become involved in Beni activities on his release and return to Dar es Salaam.[3]

The coming together of men like Kidasi, the clerk, Ramadhani Ali, the Zaramo trader, and Plantan, the Zulu *askari*'s son, meant that three key elements of the Dar es Salaam African élite were allied together inside the African Association. In some ways it might be argued that this was a development out of the Beni associations, realizing their potential for articulate combination on a pan-tribal basis. In other ways the Association's emphasis upon unity was a deliberate departure from the factional and competitive basis of Beni. Within the Association ex-leaders of both *Arinoti* and *Marini* came together. 'We have formed this Association of Africans,' they proclaimed, 'that we may unite together as brothers and follow the paths of progress in education, games, and other matters which have been followed by other enlightened people.'[4]

Beni continued to be danced in Dar es Salaam but from henceforward it was criticized as divisive. Ramadhani Ali objected in 1938 to 'the Tanga people' in Dar es Salaam who had 'separated themselves off from the mass of Africans and have built their club to dance European dances or *mbeni* or their local dances.'[5] The competition between

[1] Kidasi is named as a founder member in the papers of Kleist Sykes Plantan, see A. D. Sykes, 'The Life of Kleist Sykes', Student Research Paper, JAN/HIST/143/15, September 1968, Dar es Salaam. For his role in Arinoti see, Censor's reports, 15 September to 31 October 1919 and 16 April 1920, Sec. 075–186, N.A., Dar es Salaam.

[2] Interview with *Mzee* Thabit bin Ismaili, September 1968.

[3] A. D. Sykes, op. cit.

[4] John Iliffe, 'The Role of the African Association', p. 3.

[5] This quotation is an extract from a letter by Ramadhani to *Kwetu*, 4 November 1938, as translated by John Iliffe, op. cit., p. 9.

Marini and *Arinoti* was attacked for creating an artificial enmity among Africans who should 'combine to help one another'.[1]

And just as the ideas of the Islamic Reformers have come to colour the opinions of ex-Beni dancers in Mombasa, so these proto-nationalist criticisms have coloured the view of ex-Beni members in Dar es Salaam. 'I think it is a good thing that Beni was abolished,' says Urban Tamba, 'for it divided us Africans and so made us an easy prey of colonialism'.[2] *Mzee* Thabit bin Ismaili 'still loves the idea that he was once an Arinoti', but he says that 'later this dance proved to be very destructive. Instead of being the greatest influence of unification I had ever seen it turned out to be the greatest dividing force I had ever seen! One African group was set against another, they fought and tried to bewitch the other . . . The colonialists enjoyed that. They knew as long as he talked in terms of "I am Arinoti, you are Marini", we could not conceive a concerted action against them . . . I lost my brother in a fight against the Marini.'[3]

Of course, we must be careful not to read too much back into the 1930s. These oral memories have clearly been coloured by the experience of the radical nationalism of the 1960s, as when *Arinoti* is compared to TANU as the poor man's association. The African Association in practice did not achieve much unity, being divided between clerks and traders, and in any case was always in danger of being a mere club for the élite, while the Beni associations in their hey-day had contained a much more varied membership. Indeed, it was sometimes hard to distinguish between a branch of the African Association and an élite dance club. An intelligence report of 1936 describes the Dodoma branch of the African Association as a 'dance club which meets about once a week and whose members ape European styles of dancing and dressing'.[4]

Probably in the 1920s and 1930s the most damaging criticism of Beni was on the grounds of its extravagance rather than on the grounds of its disunity. Nothing so clearly illustrates this strand of élite criticism of Beni as an article from the Swahili magazine, *Mambo Leo*, published in March 1928.

[1] This quotation is from an interview with Rawson Watts printed in the *Tanganyika Standard*, 14 October 1930, Iliffe, op. cit., p. 3.
[2] Interview with Urban Tamba, 14, 17, and 28 September 1968.
[3] Interview with *Mzee* Thabit bin Ismaili, 15, 25, 30 September 1968.
[4] Extract from the bulletin of the Political Intelligence Bureau, September to November 1936, SMP 19325/1/53, N.A., Dar es Salaam, cited in Iliffe, op. cit., p. 13.

Dances! Dances! Dances! They are the ones which bankrupt us. I opened my mail-bag the day before yesterday and took out a very thick heavy letter. I thought: 'Aha, I have got something worth reading today!' But when I opened it I found three pages full of a dance story which took place in a certain town. The letter told about the food, tea and biscuits, and mineral waters and many other oddities which the dancers consumed; also it contained details about the clothes worn by the dancers, the different types of trousers and shirts, and at the end of the letter the writer finished it by asking God to embellish the dancers! After reading this letter, I thought: 'These people have spent much money uselessly!'

Then I looked for another letter, and chose another thick one, only to find many pages full of stories about dancing competitions in a certain town. The competitions took three days, and each day the competition intensified, until the last day when the competitors met in a hotel booked for such functions. Then I was grieved very much to think how these fools spent their money on useless projects to gain cheap popularity.

Lately I visited a town and I came across a group of people sitting in a clearing. I approached them and found the whole place decorated with multi-coloured papers, with many pressure-lamps hanging around the place . . . I saw a crowd of women dancing, all wearing uniform, decorated with bangles and other trifles, and the whole place was filled with a strong, sickening perfume!

Then I thought: 'Now, who has bought these women's clothes; who has bought these bangles and other trinkets; who is meeting the expenses of the pressure lamps?' I grieved. From that day, the many letters I have read have been about dances only, and to make it worse, it's not like the old traditional dances which incurred no expenses, but these are imitative dances which require plenty of money. I realized that the fashion was growing more and more.

The day before yesterday a certain person came to me for a small financial loan. He said that he had no money, and he didn't have even a morsel of food at home . . . He came to borrow only seven days after he received his monthly pay. I thought: 'Has this man spent his money already?' Then I realized that this was the result of dances!

I have no more to say about this because I am sure all my readers know what I am driving at. But among those who feasted at the dance, how many have denied their children food so as to appear seemingly great? Among those who wore such stupid and dandified clothes, how many have left their wives and children to go in rags? . . . Among those who danced under the light of pressure-lamps, how many haven't even a single cent to buy a candle-stick or paraffin with which to illuminate their houses?

Many brag, saying: 'Wau! last night is worth remembering; even Europeans came to watch our dancing!' Yes, true, but what were the Europeans thinking when they were watching the dancing? Come on, gentlemen abandon these nonsensical bankrupting dances. The far-sighted people of the world are laughing at you and looking at you with scorn because of your folly![1]

Beni in the towns of the Tanganyikan interior: the rise of communal welfare societies

The desertion of the élite need not, of course, have meant the end of urban Beni in Tanganyika. Indeed, it is obvious from *Mambo Leo* that Beni was flourishing in some Tanganyikan towns in 1928. The interesting thing, though, is to ask which towns these were and to ask what had happened to Beni elsewhere. It seems that Beni flourished in the smaller settlements of the Tanganyikan coast; survived in Dar es Salaam; and died in the towns of the interior.

In the smaller settlements of the coast Beni flourished because it was still able to play its original role. Pangani, which remained a lively Beni centre into the 1950s, stood in something of the same relation to Tanga that Lamu did to Mombasa. Tanga grew into a modern port; Pangani remained a small Swahili settlement. So when R. S. Tanner was District Commissioner in the late 1950s, he found that Beni still expressed 'an intense but harmless rivalry' between two competitive societies 'which could not exist without each other'. In the 1950s these two societies were named *Beni* and *Mkwaju* and seem to have corresponded to the same sort of division which initially existed between *Marini* and *Arinoti*. *Beni* possessed brass instruments; *Mkwaju* only possessed cymbals. *Beni* members boasted that they were 'superior' to their rivals. The two groups wore sailors' or red-cross uniforms but there were constant changes and innovations. Tanner, observing the situation with a sociologist's eye, noted that many members of both societies were widows or divorced women and that most members of both societies were Swahili.[2]

Competitive Beni societies were noted also at Bagamoyo and at Lindi; in the Rufiji delta and at Kilwa. When Peter Lienhardt worked

---

[1] 'Maongezi ya Mtengenezaji', *Mambo Leo*, no. 63, March 1928, translated from the Swahili by George Mkangi.

[2] Interview with R. S. Tanner, Nairobi, 10 January 1968.

on the Tanganyikan coast in the 1950s he found that the old principle of locational competition was as important as ever in the coastal towns and villages.

In German times in Tanganyika there was costly display, paid for out of bonuses the Germans gave to their African troops. Feasts were held and the supporters of each of the rival dances led the cattle they were to slaughter for the feast around the quarter of the village where their rivals lived. Later the party paraded again carrying the heads of the slaughtered animals on sacking upon their own heads and wearing the skin on their backs . . . Today the rivalries of football teams and their associated dance-bands provide entertainment for everyone. Football has become very popular in Tanzania. In 1959 there were two groups of football clubs spread right along the coast. At that time they were called 'Yanga' (short for 'Young Africans') and 'Sunderland'. Every place that was big enough to produce two teams had one of each name . . . Each football team has its own dancing club, and the dance-bands compete just as vigorously as the footballers. They arrange their dances on the same night for the express purpose of seeing which can attract the most supporters. A musician may be asked to come and live in a village with a room provided, a regular wage, and perhaps a girl friend, just in order to help one of the dance-bands to beat the other. Younger strangers coming to the village are offered club colours by the girl supporters. Dancing clubs have a protocol over the type of dress to be worn, requiring the women to wear dresses . . . and the men to wear European trousers rather than robes . . . Protocol is taken so seriously that fights break out when people try to come into a dance dressed in the traditional fashion . . . Many of the older villagers involve themselves in the affairs of the modern football and dancing clubs. They can use the clubs to increase their influence and cultivate their personal rivalries, as well as amusing themselves with their juniors' successes.[1]

This is plainly still the world of Beni and obviously there have been complex interactions between bands and football over the decades. At one point in the progression it would no doubt have been more accurate to write of each dance association having its own football team rather than the other way round. In some places, at least, *Yanga* was a Beni society before it was ever a football club. But at all times from the 1920s to the present the competing bands and teams have expressed

[1] Peter Lienhardt, *Swifa ya Nguvumali. The Medicine Man*, London, 1968, pp. 16, 18.

99

'the passionate spirit of rivalry . . . prevailing so openly throughout coastal society, a part of the coastal character and of the structure of the society itself'.[1]

By the 1930s Dar es Salaam had ceased to be a Swahili town in any simple sense. Beni did not survive there in the way it survived in Pangani or Lindi, but it did survive. It seems to have done so because it was useful to the migrant workers even if the Dar es Salaam élite had abandoned it. Like Mombasa, Dar es Salaam was a growing town despite economic depression, and conditions for the Africans who came to work there were very bad indeed. Beni came to be employed as one of the ways in which these migrants organized themselves into communities despite the odds against them.

This can be seen well enough from the men whom Mr Chijumba interviewed about Beni in 1968. Admittedly they had all been members of *Arinoti* rather than of *Marini* and might therefore have been expected to be newcomers to the town. But there is a difference between them and earlier *Arinoti* leaders like Zibe Kidasi. *Mzee* Thabit bin Ismaili came to Dar es Salaam from the Kilwa district in the late 1920s when he was ten years old. His father became 'King' of *Arinoti* and his maternal uncle became 'King' of *Marini*. The family was not a wealthy or influential one in any way. *Mzee* Thabit himself made his living as a *dhobi*-man, washing and ironing clothes. His description of the Beni rivalry in Dar es Salaam in the 1930s and 1940s brings out how closely it was by then connected with the business of finding accommodation and building up a community. 'The relationship between *Arinoti* and *Marini* was one of enmity. Members of different groups could not rent rooms in the same house or have any other social function together except when it involved competition.' Beni was still not divided on ethnic or regional lines: the lodgers in one house might be drawn from many different tribal backgrounds but all become members of *Arinoti* or *Marini*, and it seems that leadership positions in this period were often taken by landlords, whose income from other trades was supplemented by rent and who had the immediate following of their tenants.[2]

Beni survived in these different forms on the coast, but in the towns of the interior it had died out completely by the 1930s. In some of the smaller administrative centres – a place like Mkalama, for example – this collapse was certainly due to the withdrawal of government em-

[1] Lienhardt, op. cit., p. 16.
[2] Interview with *Mzee* Thabit bin Ismaili, Dar es Salaam, 15, 25, 30 September and 2 October 1968.

ployees, who had been responsible for Beni's establishment in the first place and who had kept it going almost alone. But this was not true of larger and longer established towns like Tabora or Ujiji where Beni had come to take a much more significant role than merely that of an élite diversion imported from outside. The African proletariat of these towns was deeply divided and the Beni competition had come to express their rivalry. The withdrawal of the clerks was not reason enough in itself for the disappearance of Beni from Tabora and Ujiji.

There seem to be two reasons for the collapse of Beni in the towns of the interior. The first of these was the economic distress of the early 1920s which coincided with the withdrawal of the clerks and made it very difficult for anyone else to run Beni on any sort of scale. In the Tabora Annual Report for 1920 'a total collapse of trade' was recorded for the last months of the year; at Kondoa Irangi it was reported that 'very many petty traders' had 'gone to the wall'. Similar reports were made for other towns. And whatever economic recovery they made in the later 1920s was aborted by the world slump, so that reports of the early 1930s speak constantly of unemployment and privation.[1]

Now, it is true that Beni survived in Lamu through just such periods of economic decline and depression. Moreover, in so far as Beni had always acted as a sort of mutual aid association it might have been expected to become more rather than less relevant in times of distress. The second reason why Beni seems to have come to an end in the difficult times of the 1920s and 1930s was that the leaders of the African factions in towns like Tabora and Ujiji made a deliberate choice to move to other and more effective forms of community organization.

The clearest evidence for this comes from Ujiji. The African population of Ujiji was divided into two bitterly competing groups. One was made up of so-called Manyema, people from the Congolese side of Lake Tanganyika, who had originally been brought to Ujiji as slaves. The other was made up of freemen who had migrated to the town from the rural areas to the east of the lake. The Manyema prided themselves on the greater purity of their Islam; the freemen prided themselves on not having been slaves. Competition between them was sharpened by the economic stagnation of the town and by the desperate shortage of jobs. When the British took over Ujiji this bitter contestation was expressed through the *Arinoti–Marini* rivalry; by what one British officer described as 'the original ngomas, with their ridiculous

[1] Annual Report, Tabora, 1920–1; Annual Report, Kondoa Irangi, 1920; Sec. 1733/5, N.A., Dar es Salaam.

addenda of Sam Browne belts and Major-Generals'. Writing in 1932 this officer remarked that 'like most administrative officers in the past I declined to take seriously the original ngomas'. But, he added, 'it would be foolish not to take notice of the powerful associations which have descended from them.'[1]

What these 'powerful associations' were and how they developed was partly illuminated by the tragically uncompleted research of E. L. K. Kabbembo, who was killed in a car crash while working on the faction history of Ujiji–Kigoma. According to the rough notes of his interviews, the two 'powerful associations' of Ujiji were the Kongo–Arabian and the Watanganyika, the first representing the Manyema faction and the second representing the Tanganyikan freemen. These associations were founded in 1924, replacing the previous dance societies.

Just as Beni itself was first founded in Mombasa because of the impression made upon a visitor from that town by what he saw in Zanzibar, so also the Kongo–Arabian Association owed its inspiration to *Mzee* Songoro's visit to Zanzibar in 1924. But *Mzee* Songoro, an elder of the Manyema, was not impressed by the Sultan's band or by the Beni societies of the island. What impressed him was the more formal self-improvement associations he found in operation.

> He was very much impressed with how the people in Zanzibar lived. They stayed together helping each other; he thought Zanzibaris were much more civilized than people in Ujiji. *Mzee* Songoro found Associations in Zanzibar and from Zanzibar he brought the idea back. He called a public meeting; people met under the mango trees of *Mzee* Kandusi, an Arab. On that day they danced, ate, and enjoyed themselves like anything. Immediately the descendants of the slaves decided to form the Kongo–Arabian Association. Then the 12 tribes of the Watanganyika decided to meet. They collected money, opened a co-operative shop . . . They asked for permission to build a house office.[2]

These developments did not transform factional politics in Ujiji. The two Associations still mocked each other. 'Each group claimed to be more important than the other. They used dirty language to each other. Watanganyika used to tell Kongo–Arabian, "You are slaves". And the latter who had been Moslems for a long time would reply "You

---

[1] Annual Report, Western Province, 1932.

[2] Draft notes by Mr Kabbembo, 'Research – Ujiji Project: Urban politics, 1900-68', 26 March to 6 April 1968.

are still very uncivilized".' This rivalry continued to be expressed through dance. The Watanganyika particularly liked the *Changani* dance; the Kongo–Arabian performed a dance of the same name as that of their Association. 'There were a lot of *ngoma* competitions.' And in 1932 this rivalry flared up into a spectacular street fight in which men were killed.[1]

The two Associations were sometimes described, in fact, as *ngomas*. But British officials were quick to point out that 'both are more than a dancing society, each approximating to a co-operative'.[2] The constitution of the Watanganyika has been preserved in the Tabora District Book and it is a revealing document. The founders of the Ujiji Associations had obviously not accepted the argument for African unity instead of factionalism which the élite was urging against Beni; but equally obviously they *had* accepted the arguments for self-help and economic enterprise.

The constitution of what was called 'The Unity of Lake Tanganyika Nations Association, Ujiji', began by defining the sort of mutual aid functions which Beni had in fact fulfilled for its members:

> We made this society which is called Tanganyika on the purpose of relief in any distress, i.e. in case of sickness or death . . . We are bound to help anyone in right distress.

But the constitution sternly announced a Puritan ethic, far removed from the carnival atmosphere of Beni. 'Drinking, playing cards, or fighting or adultery' were 'cases we cannot assist to'. Moreover, the prevailing tone was very business-like. 'We made an effort to collect some money to continue the above-mentioned cases, and we have put some money in the Savings Bank as our deposit and we draw this money from the Bank if we have not sufficient money to cover the difficulties which can develop among us.'[3]

The business-like proceedings of the Associations are testified to by the District Commissioner's account of them:

> The Tanganyikans have a meeting house valued as sh. 1500/- and funds amounting to sh. 2000/-. The Arabiani's head-quarters is valued as sh. 800/- and their available fund at approx. sh. 600/- . . . The Tanganyikans have opened a shop in Kigoma and also in

[1] Kabbembo notes.
[2] 'Tabora *ngomas*', Tabora District Book.
[3] Constitution of the Unity of Lake Tanganyika Nations Association, Tabora District Book.

Tabora – a large and respectable looking building with an advertisement board – and all members are expected to purchase necessities at these shops, the profits . . . going to the general funds.[1]

It was little wonder that the British authorities were impressed and took these Associations more seriously than Beni. After the affray of 1932 had been mediated, great care was taken to balance the two factions within the internal government of Ujiji–Kigoma and in 1941 the leaders of the two Associations were jointly appointed as the local Native Authority.[2]

The two Associations spread from Ujiji to Tabora, where they were similarly organized. In 1919 there had been branches of the *Arinoti* and *Africa* Beni societies in Tabora, the first calling itself a German and the second calling itself a British band. They had been supported by the 'better class of Swahili . . . all men in employment', including 'Native Police clerks and Police'.[3] By 1933 the memory of Beni was so faint in Tabora that when the Assistant District officer discovered that a form of the dance had become popular in the southern rural areas of his district he had no idea that it had once existed in Tabora town, and vaguely surmised that 'as far as can be discovered the *ngoma* comes from the coast'.[4] In Dodoma, also, the Kongo–Arabian and Watanganyika Associations seem to have replaced Beni. In fact, they spread also to Dar es Salaam but there they could not hope to monopolize faction politics; they co-existed alongside Beni and many other 'tribal' clubs and dance societies, and alongside the African Association.

In this way many people who had once been involved in Beni moved on to other organizations. Some of these, like the African Civil Servants Association, concentrated on more effective representation of an élite and did not bother with a wider following; others, like the African Association, stressed unity but could not attract as wide a following as the Beni societies or other frankly factional groupings; yet others, like the Ujiji Associations, did not concern themselves with unity or with élite trade unionism but sought to improve the economic condition of their followers. All of these developments could be regarded as representing an advance over the 'false consciousness' of Beni; as being more rational, more pragmatic, more forward-looking.

[1] 'Tabora *ngomas*', Tabora District Book.
[2] Annual Report, Western Province, 1941.
[3] Assistant District Superintendent, Police, Tabora to Sec., Admin., 3 October 1919, Sec. 075-186, N.A., Dar es Salaam.
[4] 'Beni or Dundo Dance', Tabora District Book.

Still, we must remember that Beni did continue; there was still need for it. None of these other attempts managed to meet the needs of the migrant worker in Dar es Salaam. Moreover, the slightly priggish emphasis upon thrift and industry which characterized these strivings towards 'true consciousness' lacked the nourishing dimension of carnival. Stripped of its élite leadership, Beni in Dar es Salaam continued to provide this dimension; it offered a heightening of experience and pleasure which was worth the time and money spent on it; it offered a running commentary on the whites, on the African élite, on other groups of migrants. By contrast with the life-styles and aspirations of the fox-trotting élite, Beni's music and costumes no longer seemed so much an imitation of Europe. Beni in Dar es Salaam was a sort of populist amalgamation of European themes and African assumptions; in terms of cultural expression, at least, it perhaps came closest of all to being appropriate to the actual situation of most Africans in the city.

4 *Beni in the Diaspora between the Wars*

Beni in the Tanganyikan countryside, 1919–39

By the 1920s the Beni dance mode, which had originated in a very specific cultural context at a very specific time, had already shown remarkable adaptability. Beni certainly did not remain restricted to 'classical' Swahili environments and even within them its relevance did not remain restricted to conceptualizing the significance of early colonial rule. Beni had proved attractive to people in the polyglot new towns and in the rural areas; it had responded to the situation created by the First World War and to the situation created by the re-establishment of British colonial rule. In the 1930s this versatility was even more strongly marked. Beni proved an apt vehicle for reaction to and comment upon the development of Indirect Rule conservatism, the renewal of missionary paternalism, the stultifications of the Great Depression. It was carried to still further environments and adapted even more radically.

Almost everywhere it went Beni was thought of as innovative and prestigious but often this had little to do with overt European or Swahili elements in the Beni mode. The Swahili elements faded as Beni died out in the up-country towns of Tanzania and as rural Beni became more and more a thing of its own. Nor was Beni thought of as a 'European' dance. By the 1930s the main European agents in the rural areas were seen as enemies of modernizing change – to take an example relevant to Beni, the wearing of 'modern' clothes, such as long trousers and shorts, was opposed by most missionaries. To dance Beni was not to 'ape' but to defy this sort of European presence.

At the same time, while Beni was thought of as innovative the breakdown of the urban supervisory network allowed each rural area to adapt the Beni mode to its own particular and successive needs. Because of the multitude of rural situations in which Beni appeared and their unevenness, this adaptation process is impossible to describe fully. I seek merely to illustrate it here. I seek first to make some generalizations about the way in which Beni was used to meet some widespread needs of the Tanganyikan countryside. Then I wish to take one or two examples of the way in which Beni was adapted to the particular needs of individual rural environments. Finally, I wish to discuss those cases where the fullness of the adaptation of Beni was expressed through a change of its name and its emergence as the characteristic dance of a particular rural population.

The adaptation of Beni to rural needs: Islamicization

Beni had always flourished in Tanganyika in environments which were essentially Islamic – on the coast and in the towns of the interior – though many Christians had become members. Now, as Beni spread into the countryside, it was often made use of to meet a new kind of Islamic need. The years after the First World War witnessed an expansion of Islam in many Tanganyikan rural areas, which in some cases confirmed and in others produced a communal, 'tribal' Islam which was very different from the Islam of the coast. These 'tribal' Islamic communities showed an admirable independence of mind, maintaining many of their own customs and repudiating any idea of the infallibility of coastal law and culture. But there were some aspects of 'traditional' cultures with which a devout Moslem might feel uncomfortable and among these were traditional ritual dances. Beni seemed satisfactorily Islamic, with its coastal origin and its Swahili songs, but not oppressively so.

As a result there seems to have been a connection between the expansion of rural Islam and the spread of Beni. 'The rise to power of Beni coincides with the increase of Islam,' wrote an administrator from north-western Tanganyika, who believed that the Beni societies were 'excellent organizations . . . prepared for the seed of Muslim propaganda from without'. In Bukoba district Beni was banned because its Islamicizing influence was feared by the missions.[1]

We might be tempted to dismiss this as the opinion of alarmist administrators who had not distinguished sufficiently between the coastal origins of Beni and its lack on the coast of any defined ideological content. But there is evidence from the African side also. The Ngindo peoples of south-eastern Tanzania became almost completely Islamicized in the period following the Maji Maji rising of 1905. Crosse-Upcott, who has written the major ethnographic study of the

[1] Annual Report, Bukoba, 1920–1, Secretariat. 1733/11/4, National Archives, Dar es Salaam.

Ngindo, tells us of the dilemma posed to the Islamic teachers of that area by the traditional dances:

> As for devil dancing, it is not the detraction from God's unity that prompts scruples, but rather the threat to competing Islamic services. A preacher told me of the enormity of the temptation. Whilst at his oraisons, he hears the drum-beat, disturbing his reflections, drowning his voice. Bit by bit in responding to the rhythm his limbs begin to twitch. Till eventually he comes bounding out of the mosque straight into the vortex of the dance! . . . A preacher, regarding the dance-arena as polluted ground will avoid setting foot on it for forty days . . . Nevertheless, if they personally abstain, preachers do hold dances . . . Ngindo allege the existence of an approved form of dancing known as Beni.[1]

In a much less authoritarian way there is a parallel here with the early missionary preference for the brass band over the 'pagan' dances of the freed slaves. And there is a parallel irony in the fact that by the 1920s Islamic Reformers on the coast had come to condemn a dance which was so acceptable to preachers in the interior, while Christian missionaries now supported many traditional dances and had come to dislike intensely any kind of dance which seemed imitative of Europeans.

Beni and rural needs: the aspiring young men

Beni was not only made use of in Islamic areas. It was attractive in many other places because it asserted 'modernity'. The élite of clerks and upper-class Swahili had once danced it for this reason, and when they dropped out others took it up. The rural Beni dancers were not, of course, asserting that they were at the top of the new bureaucratic hierarchy. What they did assert was a familiarity with the modern world as a result of labour migration, or of some schooling. They also asserted the right to spend their wages on modern clothes. In the coastal towns where Beni originated, the fact that young men performed the dance and the marches was balanced by the influence of older men as patrons. In some rural areas chiefs, headmen, or groups of elders extended their patronage to the village Beni groups in something of the same way. But in many rural areas Beni was a self-supporting society of young men, who were asserting through the dance their claim to influence in a society dominated by their conservative elders.

[1] A. R. W. Crosse-Upcott, 'Social Structure of the Ki-Ngindo speaking peoples', Ph.D., Cape Town, 1955, p. 239.

One good example of this comes from an account of Beni in the southern Tabora district in the early 1930s. Gone are the rivalries of *Arinoti*, *Marini*, and *Africa* bands, which had once characterized Tabora Beni; gone are the elaborate uniforms. But still present is the assertion by young men of their ability to participate in the modern world. The people in the area concerned had recently been regrouped into 'concentrations' as a precaution against sleeping sickness, and this had meant a good deal of upheaval and a crisis for customary authority. Beni became popular in these concentrations 'owing to the changes of customs and life of the people', and 'as an outlet for the spirits of the young men'.

> At Nyonga [runs the administrator's report], the *ngoma* has got a far bigger following . . . It is held in an enclosure made of stakes and surrounded by ropes. This, it is understood, is in order to prevent people who are not members of the *ngoma* entering the circle unobserved and also enable the leader to keep a check on late arrivals . . . Those who dance it are all of the young dressy type. In fact the *ngoma* is remarkable for the fact that persons who are not well dressed are not permitted to take part in it, and there is great competition among its members in this respect. There is a list kept of its members and it has leaders who are known as Bwana Kingi, Bwana Govania, Bwana Shauri, and Bwana Askari. These 'officials' sit at a table to one side of which are placed tumblers and bottles of water . . . The [*ngoma*] seen was probably attended by about 50 youths all of whom were dressed in white shorts and white shirts.[1]

The African 'Authorities' of the area tried to suppress Beni. 'On my way through Ugunda (Mtemi Mmeta's country) I observed several of the Beni enclosures near the road,' recorded the Assistant District Officer; 'they were most overgrown with grass. I asked Mtemi Mmeta about it and she informed me that she had forbidden it in her country until after the tax season as she feared that the youths would spend too much time dancing and would not look for their tax.' *Mtemi* Mbaula of Nyonga also banned the dance, but was obliged by its popularity among his young men to withdraw the prohibition.[2]

A missionary account of Beni in southern Upogoro in the late 1930s makes the same points. The young men 'show off their shorts and long trousers', elect officials known as *Kingi*, P.C., Doctor, *Bwana* Fedha,

[1] E. J. W. Carlton, Assistant District Officer, Tabora, 'Beni or Dundo Dance', Tabora District Book, January 1933.
[2] ibid.

or treasurer; and are frowned on by the African authorities. 'Old village heads complain that these dancers always ignore their authority. Actually, the young men carried things so far that the sultan prohibited the *benti-ngoma* in the Ruaha valley because of the increasing excesses and brawls.'[1] Clashes such as these were minor but still significant indications of the tensions which operated within the system of Indirect Rule.

Beni and rural needs: village rivalry

Competition *within* towns or settlements was the norm for coastal society. Competition *between* villages or clan settlements was the norm for many Tanganyikan rural societies. Beni easily adapted to this. Instead of competing associations with many branches, each village would have its own dance group, known simply as Beni, headed by especially vigorous young men, but to some extent representing the village community as a whole. These Beni groups would then dance against the groups of other villages. Such village rivalry to some extent mitigated the generational rivalry also expressed in Beni. Thus in southern Upogoro each 'valley community or larger village forms its own group', and the 'increasing excesses and brawls' were caused by inter-village competition rather than by scuffles between young men and old men.[2]

Among the Yao of the border area between Mozambique and Tanzania, where Beni had probably originally been associated with the spread of 'tribal' Islam, the dance 'was performed on a competitive basis. The competitions were run on a divisional basis – i.e. each division consisting of, say, three villages. And in fact these divisions represented clan differences. Any given division represented people from a single clan. The divisions did not represent wealth groups.'[3] In this sort of competitive context Beni songs were 'self-praise songs which praised your own clan and denigrated another clan . . . patriotic songs, praising particular norms of the clan'.[4] The competition was

---

[1] P. Kunibert Lussy, 'Some Aspects of Work and Recreation among the Wapogoro of Southern Tanganyika', *Anthropological Quarterly*, October 1953. I am indebted to Mr Lorne Larson of the University of Dar es Salaam for this reference. Mr Larson's forthcoming account of the modern history of Ulanga district will contain a full discussion of Beni development there.

[2] Lussy, 'Some Aspects'.

[3] Interview with Hussein Abdalla, Litisha, Songea District, 23 September 1968.

[4] Interview with Rajabu Athumani, Morogoro Leprosarium, Songea, 25 September 1968.

fierce. 'The competing groups used witchcraft to overcome the rival group in performance.'[1] And competition was seen as the very essence of the dance: 'competition tended to beautify the songs and thus raised the standard of performance because each competing group wanted to do better than the other'.[2]

There are many other examples of this sort of village or clan competition in the rural areas. But although competition 'tended to beautify', rural Beni was nothing like as elaborate as the *Marini–Arinoti* confrontations. An account of Beni dances in Upogoro shows how modified both costumes and instruments had become.

> A powerful drum about two metres high, so that a special platform of table height has to be erected next to it for the players, is put up in the middle of a clean swept place beneath a nice shady tree or in a village. The drum is beaten with a drum-like stick like that used with a kettle-drum. The left hand of the player plays variations of the tone on the vibrating drumskin and plays a soft accompaniment. Next to the large drum there is another smaller one, and nowadays one also finds tin cans as further noise instruments. The dancers arrange themselves in a large single circle among the drums. They are decorated and have their hair dressed, wearing bright scarves around their heads . . . As they dance the shrill notes of a football whistle sometimes sounds, and now and then the roaring of antelope horns. When the crowd sings and the drums accompany softly, the single row of dancers moves shuffling along until the rhyme of the song is finished. Then the big drum sets in with all its might. The dancers turn towards it, swinging in their hands the tail of the gnu or coloured handkerchiefs, swaying and rocking their bodies to the rhythm of the music.[3]

The development of Beni in particular rural environments

It is easy enough to see that Beni met these general needs of providing a dance suitable for rural Islam, allowing for the expression of the aspirations of young men, and articulating village rivalry and interaction. The working out of Beni history in any one particular place is considerably more difficult. In the towns of the Kenya coast Beni was a continuous affair, even if there were times when it was more and other times when it was less prosperous. In the rural areas, though,

[1] Interview with Jawadu Salehe, Morogoro Leprosarium, 21 September 1968.
[2] Interview with Hashim Mohamed, Morogoro, 27 September 1968.
[3] Lussy, 'Some Aspects', p. 123.

Beni was spasmodic. It would be taken up at one time and in one form to meet one need, or merely as a fashion; then dropped; then taken up again in another form; then dropped once more, and so on. Thus the so-called *Benti* of southern Upogoro in the late 1930s, descriptions of which I have quoted, was not the end result of a single continuous process of Wapogoro adaptation of Beni. In fact it was the third wave of Beni in the area. In the early 1920s there had been what Lorne Larson calls 'the *Beni–Arinoti* period'; in the later 1920s there had been what he calls 'the *gwaride* period'; and in 1936 *Benti* 'was introduced again . . . by people who had been working on the Central Railroad.'[1]

Rural adaptation of Beni was thus a business of many stages. Each form of Beni, as it entered a district in these successive waves, was in itself different; *Benti*, when it came into southern Upogoro, was already the result of a series of adaptations made elsewhere which had carried it a long way from *gwaride* or *Beni–Arinoti*. And then *Benti* was further modified by the Wapogoro. All this makes it difficult to see Beni history in any one district as part of a coherent development of dance and musical forms.

This perception can only be achieved through a full-scale study of the total dance history of various eastern African societies. I have not myself made such a study but other scholars have begun to do so and in what follows I am dependent on them. The possibility of integrating Beni into a more general dance history is stated by Henry Anyumba in a tantalizingly brief passage. '*Mbeni* dances of Machakos district . . . have succeeded in the last thirty or so years in incorporating in their organization sharply contrasting elements partly deriving from external influences and partly from the traditions of other dances particularly *Nguluku*. Flexible convolutions – followed by rigid formal movements, and static stance with mobility, have been exploited quite effectively, in a way probably very different from earlier songs and dances.'[2]

Until Anyumba gives us a fuller study, however, the most detailed musical history available for an eastern-African people is Gerald Hartwig's discussion of Bukurebe. Bukurebe is an island in south-eastern Lake Victoria. Before the colonial period its musical history is notable mainly for the monopoly exercised over song and dance and over the use of certain instruments by older men. Some songs were

[1] L. E. Larson, 'The African Voice: Protest and Improvement in the Ulanga District, 1945–54', History Research Seminar paper, 1 December 1972, University of Dar es Salaam.
[2] H. O. Anyumba, 'Historical influences on African Music', in B. A. Ogot, (ed.) *Hadith* 3, Nairobi, 1971, pp. 199–200.

limited to the leaders of the bands which hunted buffalo, hippopotamus, and elephant; others were the property of fishermen. Of the long-standing Kerebe instruments only the flute could be used by almost everyone. Kerebe drums were associated with the royal clan and used only for ritual and ceremonial occasions. The *enanga* zither, and the song styles that went with it, were the property of the elders, who drank their beer and told tales of the past to the music of the *enanga*. Young men were not allowed to participate in these sessions of reminiscence: still less to play and sing. Nor could the young men take part in the various *ngomas*, or games, as Hartwig calls them, introduced from outside Bukurebe in the nineteenth century, some of which involved dancing to a new sort of drum. 'The age of the participants excluded younger people. For men this meant that those of under thirty-five years of age did not participate in proper games . . . During the last years of the nineteenth century the young people had to be content with the flute, while their elders exhausted themselves playing *make, someke,* or *akasimbo.*'

All this is a world away from the atmosphere of rural Beni, danced to a drum by the young men. And Hartwig does indeed show that a dramatic transformation took place in Kerebe musical and dance practices in the twentieth century. The old controls broke down; an 'age of dance' had begun, dominated by the young. The interesting thing for our purposes is that although Beni played a part in this development, it only arrived in Bukurebe after the era of the young man's dance had been vigorously under way for years. Hartwig sees the key innovation not as Beni but as a 'game' introduced in 1907 by one Lukondo. Lukondo enjoyed royal patronage and 'once Lukondo's game had so completely captured the imagination and enthusiasm of the Kerebe, the advent of other games followed in a literal deluge . . . entertainment through the medium of games was not only restricted before 1900 but it was also on a very limited scale. By 1920 games dominated the lives of the majority.' Beni itself was not introduced until the 1920s.

Hartwig sees the 'deluge' of *ngomas* as a product and a sign of the radical transformation of Kerebe society. The authority of those who had monopolized music had collapsed.

New musical innovations appeared before the European colonial era with the senior members of society monopolizing the new form of entertainment . . . The dominant minority in Kerebe society . . .

established the acceptable goals for the Kerebe . . . With the advent of colonial rule, the means for advancement were altered. The autocratic domination of the minority was lessened. Wealth could be achieved by raising cash crops. Former external pressures, threats as well as opportunities, became a thing of the past. The previous system with all its demands was replaced by an era of greater relaxation. There was more time for enjoyment and the Kerebe threw themselves into games with abandon. Music and dancing became the consuming passion of the majority . . . Drums, usually replicas of the royal drums, dominated the games; they ceased to be a royal monopoly.

Even the *enanga* zither ceased to be a monopoly of the old:

The role of the *enanga*'s music commenced its alteration from one of reminiscence to one of pure entertainment . . . A drastic upheaval in Kerebe society contributed to the alteration of the *enanga*'s role. The colonial era introduced two profound elements that contributed immensely to destroy the former social foundations: cash crops and Christianity . . . Cash crops produced money that gave individuals an independence hitherto impossible to attain. For its part, Christianity . . . proceeded through the schools to undermine . . . parental authority . . . Within a decade after the missionaries had arrived in Bukerebe in 1895, the old social order was irreparably damaged . . . The newly found independence and freedom of the younger Kerebe was seen in their use of the *enanga* . . . the role of the *enanga* changed to a form of amusement that could be utilized during any festive occasion, played by young and old alike.

In this situation of the collapse of the old social forms, Hartwig believes that the *ngomas*, or games, ceased to be merely a 'form of amusement' and became 'a way of life', providing missing incentives and solidarities. The idea of competitive *ngomas* was introduced from Usukuma some time before 1914. While on the coast Beni developed within a competitive tradition which was centuries old, in Bukurebe the competitive dance had been introduced only a decade before Beni's arrival.

Hartwig thus describes the competitive *ngomas* which preceded Beni:

Competing games, always two in number, selected a mutually agreeable time and site. Each game was assigned a location approximately one half mile in distance from the other. Playing and dancing began at noon and stopped around five o'clock . . . The winning game was determined by the number of observers who happened

to be watching one of the games at the end of the afternoon . . .
Each game maintained its own internal organization complete with
officers assigned to specific duties . . . Unlike nineteenth-century
games, children could and did join these new ones . . . Each game
resembled a welfare society. If any member needed the assistance
of his companions for tax payment, the construction of his house or
the cultivation of his fields, the aid was forthcoming . . . Two or
three-day fêtes became common, usually on weekends.

Given all this, Hartwig feels justified in calling the period between
1910 and 1950 'the era of the dance', in which 'games dominated
Kerebe life' and 'the freedom acquired as a consequence of the old
order's decay was channelled effectively into a new and vigorous way
of communal life, one based simultaneously on fierce inter-group
rivalries and compassionate intra-group relations'.

In other places, it seems that Beni itself was the major new form
through which this kind of change took place, and Hartwig's analysis
helps us to understand more fully what was involved in the participation
of young men in rural Beni. But in Bukurebe, where there were so many
other *ngomas*, Beni assumed a rather different character.

Beni appeared around 1920 [writes Hartwig]; its founder was a
veteran of the war. Significantly the group used Swahili rather than
Kisese or Kijita. The followers differed from others in their dress
as well. White shirts and trousers were necessary apparel – shirts
were never laid aside as a smart appearance was part of the game.
It remained aloof from other games, never competing against them,
separated distinctly by language and dress. Beni flowered briefly,
then ceased to exist when an outstanding singer died. The game itself
did not die. It merely slept until about 1939, when former members
reorganized the game and it sprang forth with renewed vigour.
Though presently in decline along with all games, its demise will
be more gradual because of its modern aspects, particularly language
and dress. It remains popular in the eyes of the educated youth in
contrast to other games that are regarded as being sadly out of date.[1]

The assimilation of Beni under other names

Hartwig's account, rich as it is in its implications, is not typical for all
rural societies. Beni did not everywhere remain 'aloof'. In some rural
areas it became so completely assimilated that its 'alien' characteristics

[1] Gerald W. Hartwig, 'The Historical and Social Role of Kerebe Music', *Tanzania
Notes and Records*, no. 70, 1969, pp. 41–56.

were almost entirely forgotten. Usually this assimilation was accompanied by a change of name; and under the new name the dance often came to be thought of as especially, almost traditionally, characteristic of this or that rural area. This was a process that took some time to mature and it seems that it was not until the 1930s that these Beni mutations emerged in their final shape.

Some arose in Tanganyika itself. Among the Mwera of southern Tanganyika 'the Beni dance was changed into *Chikosa* which is being enjoyed even today'.[1] In southern Tabora at the end of the 1930s Beni was becoming known as *Dundo*; in Ulanga at the same period the dance was spreading in the last of a series of waves of expansion, but this time under the name of *mlangimlangi*.[2]

But the most spectacular mutations took place outside Tanganyika where it was more easily possible to escape from the tug of the 'distinctly separate' language of Swahili. In some areas of the Northern Province of Northern Rhodesia Beni turned into *Kalela*. This did not happen quickly. Up to the mid-1930s Beni itself was danced in the mining towns of Northern Rhodesia by workers from almost all the African societies of the Northern Province. But around the year 1930 *Kalela* was developed out of Beni in the Ng'umbo, Aushi, and Bisa rural districts. Clyde Mitchell's informants gave a perhaps too specific story of *Kalela*'s emergence:

> The dance called *kalela* was formerly known as *mbeni* . . . *kalela* was started by a man called Kalulu around the year 1930 on Chishi Island in Lake Bangweulu. The inhabitants of this island are of the Ng'umbo tribe.[3]

Soon *Kalela* was being danced by Aushi workers in Elisabethville[4] and by the late 1930s it was being danced by Aushi, Ng'umbo, and Bisa teams on the Copperbelt. Informants today remember *Kalela* as especially characteristic of the Bisa, and remember Beni not so much as the fore-runner of *Kalela* but as a dance which remained especially characteristic of the Bemba. These same informants make a distinction in style also. *Kalela* as danced by the Bisa, they say, was very athletic and vigorous: Beni as danced by the Bemba was more

---

[1] Interview with Urban Tamba, Dar es Salaam, 14, 17, 28 September 1968.
[2] Lorne Larson, op. cit., p. 3.
[3] Clyde Mitchell, *The Kalela Dance*, p. 9.
[4] Bruce Fetter, 'Elisabethville: Secondary Centre for the Dispersion of Kalela', African Studies Association, Los Angeles, 19 October 1968.

dignified and graceful.[1] In this manner Beni and *Kalela* became in Mitchell's sense of the word 'tribal' dances.

Most important of all variations of the Beni mode was the *Mganda* dance of Nyasaland. Indeed, it may be that *Mganda* was not really a derivate of Beni at all but an independent invention. This is claimed by its historian, W. P. Koma-Koma, in his *M'ganda Kapena Malipenga*.

This is how it all started. In 1914 during the First World War, people from Usisya saw soldiers marching. While marching they sang songs and played trumpets. They all marched with the same step. When war was ended the soldiers left, so the people of Usisya tried to do what the soldiers were doing . . . After some time they discovered the idea of using gourds for trumpets . . . When they made the trumpets those who had deep voices played bass and those with soft voices played tenor. They tried very hard to make a drum that would look like the soldiers' until finally they made it. This started spreading all over Usisya, Nkhata Bay up to Nkhota-kota.[2]

The relationship between Beni and *Mganda* in Nyasaland was a complex one. Both modes certainly co-existed for a long time. It may have been that Beni was at first the more widespread and that it was subsequently replaced in many areas by the diffusion of *Mganda*; it may have been that from an early period Beni was characteristic of some peoples and areas and *Mganda* characteristic of others. Today, at any rate, *Mganda* is the dance of the peoples of what Kubik calls the 'kazoo zone' – the Tonga, the Nyanja, the Henga, the Kisi – together with the Tumbuka and the Ngoni, while Beni in its surviving form is particularly associated with the Yao.[3] But it took *Mganda* some time

[1] I am drawing here on the interviews of Arthur Turner, who collected material in Kabwe (Broken Hill) during 1972.

[2] I cite Catherine Chipembere's translation of Koma-Koma's pamphlet, *M'ganda Kapena Malipenga*, Limbe, 1965, pp. 34–5.

[3] According to Henry Chipembere, whom I interviewed in March 1973, Beni is closely associated with the Yao. There is a team of Beni dancers at Mponda's, very much under the patronage of the chief, and the dance is performed in other Yao areas as well. *Mganda*, on the other hand, is associated with the Christian areas of the lake shore and the islands. *Mganda* was the most popular of all dances on Likoma island, where it was accepted by the missionaries of the U.M.C.A. and where Archdeacon Glossop acted as patron of the dance. *Mganda* is still danced on Likoma today and used as the vehicle for commentary on public events.

A description of a Beni performance in Malawi in the mid-1930s may be found in Keith Coutanche, 'The Beni Dance', *Central Africa*, no. 644, August 1936, pp. 157–9. According to Coutanche 'the Beni was introduced to British territory during the early days of the East African Campaign by captured German *askaris* who obligingly taught it to their captors. Thereafter the dancing of it was encouraged (and still is) by the British authorities as a stimulus to recruiting for that excellent corps, the King's African Rifles.'

to spread and to become thought of as the special dance of Nyasas. In the decade immediately after the war Nyasa migrant workers carried Beni with them rather than *Mganda*. It was Nyasa migrants who introduced Beni into Elisabethville in 1918.[1] Beni was danced by Nyasa workers at Shamva mine in Rhodesia in the 1920s.[2]

From the mid-1930s, though, *Mganda* appears with increasing regularity as the dance of the migrant Nyasa worker. It is not plain whether Nyasa migrants went on dancing Beni, but it is certain that they danced *Mganda*. A. M. Jones was told in 1945 that for many years there had been 'separate Tonga, Henga, and Likoma teams' of *Mganda* dancers competing against each other in the Copperbelt towns. By 1940 Beni was danced on the Copperbelt by the 'Bemba', *Kalela* was danced by the 'Bisa', and *Mganda* was danced by the 'Nyasas'. Koma-Koma tells us of the links between *Mganda* and Nyasa migrant labour:

> There are many men especially in the Northern Province who go on trips outside Malawi for the sake of Mganda. Some go to work so they can get money to buy clothes for Mganda; others go out to look for European drums or small drums or anything they feel might be needed for Mganda at home. A long time ago many people liked to go to South Africa, Northern Rhodesia, now Zambia, Congo, and Tanganyika, now Tanzania. They went to all these places looking for jobs. Those who were devoted to Mganda never stayed away in these strange countries for ever but they came back home immediately they got what they went to look for . . . It has been found that after some time Mganda Boys from various groups meet in a strange country like Tanzania or Zambia. When they meet like this they still remember the old days of Mganda; they get together and rejoice for meeting again. If they are a large number they form a group of Mganda and dance like they did at home.[3]

Mganda in an urban setting could be quite elaborate. A. M. Jones thus describes a *Mganda* procession of the early 1940s:

> First may come the Regimental Mascot. When I saw it, this was carried on a cushion very sedately by a small boy . . . Then come the Officers, dressed in European suitings, very smart and brandishing canes in a cavalier manner. They dance about four abreast and burlesque with extravagant airs the British army officer – doing it

[1] Fetter, 'Elisabethville', p. 3.

[2] I. R. Phimister, 'The Shamva Mine Strike of 1927: An Emergent African Proletariat', Henderson Seminar Paper, University of Rhodesia, Salisbury, 1972.

[3] Koma-Koma, op. cit., pp. 19, 20–1.

of course in dance form and keeping time with the music. Next come the Drummers, three in number. In the centre is the big drum carried in a European manner and beaten by two sticks with the rather pompous display exhibited by the European big drummer . . . He is accompanied by two other drummers beating on African drums of the familiar pounding-mortar type. Behind these is a body of Trumpeters . . . One man acts as a Doctor . . . There is also a party of Stretcher bearers with stretcher . . . Accompanying the Procession is a Constable. He is an important person whose duty it is to see that everyone dances properly and that there are no squabbles . . . At the Headquarters . . . are two very important people. They are the King and his Secretary. The King is in command of the whole show, changing the dancing or announcing an interval for food, and so on.

Jones regarded rural *Mganda* as a poor relation of this urban splendour. 'They do only a small part of the sum total of dance steps belonging to the full *Mganda*. The Procession is so attenuated as to be merely a token one.'[1] But Koma-Koma gives a useful corrective to this. So far as he is concerned *Mganda* arose in the villages, remained pre-eminently a dance of the villages, and reached the towns only by being recreated there by migrant labourers. His account stresses the vitality of rural *Mganda*:

Mganda dance is performed by men only and not by women. This dance is like the parade of soldiers. Before a group is formed they hold a meeting where they choose a king who acts as a leader of the whole group, captains and other office bearers. Before they start dancing the group has to contribute a fund for all the necessary expenses. After that they buy the following things: animal skin to be used for making the drum; gourds for making trumpets; uniforms; shakers.

One will find different Mganda groups in each different division or district. Each village has its own Mganda group. Invitation letters go between the groups inviting each other to a dance . . . When the other groups arrive it is the duty of the host group to feed the guest groups. The host group has a duty to make sure that the visitors are well received, sleeping places are comfortable from the day they arrive to the day they depart. There are times they play for three consecutive days . . . After some time the host group is invited somewhere else and this goes on until all the groups have been invited.

[1] A. M. Jones, 'African Music: the *Mganda* Dance', *African Studies*, vol. 4, no. 4, December 1945.

Boma in Nyasaland means Government but the Mganda groups use the word to mean the whole group of members or the place or field where they meet. The Mganda *Boma* is usually situated where there is a tree or trees which can provide shelter . . . The big Mganda *Boma* will take 100 or more people . . .

Right in front of the whole group they put officers. They may be 2 or 3. They lead in the dance. They dress alike and hold sticks in their right hands . . . Some officers wear complete suits . . . others wear shorts but should also have a jacket, shirt and tie, long stockings, and well polished shoes. When everybody is ready and in their places the Captain takes charge and says: 'Stand at ease, Attention, Quick March, Slope Arms, One, Two, Go'. They start singing and throw their legs just as if they did not belong to them. They all march just like one person . . . While the dancers are dancing women go inside running slowly, cheering the dancers and giving them presents, especially those who are dancing very well . . .

They try to dress themselves to look like soldiers on parade. Each group has its own name e.g. Bwaira, Koleji (College), Landani (London), Amereka, Zomba, and so on . . . The whole group or *Boma* must wear the same kind of clothes – white shirts and white shorts, black sweaters or khaki sweaters . . . They all have to dress the same . . . No two different groups are to wear the same kind of clothes.[1]

Koma-Koma emphasizes the positive values associated with this rural *Mganda*. Some men, he says, are so generous with their earnings as migrants that they will bring back uniforms for the whole *Boma*, and this emphasizes the tie the migrant feels for his home community and restates traditional values of distribution of wealth. 'Many people come to be in very close relationship because of Mganda . . . Mganda dancers co-operate with each other in different ways. They always come together when need arises . . . If there are some Mganda Boys who cannot afford to buy certain things for their guests, those who have money help to provide. They do not like to let each other down. They help each other in various ways.'[2]

The similarities to Beni are obvious. But there were some significant differences. Only men danced *Mganda* and there were no associated women's dances as in Beni. The gourd-trumpet was a characteristic *Mganda* device. Above all there was the difference in language. The

---

[1] Koma-Koma, op. cit. *passim*. He also gives a long account of the selection and installation of a King which rivals Jones's description of the procession for elaboration; pp. 21–4.

[2] Koma-Koma, op. cit., pp. 20, 26–7.

language of Beni was Swahili; the language of *Mganda* was Tonga or Henga. In this form *Mganda* was carried out of Northern Nyasaland into the Nyasa-speaking villages of the Tanganyikan shore of Lake Nyasa, and so back into the land of Beni. In these lakeshore villages *Mganda* scored a great success. This was an area of little economic opportunity but a great deal of intense missionary competition, which was exploited by the equally competitive villages to obtain large numbers of schools. The educated young men took to *Mganda* at once.

'Before the *Mganda* dance came into this area,' remembers Yakob Kaparasu, 'there were a number of local dances, namely *Lindu*, *Nkwenda*, *Magwamba* . . . *Mganda* was introduced from Nyasaland during colonial times. The dance was introduced by Nyasa people who used to come here with European administrators, e.g. Protestant Christians, teachers, and coolies of the *Ilala* steamer. The smartness of its dancers, who wore white shirts, shorts, black shoes, attracted the African Christians. They left their local dances and adopted the new dance. On the part of African Christians, *Mganda* was accepted with a total approval.'[1]

In this part of Tanzania, indeed, *Mganda* so perfectly fitted the needs of the people for identification with the wider Nyasa culture and for self-assertion as 'modern' men that it rapidly came to be thought of as their characteristic dance. Yakob Kaparasu remembers the coming of *Mganda* but he is a man of seventy. The young men who dance *Mganda* today cannot remember a time without their dance. Their fathers danced it before them; its songs are in their own language; its dress is smart but no longer obviously modelled on European soldiery. The young men know nothing of the complex history of *Mganda* or Beni, and they indignantly deny any derivation from the European military mode. They think of *Mganda* as their own traditional dance. And clearly it has become precisely that.[2]

When Julius Nyerere delivered his Inaugural Address as President of Tanzania in December 1962 he reflected on the cultural history of his country:

A country which lacks its own culture is no more than a collection of people without the spirit that makes them a nation. Of all the

---

[1] Interview with Yakob Kaparasu, Mbongo, 23 April 1968.
[2] I spoke with some dozen schoolboys at Songea Secondary School in September 1967 while they were rehearsing *Mganda*. They repudiated with indignation any suggestion of European influence, asserting that it was a dance 'as old as the tribe itself'.

crimes of colonialism there is none worse than the attempt to make us believe that we had no indigenous culture of our own; or that what we did was worthless . . . Some of us, particularly those of us who had acquired a European type of education, set ourselves out to prove to our colonial rulers that we had become 'civilized'; and by that we meant that we had abandoned everything connected with our own past and learnt to imitate only European ways. Our young men's amibition was not to become well educated Africans, but to become Black Europeans! . . .

When we were at school we were taught to sing the songs of the Europeans. How many of us were taught the songs of the Wanyamwezi or of the Wahehe? Many of us have learnt to dance the 'rumba', or the 'chachacha', to 'rock 'n' roll' and to 'twist' and even to dance the 'waltz' and the 'foxtrot'. But how many of us can dance or have even heard of, the *Gombe Sugu*, the *Mangala*, *Nyang'umumi*, *Kiduo*, or *Lele Mama*? Lots of us can play the guitar . . . how many . . . among the educated can play the African drums? . . . And even though we dance and play the piano, how often does that dancing – even if it is 'rock 'n' roll' or 'twist' – how often does it really give us the sort of thrill we get from dancing the *mganda* or the *gombe sugu* . . .? It is hard for any man to get much real excitement from dances and music which are not in his blood.[1]

There is an obvious, but superficial, irony in President Nyerere singling out *Mganda* as one of the really African dances despised by the young men who wanted to be like Europeans. But more profoundly the history of *Mganda*, or of Beni, shows that we cannot understand the cultural situation in terms of long-standing 'traditional' African dances on the one hand, and incursive 'alien' dances on the other. A visitor to Bukurebe in the 1920s might well have distinguished Beni as an 'alien' import from the truly 'African' character of the other *ngomas*, or games. Yet most of these *ngomas* were recent imports into Bukurebe and they shared with Beni a part in the cultural revolution which was bringing about the dominance of the young men in an era of dance. Conversely, what happened to *Mganda* in Tanzania demonstrated that African cultures retained an essential prerequisite of creative growth – the ability to take from and to modify 'alien' forms. *None* of the musical cultures of Tanzania remained 'traditional' in the sense of remaining exactly the same as they were in pre-colonial times. And in any case such continuity would not have marked a triumph. The

[1] J. K. Nyerere, *Freedom and Unity*, Dar es Salaam, 1966, pp. 186-7.

life of a culture resides in its capacity to change rather than in its capacity merely to survive.[1]

The missionary campaign against Beni in rural Tanganyika

The story of the missionary war on rural Beni is part of what President Nyerere calls colonialism's greatest crime, its assault on African cultural autonomy. Yet the crime of the missionaries in this case did not lie in their attempt to impose European styles upon Africans. It lay rather in their attempt to deny to Africans the ability to choose when they would adopt or adapt European styles, and when not.

As Beni spread into the 'Christian' countryside it everywhere encountered bitter missionary hostility. Some missionaries thought that Beni's elaborate networks of communication and what they saw as its mockery of whites, concealed a revolutionary conspiracy. Others thought that Beni was the spearhead of Islam. Yet others held neither of these alarmist views but regarded Beni as characteristic of the secular side of 'coasty' culture, from which they sought to protect their converts. Others yet again believed that Beni was an indication of a longing for aspects of European culture. But this did not predispose them any more favourably towards the dance.

Missionaries in the 1920s and 1930s had forgotten or repented of the days when their predecessors had tried to save the freed slaves from 'traditional' culture and from Islam by dressing them in European clothes and teaching them European music. Even on the Kenyan coast, and as early as the 1890s in which Beni emerged, missionaries were beginning to demand that their converts wear appropriate Swahili dress and that they should abandon European clothes. By the 1920s missionaries almost everywhere supported the idea of 'organic', tribal churches and they attempted to encourage or to compel their converts to honour local traditions. Missionaries now supported those traditional dances which they found to be consistent with morality and frowned upon innovations. Many of them felt and expressed the sharpest dislike for Africans who wore European clothes.

Moreover, quite apart from all these reasons for dislike, missionaries were aware that at one level at least they were in direct competition

[1] Others of the dances mentioned by President Nyerere have a history of diffusion and development equally as complex as that of Beni. A history of the *Lele Mama*, for example, would reveal the transmission of modes and ideas over many hundreds of miles and the adaptation of the dance form in many different situations. It would be difficult today to agree on a standard 'traditional' form of *Lele Mama*.

with Beni. They were competing for the loyalty of their teachers. There were not many literate young men in the rural areas who might organize Beni on any kind of elaborate scale. The obvious organizing group, indeed, were teachers in mission schools. And these teachers were everywhere experiencing in the 1920s and 1930s a sharp and almost catastrophic decline in status and income. Many teachers were attracted towards Beni as a method of asserting their right to leadership over the 'progressive' young men. But for their part the missionaries were not prepared to allow teachers to take action which implied criticism of mission policies about dress and conduct.

Hartwig tells us that in Bukurebe 'the missionaries and the Christian community confronted the games directly. The missionaries openly opposed them admonishing their community to refrain from following any of the games. An obvious reason for their antagonism centred around allegiance: seldom could an individual be a faithful follower of both Christianity and a game. Both theoretically required the total involvement of the person.' And Hartwig goes on to quote from a missionary report for 1922–3, which is almost certainly a reference to Beni:

> The majority of the country is thus divided into cliques, two especially . . . During the day they are more or less military parades, more or less costumed, but at night . . . it is then the true dance, that which they love, that which explains their fatigue of the day . . . Persons do not contradict you if you say that there is an intimate relation between the dance and the practice of religion . . . Those who are addicted to the dance no longer practise; they no longer pray, no longer take the sacrament, often no longer attend mass on Sunday . . . A curious thing, also, the leaders and sub-leaders of these dances are in general strayed Christians and former catechumens.[1]

A similar situation existed in the rural areas of Tabora district where Beni was danced in the early 1930s and where it was 'objected to very strongly by the White Fathers Mission at Uruwira and Christians are forbidden to take part in it'.[2] In Ufipa the Christian critics of Beni alleged that 'a couple of nights of Beni in any village are enough to

---

[1] Gerald W. Hartwig, 'The Historical and Social Role of Kerebe Music', p. 55. The quotation is from, Société des Missionaires d'Afrique, *Rapports Annuels*, 1922–3, pp. 326–7, in what I presume to be Hartwig's translation.

[2] 'Beni or Dundo Dance', Tabora District Book.

break up the village'.[1] In 1936 the report of the Benedictine Superiors' Conference held at Kwiro Mission in Mahenge noted: 'It should be remarked that, for some time now, a new dance called the *ngoma ya beni* has been spreading through the whole territory. It is a kind of dance society whose members pay dues, etc. This *ngoma ya beni* is a political secret society of communist origins. It is strictly forbidden for our Christians to join this society. One should take special care that the teachers do not participate in it.'[2]

But the fullest evidence of missionary response to Beni and to other associated dance forms comes from the Universities' Mission to Central Africa. The story is an absurd one in many ways – a dispute over inessentials, like the Vestarian Controversy. But it has important implications. The attempt to stamp out Beni involved a dispute over 'modernization', a dispute over *who* should possess the initiative in modernizing change. It seems worth telling the story briefly.

The Universities' Mission to Central Africa had worked in Tanganyika since the 1870s. It had important mission fields in Bondei and the Usambaras in north-east Tanganyika; in Masasi and Newala districts in the extreme south-east of the territory; and along the Tanganyikan shore of Lake Nyasa. Geographically these areas are widely separated from each other, but in the 1930s each area experienced a wave of enthusiasm for a new dance. In the north-east the enthusiasm was for *dansi*, which had belatedly spread from the Christian communities of the coastal hinterland into Bondei. Along the Tanganyikan shore of Lake Nyasa the enthusiasm was for *Mganda*. In Newala and Masasi the enthusiasm was for Beni itself. Thus the U.M.C.A. experience in the 1930s brought together three different dance tendencies: the *dansi* tendency which had grown out of the original condemnation of pagan *ngomas* by the missionaries of the Kenyan coast; the Beni tendency, which in some areas had been accepted as a Moslem alternative to traditional dance; and the *Mganda* tendency which represented the employment of the military mode by the African Christian societies of Nyasaland.

The U.M.C.A. were no happier with *dansi* than with Beni. 'African

[1] Anon, 'The Beni Society of Tanganyika Territory', *Primitive Man*, XI, nos 1 and 2, January and April 1938, p. 81.

[2] 'Bericht uber die Superiorenkonferenz gehalten in Kwiro, 11–13 November 1936'. I owe this reference and the translation from German to Lorne Larson. Larson's Dar es Salaam seminar paper, 'The African Voice: Protest and Improvement in the Ulanga District, 1945–54', contains a fascinating account of the contest between missionaries and their teachers over participation in dance societies.

youth is at the cross-roads', wrote a missionary from Magila station in Bondei in 1931. 'Very often this desire for advance shows itself merely in the assumption of European dress and of certain European customs . . . The bad old heathen dances are gone, as also are the village beer-drinks. In their place we have 'dansi', an adapted form of English ball-room dancing, an attempt at a European band, and a great deal of tippling . . . There may, perhaps, be no bad sin but *dansi* takes place at night and the whole atmosphere is dangerous.'[1] Three years later another missionary gave a lurid retrospect of the effects of *dansi*. 'All the native dances were thrown overboard, in the space of a few weeks, and fox-trotting took their place . . . Some of the teachers were the leaders of the dancing at that time . . . tragedy after tragedy . . . homes were broken, fierce quarrels and fighting took place.' The church intervened; pressure was put on African teachers; a meeting of teachers condemned *dansi*; and a declaration was published that no Christian could participate in it.[2]

It seems an odd episode in view of Samson Kayamba's conversion at Freretown school to 'the European dance, hence a Christian one, which ought to be imitated by all Christians'. But by the 1930s the U.M.C.A. had declared war on what it regarded as superficial Euro-peanization. The main motive for joining in *dansi*, alleged a missionary, was the 'inferiority complex' of young Africans. 'We would almost change our colour if we could', he cites them as saying; 'We must dress like the European and we must dance like the European, otherwise we are stamped as being "backward".'[3] There was only one sound way to deal with such an inferiority complex, so the U.M.C.A. argued, and that was to develop pride in Christianized but still African institutions. The young men who wanted to wear long trousers must have their wants redefined.

The same themes come out even more clearly in Masasi and Newala where the U.M.C.A. confronted Beni. In the 1930s the Bishop of Masasi was Vincent Lucas, famous for his attempts to Africanize Christian rites. Lucas had developed a Christian circumcision cere-mony; had Africanized the liturgy; and had studied traditional dances to determine which could be encouraged at church festivals. He was fiercely opposed to 'coasty' influences and to the impact of European secularism. Long trousers were a symbol for him too.

[1] 'Club or Night-School?', *Central Africa*, no. 579, March 1931, p. 55.
[2] 'How can I? Except Some Man Guide Me?', *Central Africa*, no. 614, February 1934, pp. 24–5. [3] ibid, p. 24.

'He let it be known at one stage,' writes Lucas's friend and colleague, Canon Lamburn, 'that he was prepared to teach any teacher who applied to him how to wear European clothing properly, but he did not approve of slovenly wearing of odd bits of European clothing. He took this line, it is true, to extremes. He insisted that the school boys at Chidya should wear the old-fashioned *shuka* as their school uniform until the boys were nearly in revolt in demanding to wear shorts. He would not allow girls to be taught sewing in school because he said that the African tradition was for men to do the sewing. These were obviously losing battles,' admits Lamburn, 'but at least he kept clear of a quick-step forced Europeanization.'[1]

Some of Lucas's losing battles were fought out on the Beni parade ground. Beni had certainly been danced in the Masasi district some twenty years before it became an issue between Lucas and his African Christians. The Masasi area had seen the last German stand in defence of the territory; the cathedral at Masasi had been used as a troop hospital; the Benedictine mission station at nearby Ndanda had been used as a major provisioning base for the German forces. There is no doubt that *Arinoti* and *Marini* competitions took place among the *askaris* of the German forces, and that the idea was picked up by locally recruited porters. When Lambert collected Beni songs in Nairobi at the end of the war many of them referred to this southern battle-field. 'She made ready to go to Masasi,' ran one. 'Goodbye mother! We have gone to Ndanda,' ran another.[2]

There is plenty of evidence that Beni continued to be danced at Lindi and elsewhere on the southern coast after the war. It was also danced among the Mwera to the north of the U.M.C.A. parishes. But it was either not danced in Masasi and Newala in the 1920s or not noticed by the missionaries. It seems likely that what happened was that Beni was danced there immediately after the war, when the returning missionaries found everything in such confusion that there was little opportunity for detailed supervision of village dances. Then it died out, only to revive in the 1930s in one of those spasms so typical of rural Beni.

By the 1930s Vincent Lucas was on bad terms with his teachers. Financial difficulties had compelled him to cut their pay and to

[1] Canon Lamburn to the author, 10 August 1970.

[2] H. E. Lambert, 'The Beni Dance Songs', *Swahili*, vol. 33, no. 1, 1962/3, p. 19; Anon, 'The Beni Society of Tanganyika Territory', *Primitive Man*, XI, nos 1 and 2, January and April 1938, p. 77.

withdraw established allowances.[1] Moreover, he and his European priests were noting with much concern the self-assurance – or arrogance as they called of it – being displayed by the new young teachers. In January 1929, for example, the Bishop's Chaplain, A. G. Blood, reported that Lucas 'had to go over to Chidya . . . to put some of the young teachers in their places who had been making a great nuisance of themselves', and described one of these men as 'an extreme instance of the "bolshevism" of the young teachers'.[2]

It was these young teachers who were most critical of the development policies of Lucas; who most aspired to furniture, and books, and 'modern' clothes; and who were consequently most affected by the cut-back of wages. It was not surprising that many of them took to Beni with enthusiasm. 'It was a wonderful dance,' recalls *Mwalimu* Isaya Pila, at one time Lucas's head-teacher at Masasi station, 'in which I have taken part myself.'[3]

Beni in Masasi in the 1930s was a very simplified affair without the *Arinoti–Marini* competition and without bugles or processions. But it still retained the Beni essentials – organization, modernity, and competitiveness – and these were enough to make it attractive. 'Anyone who could do the steps was welcome provided one dressed up nicely,' says Pila. 'They used to arrange themselves according to the dresses worn; the trousered people were in one semi-circle, followed by those wearing *shuka* and the women in the inner circle. It was only the drum-beaters and the person who blew the whistle that had to be experts – not everybody. When dancing the men would either hold their walking sticks or long pieces of material and dance gracefully.'[4]

'A clearing would be prepared,' remembers *Mzee* Amayulha, 'and temporary huts built. People danced for days and nights. Those who became sick were put into one of the huts where they were given tea. Because people liked tea they would prefer to be sick so that they could drink it.'[5] African clergy today remember the dance as 'very smart' and as 'very attractive' to educated Christians, 'the trousered people'.

[1] Blood to Spanton, 9 April 1929, Subject Files iiiE, Box 6, Masasi Correspondence 1928–30, USPG Archives, Westminster.

[2] Blood to Spanton, 17 January 1929, ibid. Blood had earlier written of a teacher's wedding in which 'the bridegroom (wore) European clothes which were happily quite a decent fit and he really looked quite respectable', so that Blood was inclined to be tolerant 'much as I dislike Africans in European clothes in the ordinary way'. Blood to Spanton, 3 October 1928.

[3] Interview with Isaya Pila, 25 September 1968.

[4] ibid.

[5] Interview with *Mzee* Amayulha, Mkomaindo, 23 September 1968.

Many mission teachers danced it and some organized dancing grounds at their schools.[1]

Yet with all these 'Christian' referents – the long trousers and the cups of tea – Beni in Masasi still carried with it the aura of Swahili civilization. 'Beni was associated with the Swahili language,' says Jabili Mchawala. 'It was sung in Swahili and it came into our area from the Coast. People who could sing in such a dance were esteemed very highly as Swahili even though his or her spoken Swahili was very poor.'[2] Beni was certainly danced as much by young Moslems in Masasi as by young Christians.

In either case the spread of Beni greatly disturbed Bishop Lucas. 'Certain new dangers are flowing in from the coast,' he wrote in 1930, 'especially so-called dances which are dangerously like Bolshevistic organizations, breeding impatience with all authority and threatening to undermine tribal organization and the courtesies of real African life.' In blissful ignorance of the remoter origins of Beni, he added: 'I am strongly tempted to set up a fife and drum band. I believe the coast heady dancing might come to be scorned by those who had learned to trip to the fife and drums.'[3]

Canon Lamburn tells us of the debate about Beni among the Masasi clergy:

> It was about 1934 when the dance first came into prominence in Luatala parish where I was then working. What we clergy noticed first of all was that there was a very bad moral influence at work, which was connected (as we knew in the confessional) with the Beni dance . . . Many of the missionaries went to Bishop Lucas and begged him to forbid the dance . . . He refused to do so. He said that it was of no avail to forbid such things until such time as the conscience of the African Christians themselves had been aroused to the evil of the matter . . . I had to face the trouble of the malign influence of the dance at Luatala throughout most of 1935. Meanwhile Bishop Lucas, as usual, had gathered more accurate information about the dance itself. He discussed the matter with me, and told me that he had found that the dance was organized with no little administrative skill, and that there was a whole hierarchy of officers in the dance guild, known by names such as Admiral or General; there was also a Queen who had a position of great

---

[1] Interviews with Archdeacon C. Kasoyaga, Father A. Bakari, Asst. Bishop M. Soseleje, Masasi, 25 September 1967.
[2] Interview with Jabili Mchawala, 17 September 1968.
[3] Masasi Diocesan Report, *Central Africa*, no. 570, June 1930, p. 116.

importance . . . At the dance itself one of the officers sat in the middle dressed in European clothes, and behaving in a parody of the white man's manner, while round him danced the threatening hordes of dancers. Bishop Lucas thought that the meaning of the dance was simply vengeance on the white man, and that the organization of the dance, though not in itself subversive, was at least an organization ready to be adapted to subversive aims. It was about 1937 that a meeting of the clergy, with a large African majority, unanimously asked the Bishop to forbid this dance to Christians. Having got that vote, Bishop Lucas did forbid the dance.[1]

Some missionaries were privately sceptical of Lucas's interpretation of Beni – some of them having seen the weekend processions in Mombasa.[2] But the parish log-books of the Masasi diocese are full of the contest between Beni and the church. The clergy saw Beni as part of a profound generational tension. 'Native dances are precious,' wrote the European priest in charge at Lukwikwa parish in July 1938; 'they can entertain everyone during a Church festival. But this Beni appeals only to a very few young people.'[3] 'The elders said that this dance should never be performed in their area,' noted Father Robert Namalowe in Mpindimbi parish in June 1937; 'the young men should look for another kind of dance . . . But the young men misbehaved right in front of the elders by saying firmly, "We shall perform Beni".'[4]

The missionaries believed that they could act against Beni with the support of most of the village head-men and clan-heads. In the later 1930s very vigorous steps were taken against the dance. We can follow this most clearly in Masasi parish itself. After the ban on Beni in 1938 the priest in charge at Masasi read 'the Bishop's letter on Beni' to the elders of the parish 'and they all agreed to help in stopping the dance'.[5] Beni dancing platforms everywhere in the parish were pulled down. 'The new Beni *kiwenja* at Mkuputa has been wrecked; it still has its opening decorations clinging to the wreckage,' noted the parish priest in November 1938. 'The Mwachiko one is also laid low and the Mkuti one appears to be no longer in use, but I suspect that this one has been moved to a less conspicuous place.'[6] In May 1941 Beni revived at

[1] Lamburn to author, 10 August 1970.
[2] Interview with Leader Stirling, Soni, 3 October 1972.
[3] Entry for 11 July 1938, Lukwikwa log-book, November 1937 to February 1944. Original in Swahili. The Masasi log-books are deposited in the Library of the University of Dar es Salaam.
[4] Entry for 18 July 1937, Mpindimbi log-book, 1935 to 1937. Original in Swahili.
[5] Entry for 30 October 1938, Masasi log-book, July 1938 to February 1941.
[6] ibid., entry for 6 November 1938.

Mkuti. 'On Saturday night I heard the Beni dance at Mkuti and on inquiry on Sunday I learnt that there had been a *chama* erected at Mkuti with leaders Viktor Mtendasye, Charli Rutemba and Niklas Sindi. I closed the school immediately and sent Mwalimu George Matemwe to teach at Mkomaindo. I sent word to the Mwenye [clan-head] that the school would remain closed until he with the players came to the Bishop or his representative the Archdeacon to apologize and to ask for guidance. They came today and I sent them to the Archdeacon. After much discussion they agreed to stop the dance and I sent a note to the teacher telling him to start school again.'[1]

It was shrewdly effective to strike at this modernizing dance by closing the schools. But this dramatized the dilemma of the African teachers. Many liked Beni and had danced it. Now they found themselves in the middle between the church and their fellow Christians. *Mwalimu* Mwika Twanje of Liloya parish recorded his predicament in the log-book:

> After leaving the father's company I had the company of Raphael Sungununu, the Beni dance leader. On the way he filled me with blame, alleging that I was an evil man and that I was the person responsible for the banning of the Beni dance in Liloya. He went on to allege that I am the person who asked the Europeans to ban the dance . . . He gave a spate of words against me and he said the Liloya would be the sufferer because of me.'[2]

One or two of the teachers resolved their dilemma by resigning from the service of the church and continuing to dance Beni.

This tragi-comedy is remembered by some Africans in Masasi with a particular bitterness. *They* did not see Beni as a quasi-Bolshevist organization with subversive aims. Its banning seemed to them to be a gratuitous demonstration of paternalism; a spectacular proof that the priests did not want the men to wear trousers. 'The main object of Lucas's ban,' says *Mwalimu* Isaya Pila, a man who had worked with Lucas since before the First World War and who had been involved in running the very first of the Christianized initiation rites, 'was mainly because he saw a resemblance between the dance and their dance in Europe. Since he had this superiority complex he felt that Africans were trying to advance culturally, so he banned it.'[3] And *Mzee* Amayulha tells a splendid story, myth in its relation to the facts of

---

[1] Entry for 13 May 1941, Masasi log-book, February 1941 to August 1944.
[2] Entry for 18 November 1937, Liloya log-book. Original in Swahili.
[3] Interview with Isaya Pila, 25 September 1968.

Beni history, but very revealing of the way in which many Africans in Masasi saw the ban. 'Beni was abolished by the Europeans on the excuse that they had allowed it because they were rejoicing for their victory in the war and now that war was over there was no more need for Beni. Together with Beni, shorts were also discouraged. The Europeans abolished them on the grounds that they had allowed them in order to enable people to run quickly on the battlefield but that now the war was over shorts should not be worn!'[1]

So the U.M.C.A. banned *dansi* and Beni. But the fate of *Mganda* on the Tanganyikan shore of Lake Nyasa was quite different. Though *Mganda* was in so many ways similar to Beni it came to the U.M.C.A. stations on the lake from Christian Nyasaland rather than from the Islamic coast. 'The people of Manda received *Mganda* with great approval,' recalls *Mzee* Florian Ngalawa, 'both among the ordinary Christians and the missionaries. It is played during the day and the players are smartly clad. This counter-balanced the indigenous dances.'[2]

The missionary enthusiasm for *Mganda* was strikingly expressed in 1942, when an account of Easter celebrations in the lake-side villages appeared in *Central Africa*, whose columns had previously resounded with condemnations of *dansi* and Beni.

The Christian villages in East Africa during these six weeks of Lent are strangely quiet. The wild, delirious, exhilarating throb of the drums is stilled . . . On Easter Sunday out come the drums ready prepared after six weeks of unwonted silence to beat out the stupendous message. Half an hour after the great congregation has come out from High Mass half a dozen villages have their dances in full swing. On and on it goes . . . the hardly varied tune and heavily marked rhythm . . . grips the beholder till he feels that he too must join in and dance. Dance out with every movement of his body the inexpressible wonder which is in his soul . . .

In Bantu Africa, Livingstone said, you do not ask a man what is his religion, but what does he dance? This is true today, and if it is the great Christian *Mganda* he does not dance at all in Lent. But on Easter Day he dances out again the mighty news of a Chief who died for His people and rose again on the third day.[3]

The Christians of the lake-shore soon came to think of *Mganda* as a wholly appropriate way of expressing the values of their overwhelm-

[1] Interview with *Mzee* Amayulha, 23 September 1968.
[2] Interview with Florian Ngalawa, 24 April 1968.
[3] 'The Sun Dance', *Central Africa*, no. 712, April 1942, pp. 34–5.

ingly literate society. *Mganda* came to serve the needs of an inland coast, almost as confident in its superiority in modernizing culture as had been the Swahili towns in which Beni arose.

Beni and its derivates in the industrial towns of Central Africa

One of the many paradoxes of Beni history is that just as the dance was dying out in the towns of the Tanganyikan interior it was coming to play an important role in the new industrial towns of Central Africa. But this new urban Beni was very different from the old. In Tanganyika the town had been the original home of Beni and the dance had then been exported from the towns to the countryside. In the Rhodesias Beni only reached the towns after it had been filtered through the rural environment. In the towns of Tanganyika Beni was the expression of a supra-tribal culture. In the towns of the Rhodesias Beni and *Kalela* and *Mganda* arrived as the expressions of the identity of regional groupings – the 'Bemba', the 'Bisa', the 'Nyasas'. In the Tanganyikan towns Beni was controlled by an élite of clerks and government employees. In the Rhodesian towns such men did not participate in Beni or *Kalela* or *Mganda*, which were danced by miners and domestic servants and 'lorry boys'. And over and above all these differences, of course, was the difference of the industrial towns themselves. Mombasa was becoming a polyglot modern city but Beni had risen in Mombasa at a time when it was still essentially a Swahili town and this shaping influence continued to be felt. The towns of the Copperbelt and the mining compounds of Southern Rhodesia possessed no such African urban tradition. *Beni*, and *Kalela*, and *Mganda* had to be the dances of migrant labourers or nothing.

The specialization which produced *Kalela* as essentially 'Bisa' and *Mganda* as essentially 'Nyasa', while Beni became essentially 'Bemba', did not mean that these 'tribal' entities competed with each other through dance. Competition took place *within* Beni, within *Kalela*, within *Mganda*. In the early 1930s Beni competitions were danced between different teams formed by the 'Bemba-speaking' migrants. Jones describes how *Mganda* competitions took place between 'separate Tonga, Henga, and Kikoma *Mganda* teams . . . Each team had a separate procession, drums and dances, in fact, a separate show. Each team will have its own King, Secretary, etc. The Kings will all sit together and one King is chosen by the competing teams as the supreme arbiter. The dancing *in situ* is arranged in rotation, the retiring team going outside the ring of spectators to practise its next "turn".'[1] In the same sort of way Mitchell writes of *Kalela* teams made up of 'the N'gumbo under Chief Mwewa', 'the Aushi from Chief Milambo's area', 'a composite Bisa *kalela* team drawn from all chiefdoms recognizing the paramountcy of Chief Kopa', and a breakaway Bisa team formed 'with the object of praising Chief Matipa'. 'Each dancing team is organized in the same way . . . At the head is a "king", elected by the members of the dancing team to be the general organizer and administrator of the team. He is also their treasurer: the team members pay their subscriptions to him when they go to another Copperbelt town to compete with other *kalela* dancers, or whenever they hold a feast.'[2]

At the same time, though, there was an indirect competition with all other kinds of dance, which comes out very clearly in Mitchell's account. 'A casual stroll through the Management Board Location on a Sunday afternoon is enough to demonstrate the overwhelming popularity of *Kalela* over all other tribal dances with the African spectators. While there may be a handful of people watching other dances, the *Kalela* arena is thronged with spectators who obviously are enjoying themselves.'[3]

Competition among Beni or *Mganda* or *Kalela* teams was often more of a method of establishing friendly relations with fellow 'homeboys' than an indication of serious rivalries. But sometimes this competition could lead to violence, just as the rivalry of the Beni moieties did in the Swahili towns. The remarkable urban missionary, R. J. Moore, describes a performance of *Mganda* in a Northern Rhodesian urban location in the late 1930s:

Above the hubbub a noise like a drum and comb band is heard. There is another diversion as the Angoni band very impressively marches in. People throng to watch. It appears like a comic opera, but it is serious. They come in columns of four, led by a captain flourishing a wooden sword. They all wear paper pill-box hats and silk sashes. Four rows of buglers blow their instruments made from gourds. The big drum booms, rows of 'soldiers' follow. The whole thing is half dance, half parade. They advance in perfect step, two paces, and point their canes to the right, back a pace and point them to the left; then march a few paces, and do it again. The band goes

[1] A. M. Jones, op. cit.
[2] Clyde Mitchell, op. cit., pp. 2–3. Mitchell is here describing the situation as it existed in 1951.
[3] ibid., p. 5.

in one direction and the block of men in another; they finally unite again at the other side of the ground.

'They're the fellows who had a competition with the Tumbuka in the compound,' someone says. 'It ended in a fight. You should have seen the compound native police sweating away, taking metal pipe ends and bicycle chains away from the fighters. But as soon as they threw them away, someone else picked them up. There were two Europeans watching; it was no concern of theirs. A fight in the villages would have stopped if a European came along. It's different here, isn't it?'[1]

It was Moore who made the most thorough and compassionate analysis of the Copperbelt environment of the late 1930s and early 1940s in which Beni and *Mganda* and *Kalela* thrived. The keynote of his analysis is precisely the realization that 'it's different here'. Europeans expected the urban African worker to live as simply and economically as the 'traditional' villager and to make 'traditional' provision for his welfare. Yet this was impossible. Even in the villages, Moore wrote, 'if the country man has a few shillings left after paying tax he invariably spends them on "luxuries" such as clothes . . . Even in very remote places a man manages to collect a few shillings . . . the cloth is purchased and his simple needs are met for a year. Shorts and shirt are made, worn and continually patched.' Unlike the U.M.C.A. missionaries in Masasi, Moore did not deplore these developments or regard them as mere emulation of the Europeans. 'Luxuries of fifteen or twenty years ago,' he wrote, 'are now necessities.' And in a striking passage he emphasized the many practical and functional reasons for African expenditure on modern clothing:

> Some employers argue that the Bantu do not need to be cluttered up with all our sartorial adornments; that because the African can play football without boots and live with scanty clothing he need provide himself with little more than a loin cloth . . . [But] a man going to work in all weathers needs a raincoat . . . the school teacher cannot walk to his work with his clothes under his arm and stand shivering before a hilarious class. The changed life of a full time worker calls for many of the minor accessories of civilization for which allowance is seldom made. The African urban dweller today,

[1] R. J. B. Moore, *These African Copper Miners. A Study of the Industrial Revolution in Northern Rhodesia with principal reference to the Copper Mining Industry*, London, 1948, pp. 52–3. Moore worked as a missionary on the Copperbelt from 1933 to his death in 1943.

whatever his work, can no more exist without a smart rig-out of clothes than he could have managed yesterday without bow and arrow.

African workers, Moore asserted, experienced 'a constant thwarting of their ambitions owing to their low wages'. They saw that a few privileged African clerks were able to achieve these ambitions – 'on entering a *boma* office to buy a stamp or post a letter, the African sees a fellow-being immaculately clad in white drill suit, with a tie and shoes'. They envied these men. But above all they resented 'the limitless resources and wealth' of the Europeans; the careless expenditure of those who demanded such austerity from their African employees. In this context the 'very smart European suitings', the silk sashes and pill-box hats of *Mganda*; the 'well-pressed grey slacks, neat singlets, and well-polished shoes' of *Kalela*; were affirmations of the right to live conveniently and with dignity in the 'different' world of the towns.[1]

Moreover, African workers were obliged to create for themselves a sense of community and some sort of mutual help organizations. The dance associations functioned in varying degrees as mutual assistance societies. One of the variations of Beni which appeared on the Copper-belt was *nyakasanga*, a form of the dance which had developed among the Luvale, Luchazi, and Chokwe. C. M. N. White describes how the *nyakasanga* teams 'contribute to assist members in distress, pay a fare back to a rural area and buy some goods to take back with him if a member is destitute, pay for a box as a coffin to ensure that a member dying in town has a proper funeral'.[2] Koma-Koma emphasizes the exchange of gifts and food and the clubbing together of members to fit out the King and other officers with appropriate smartness which characterized both rural and urban *Mganda*.[3]

In the Southern Rhodesian mining compounds, indeed, it was often difficult to draw a meaningful line between dance associations and more formally constituted welfare societies. Inquiring into Beni in the early 1920s the Southern Rhodesian authorities discovered that it performed a number of mutual benefit functions. At the same time, one of the most active of the formal Burial Societies turned out to be structured almost exactly on Beni lines. This was the Port Herald Burial Society, which was founded in Salisbury in 1918, and which had branches at Bulawayo, Umtali, Gatooma, Umsweswe, Gwelo, and Shamva. 'The

---

[1] Moore, op. cit., pp. 63, 67, 75.
[2] White's account of *nyakasanga* is cited by Mitchell, op. cit., p. 20.
[3] W. P. Koma-Koma, *M'ganda Kapena Malipenga*, pp. 26–7.

society was structured hierarchically, with a King at the head, and other titles included the "Governor", the "General" and the "Doctor". . . . While the member designated as "Doctor" did not do actual medical work himself, his duty was "to visit all members daily, and if he finds any of them sick he is to see that such persons' condition is brought to the notice of his employer".'[1]

Bruce Fetter emphasizes this aspect of Beni in his account of the dance history of Elisabethville:

> Mbeni was a useful tool for adapting to new conditions in Elisabethville. Europeans were now in full control of recruitment; as a result, chiefs had few contacts with the men who went to the city. Thanks to lower death rates and improved living conditions, many Africans decided to remain at work for Europeans rather than returning to their villages. The ethnic character and political organization of the Mbeni association and its imitators such as Kalela, offered a means of survival in the city. Men from the same region used the clubs as a means of sharing their resources, burying their dead, and offering hospitality to newcomers . . . The associations, in caring for new arrivals and for the sick, were performing important social functions on which the Belgian government and companies were unwilling or unable to spend money.[2]

Beni and African protest in the industrial towns

Wherever Europeans came across Beni they were suspicious of it. The British were hostile to Beni in the Tanganyikan towns; the missionaries were hostile to it in the Tanganyikan countryside. But in the new industrial towns and mining compounds Beni aroused the most alarm and suspicion of all. The mining companies feared that any organized association of Africans would increase the danger of strikes; the colonial administrations were worried by the security danger in the congested and unpredictable compounds.

Thus the Belgians were hostile to Beni in Katanga. 'During the Depression,' writes Fetter, 'the dance associations continued to play an important role in the welfare of Elisabethville's Africans, but they encountered increasing opposition from Belgian authorities . . . In 1934 the territorial administrator for Elisabethville banned public

---

[1] I. R. Phimister, 'The Shamva Mine Strike of 1927: An Emergent African Proletariat', Henderson Seminar Paper, University of Rhodesia, Salisbury, 1972, pp. 28–9.
[2] Fetter, 'Elisabethville: Secondary Center for the Dispersion of Kalela', pp. 3–4.

dances, a blow which deprived the associations of their raison d'être.'[1] In Southern Rhodesia the Chamber of Mines was alarmed at reports of organized drill among African mine-workers – in fact performances of Beni – and expressed the fear that the dance societies might become 'the basis of labour movements'.[2]

Such fears found their most lurid expression in the work of the right-wing journalist, Daniel Thwaites, who sounded an alarm in 1936 over the dangerous potentialities of African nationalism. Thwaites described the Beni societies of the Belgian Congo and Angola as devised by a 'master mind' to attract the support of urban Africans and to play upon 'all the weaknesses and all the aspirations of the natives . . . [affording] opportunity for dressing and mimicry, for mercenariness, love of debauchery, the passion for shows'. In Thwaites's view Beni and its mutations constituted 'a cancerous growth of racial hatred deliberately cultivated on modern lines by a master mind well versed in native lore, with a profound knowledge of how to make the complicated appeal to native psychology, of how to blend subtly the native's primitive aspirations to belong to a secret society, feed his animal appetites and gratify his aspirations to ape the white man'. Thwaites interpreted the use of Belgian and Portuguese titles by the associations in the Congo and Angola as preparatory to a take-over. 'The object of the society is to provide a native understudy for all known white men whether in Belgium or the colony itself . . . from the head of the state down.' When they were ready the leaders of the association would strike; the downfall of Belgian rule was toasted at each dance; and at Loanda there had already been an attempt to poison the European population so that their understudies could take over.[3]

After this stirring stuff it comes as something of an anti-climax that Beni can be reliably connected with so few instances of protest in the Central African towns. Beni was danced by the Nyasa miners at Shamva and is remembered as having been 'important', but the most recent study of the Shamva strike of 1927 concludes that Beni played no part in its organization.[4] Clyde Mitchell found no protest dimension to *Kalela*.[5] Oral tradition so far collected in Central Africa emphasizes the 'tribal' and mutual aid roles of Beni but has nothing to say about

[1] Fetter, op. cit., p. 5.

[2] Phimister, op. cit., p. 26.

[3] Daniel Thwaites, *The Seething African Pot. A Study of Black Nationalism*, London, 1936.

[4] Phimister, op. cit.

[5] Mitchell, op. cit., p. 12.

protest. Clearly the dance associations were not primarily or essentially protest organizations, except in so far as the efforts of African workers to make a place for themselves in the towns were a manifestation of the creative side of protest.

But the Beni dancing teams did play a part in the most spectacular of Central African industrial protests – the Copperbelt upheavals of 1935. The manner in which they did so is very revealing of the significance of Beni in the life of African workers. Before 1935 the existence of the Beni associations had gone almost unnoticed in official reports and correspondence. Then, at the height of the disturbances, the discovery of 'uniformed' men, of banners, and of other mysterious symbols had caused a momentary alarm. For a moment there were fears of a paramilitary conspiracy.

The Russell Commission, which inquired into the 1935 riots in the calmer atmosphere which followed them, received plenty of evidence about the Beni associations of the Copperbelt. But in reaction to the earlier panic, the Commission played down the role of Beni. It identified another scapegoat and in its final report named the Watch Tower movement as the main source of sedition and disturbance.

The Commissioners were certainly correct to regard Beni as primarily concerned with recreation and welfare. They were certainly correct to regard Watch Tower as much more explicitly ideological. Yet there can be little doubt that in fact the Beni societies were much more deeply involved in the organization of the strikes than was Watch Tower. Ian Henderson, who has made the most recent study of the upheavals, has summed it up in this way: 'The clerks, mainly Nyasas, provided the initial impetus and some worldly knowledge; the strike was then spear-headed by the Mbeni and the Bemba.'[1]

In an earlier, East African, stage of Beni history the clerks would have been leading members of the associations and could have used them directly for communication and planning among themselves. In the 1930s and on the Copperbelt the clerks had no time for Beni, except as a means of communicating with the underground workers. 'The Mbeni was a society mainly composed of Bemba-speaking peoples from the Northern Province,' writes Henderson, 'who formed a majority on the mines . . . The Mbeni society was genuinely a dance society that met to give its members amusement . . . But it was also an organization which, in the 1930s at least, was run by men of prestige and standing among their fellow workers. As such it offered them

[1] Ian Henderson, 'The Copperbelt Disturbances, 1935 and 1940', forthcoming.

recognition of their superior ability or education outside the tribal context . . . It had a ready-made organization which covered Luanshya/Roan, Kitwe/Nkana, and Mufulira. The King, the Governor, the Doctor, and other officials were chosen from among the powerful men in the towns, who had leadership qualities and who had earned the respect of their fellow workers.'[1]

Through Beni, then, the Nyasa clerks were able to make contact with men who commanded considerable influence over the Bemba miners; who were in correspondence with each other; and whose dance performances drew great crowds to whom instructions could be given. So at Mufulira the tax increase was announced on one day, and 'by the next day the clerks were in contact with the Mbeni dance society, and the African workers were on strike'. 'The afternoon of 12 May passed in dancing and drum-beating. Blacklegs were assaulted . . . William Sankata, King of the Mbeni, and two officials, Ngostino Mwamba and James Mutali, seem to have done the organizing.' Beni was also involved, though less centrally, in the strikes at Nkana and Luanshya. 'Mbeni songs were sung at strike meetings at Mufulira,' writes Henderson, 'and the Mbeni cross was used on strike notices at Nkana.' Thus, he concludes, 'though the Nyasa clerks were useful to the strikers as slogan writers and advisors, the strike was led by powerful Bemba militants on all three mines, most of them Mbeni officials'.[2]

These men were not militant *because* they were members of Beni. Nor did they join Beni because they were militant. It was not Beni but the economic and social problems of the Copperbelt which made most Bemba miners and their leaders into militants. But these men were *leaders* partly because of their command of the dance associations; their leadership qualities had been recognized by their election to Beni high office. Beni may have been abandoned by the educated élite but it was still a school for leadership; an expression of rational needs rather than an irrational 'Cargo Cult' mimicry; and an expression of creative vitality.

[1] Henderson, op. cit.
[2] ibid.

5 *The End of Beni*

Introduction

With a few exceptions Beni died out by the 1960s – died in Lamu as much as in the rural areas of Central Africa. In a variety of local adaptations variants of Beni continue to exist today but Beni as a distinct, recognizable, and related genre is dead. Roughly speaking the death of Beni coincided with the death of formal colonialism in eastern Africa. It is tempting to suggest that Beni came to an end because it was no longer necessary or fitting to emulate Europeans; that Beni was discarded because it was too obviously part of an era of cultural emasculation. The evidence and arguments already presented, however, make it very difficult to advance such a simplistic view. In many places Beni and its derivates had come to be thought of as fully African – indeed, as characteristic of aspects of local culture. In other places Beni was seen as at least in cultural opposition to the whites. Almost everywhere the modifications made in the Beni mode had shown a continuing cultural vitality which makes the idea of emasculation suspect.

Yet there seems to be some connection between the very minor process of the death of Beni and the major process of decolonization. Decolonization was partly brought about by, and in turn accelerated, a more general process of secularization, of increasing cultural autonomy and initiative. The difference between the experience of the First and the Second World Wars is in point here. The First World War had a tremendous impact on Beni, stamping a military character upon its symbolism and resulting in an enormous diffusion of the Beni mode. The war was intensively fought on an African field of battle in which an African *ngoma* seemed especially relevant, and its consequence was a re-assertion of European paternalism. The Second World War was very different. The young men who were caught up in it saw action far outside eastern Africa and returned with memories of all sorts of new cultural experiences. A minor result of this was that the war gave little or no stimulus to Beni, and that often the returning ex-soldiers introduced newer forms of dance and music which they had encountered on their travels. A major result was that the contest which once again broke out between missionary paternalism and the cultural tastes of the young men was now more fiercely contested on the African side.

Lorne Larson's work on Ulanga district is very significant here. In Ulanga Beni had been danced right up to the beginning of the war. But when the young men returned from the war they brought with them a development of *dansi*. Larson writes:

> One of the easiest things to trace of the *askari* heritage was a new dance movement which swept the district – *danzi*, European-style dancing . . . While on military service, *askaris* had learnt European-style dancing in entertainment centres, and a few of them had learnt to play the guitar. Philomoni Hasani Namkipa, reputedly the most popular guitar player in the period under discussion, recalls how *askaris* based in Nairobi were given the opportunity of adult education classes, and that he and many others opted for music lessons. There, he was taught by Italian internees who eventually made him a guitar which he brought back to the Ulanga district, where over the years he played dances throughout the district and in Morogoro and Kilosa, exchanging musical skills and knowledge with other ex-*askari* musicians. Spread by the talents of these musicians, *danzi* became an instant success – even in the remotest parts of the rural areas.[1]

Larson uses this as one instance of a more general process of innovation by ex-*askaris*. He goes on to show how the innovation was bitterly contested in the post-war years by missionaries in Ulanga, who repeated the earlier tragi-comedy of the Masasi attack on Beni. But the point now was that time was against the missionaries. They might still continue into the 1950s to discipline teachers who took part in *dansi* or to forbid Christian congregations to do so. But the whole nature of their relationship to African society was changing. Partly, of course, this was the result of decolonization which made it very difficult for white missionaries to lay down the cultural law. But in addition it was the result of the process of secularization, which even before independence had broken the missionary monopoly of education and provided alternative sources of employment for young men who wanted to defy the missionaries. And it was the result of the process of widening communications, particularly through the radio. As

[1] Lorne Larson, 'The African Voice: Protest and Improvement in the Ulanga District, 1945–54', p. 6.

Larson comments, the fuss over *dansi* seems very odd only twenty years later; 'modern' dancing is taken for granted today by 'the post-Independence generation with its ubiquitous transistor radio and the popular acceptance of the "Congo Jazz" music tradition'.[1] The point, of course, is that the 'popular acceptance' of Congo Jazz has struck a blow not only at missionary cultural colonialism but at Beni as well.

The movement of the Beni mode across the whole of eastern Africa was a spectacular enough diffusion in itself. But by comparison with the movement of today's musical fashions it was very slow. In the newly open cultural situation in eastern Africa, fashion became the main executioner of Beni. Fashion did not so much affect those manifestations of Beni which had come to be valued as 'traditional', but wherever Beni itself was still danced because it was thought to be 'smart' it was very vulnerable to fashion.

The last days of Beni in Lamu

In the long run, it seems, these generalizations are applicable even to Beni in Lamu. Still, Lamu remained a very different cultural environment from the up-country areas. For one thing Lamu cultural manifestations had never been under missionary supervision. For another the concept of fashion had a very different history in Lamu. Throughout the nineteenth and early twentieth centuries Lamu dance and musical culture had been nothing if not responsive to fashion and since fashions were carried directly to Lamu by sea the town had experienced and responded to a very great variety of new modes. The remarkable feature of Beni in Lamu had been its capacity to absorb each new fashion in turn and yet to continue to remain recognizably Beni. While Lamu dance and music remained geared essentially to *collective* assertions of fashionableness, Beni could still flourish. What undercut Beni in Lamu, so it seems, was the individualization of music fashion, once again connected with the popularity of the radio, though in this instance it was not so much Congo Jazz as the modernized music of the Middle East which achieved popular acceptance.

These factors of cultural individualism, of contact with the wider Islamic world, and at the same time a variety of secularization, came to transform Lamu musical life by the 1960s. But the pace of change was slow and in the 1950s Beni enjoyed a very real, even if deceptive, flowering in Lamu and its hinterland.

[1] Larson, 'The African Voice', p. 6.

It will be remembered that by the 1930s control of the big Beni associations in Lamu had passed out of the hands of the plantation-owning aristocracy and into the hands of a more 'popular' leadership. This new leadership had had very little chance to show what it could do, however, because of the financial crisis of the depression years. The coming of the Second World War had a further restraining effect on Lamu Beni. During the first two years of the war, while fighting was in progress in Italian Somaliland, all *ngomas* were banned in Lamu town, though they were danced again as part of the rejoicings over the capture of Mogadishu and Kismayu.[1] Nor did the war bring any economic stimulus to Lamu, which became in Dr Salim's words, 'even more isolated from the rest of the country'. Little appeared to have changed in Lamu – 'the old unhurried routine remained virtually undisturbed'.[2]

Some people have tended to explain the persistence of Beni in Lamu into the 1950s as a result of this unchanging conservatism and sluggishness, and it seems to be true that the end result of 'modern' influences on Lamu has been the decline of Beni. But this is a question of the nature of change. Change and vitality *within* the assumptions of Lamu collectivity were good for Beni; change *away* from them undermined it. The flowering of Beni in the 1950s was certainly not a result of continued stagnation. It was the result of a renewed economic vitality which gave new vigour to the institutions of the town.

In the early 1950s the copra trade improved; the cattle trade with the Somali flourished. This economic progress was accompanied by the first signs of intellectual and political change. 'Even in Lamu,' writes Dr Salim, 'the [Mau Mau] emergency was having more influence than that of economic benefits. The "sleeping hollow" of the coastal strip was feeling more and more part of a wider entity . . . A section of the younger generation learnt readily and avidly to listen . . . to anti-British and anti-colonial broadcasts from Bombay and Cairo.'[3]

Eventually the involvement of the young people in the wider post-war world brought an end to their involvement in Beni. But this did not happen in the 1950s. With the revival of trade more money became available for the costs of carnival; with the boom in the cattle trade

---

[1] A. A. M. Lawrence, 10 November 1941, 'Lamu and the War, 1939–41', a minute now among the collection of documents in the library of the Curator of Lamu Museum.

[2] A. I. Salim, 'The Swahili-speaking communities of the Kenya Coast, 1895–1965', pp. 443–5.

[3] ibid., p. 454.

more cows became available for competitive slaughter at Beni 'picnics'. In 1952 the Lamu Annual Report, beginning to detect signs of a renaissance in the town, commented that 'it was encouraging to see a revival of weekly processions of the three town bands members of which have considerable musical talent but lack an experienced bandsman to train them properly'.[1]

The 1950s became a great time for Lamu Beni. The new world did not seem such a different place from the old world after all. The symbols of colonial authority remained much the same. In 1954 the Kenya Police Band arrived in Lamu, 'astonishing the local population by its bearing, its precision, and its musical ability'. In 1954 also there were 'signs everywhere of a re-awakening that perhaps reflects the renaissance which is now apparent throughout the Arab world'. This did not undercut Beni either, since the dance was well integrated into Lamu's Islamic festivals. It was undoubtedly danced at the *maulidi* festival, celebrated in 1954 'with Lamu's accustomed abandon' and attended by pilgrims from Mogadishu, Mombasa, Zanzibar, Dar es Salaam, Tanga, and Kismayu.[2]

The climax to this renewed era of festivity came in 1956. Several thousand visitors attended *maulidi*, while in July 'another Lamu social occasion, of a very light-hearted nature, took place'. In that month of the year, wrote the District Commissioner:

> Lamu has a large population (sailors, in particular, mostly being at home here prior to their cruises) so the population is able to utilize its surplus energy in processions and music. For these processions there are two main rival teams, the 'Scotch' (from the north part of the town) and the 'Kambaa' (from the south), each with its own band (mainly trumpets and drums). Between these two teams there is considerable rivalry; in fact, care has to be taken that there is no head-on collision in one of Lamu's narrow streets, as neither is disposed to give way to the other. The processions go in for fancy dress, upon which the ingenuity exercised is remarkable. On the night of the 15th, the two teams had a special parade at the conclusion of which the District Commissioner was called upon to judge which was the best. Many of the costumes were cowboys (as could be expected) but the Scotch, in particular, in addition produced certain costumes of astonishing originality, including a squad of peers in full array, none lacking the Order of the Garter! The Scotch thus won the costume prize easily but the Kambaa won the

---

[1] Lamu Annual Report, 1952.   [2] ibid., 1954.

prize for the band. Both bands were then called to the front and played God Save the Queen.[1]

These Beni processions of the mid-1950s are remembered vividly in Lamu. Men now in their mid-twenties remember seeing the processions as children; remember the flaring pressure lamps at night, the cattle heads carried on poles, the lavish expenditure once again possible after hard times. Men now in their late thirties and forties treasure photographs of themselves dressed in the costumes that won the prize for the *Scotchi*.[2]

The renewal of carnival made a deep impression on many visitors to Lamu as well. Even in its last days Beni had the capacity to expand. It was in the mid-1950s that Beni came to Faza and the Bajun villages north of Lamu for the first time. Faza village was divided into two competitive moieties, Kwatongani and Kwatini. It was the men from Kwatongani who first out-did their rivals by importing Beni. Previously the two factions had competed at *Goma*, *Ndongwe*, and *Kidurenge*. But sailors and boatmen from Kwatongani had witnessed and participated in the Beni processions in Lamu, had learnt how to play the instruments and how the dance was organized. They bought a big drum from the *Yangi* Beni of Lamu; a kettle drum was obtained from Nairobi; a patron was chosen – *Bwana* Ulaya, a boatman on an *Mtepe* dhow; and they practised the dance. When ready they paraded in three files, the front line wearing 'full suit', ties, shoes; the middle line wearing long white trousers and white shirts; the rear line wearing black trousers, red shirts, and khaki hats, like cowboys. The leader of the dance carried a cane and went up and down the lines inspecting his men.

The innovation was a tremendous success. The Kwatini faction was dismayed by the effect of the booming big drum and by the crowds who gathered to watch Beni being danced in Kwatongani location. The Kwatongani men called their new dance team *Rarua*, implying that they were ready and able to tear down anything that got in their way.[3]

[1] Lamu Annual Report, 1956.

[2] I was shown the family album of Ahmed Bwana Mkuu, who works as a doctor and circumcisor. In the album, along with photos of weddings and family celebrations, are three pictures of Beni in the 1950s, showing Ahmed himself in full Scottish dress and two of his friends as peers.

[3] Interview with Omari Badi and Bunu Madi, Kwatongani, Faza, 20 October 1971. Omari Badi, now a councillor on Lamu Council, was a youth leader of *Rarua*; Bunu Madi, now a boat-owner in his 50s, was an organizing elder. During the interview they expressed a key axiom of coastal Beni. *Rarua* did not compete with Beni groups in Chundwa or other villages because 'in dances one competes *within* villages not between them'.

Kwatini had to find a reply. At first they hired drummers and a big drum from the Lamu *Scotchi*. Then a migrant from Kwatini, who had prospered in Nairobi, took pity on his location mates. This was Omar Mohamed Khatmiy, who ran a hotel in Nairobi and who had been detained by the British for supplying members of Mau Mau with food. Politically conscious and an enthusiast for modern education, without which he was convinced that his coastal people would fall far behind, he now remembers Beni as mere foolishness. But in the mid-1950s, 'for the sake of my people', he bought a big drum and a kettle drum at an auction in Nairobi and sent them back to Kwatini.[1]

The men of Kwatini then formed the *Kingi* association. Under the command of Ali Kombo they marched in three lines wearing kilts made of *kikoi* cloth, shirt, and cloak. But, alas, the drum from Nairobi proved a humiliating disappointment. It was too small. Its beat was drowned out by the boom of the *Rarua* drum. *Rarua* informants boast that one encounter was enough; after that humiliation, they say, *Kingi* never danced again. In fact the confrontation was longer drawn out and climaxed in tragedy.

In May 1956 the taunts of *Rarua* proved more than the men of Kwatini could endure. A fight broke out between the two Beni groups, and later, after the fight had broken up, one of the Kwatini men went in search of one of his rivals, 'who died'.[2] 'To indicate how dangerous dances of this nature can be,' reported the District Commissioner, 'a riot occurred at Faza on 3–4 May between two teams, "Kingi" and "Rarua", and a man was killed. As a result of this permission was withheld for further dances at Faza for some months.'[3]

In fact there was never another competition between the *Kingi* and *Rarua*, even though Beni as a mode of dance survived into the early 1960s. Meanwhile Beni in Lamu was beginning once again to falter. In 1957 'the usual dancing and Band competition took place in Lamu' but 'the award of only one prize for costume, dancing, and band seems to have caused some concern, jealousy, and *fitina*'.[4] In 1959 the Sultan of Zanzibar paid a visit to Lamu and his band played a concert on the sea-front. But despite this reminder of old times, Beni was flagging. Between 1957 and 1961 there was no full-scale competition between *Kambaa* and *Scotchi*. In 1961, 'after four years the dancing competition

---

[1] Interview with Omar Khatmiy, Kwatini, 20 October 1972.
[2] Interview with Mohamed Othman, Faza, 20 October 1972. Mohamed Othman is keeper of what remains of the *Kingi* drums.
[3] Lamu Annual Report, 1956.
[4] ibid., 1957.

between the two "Bands", *Kamba Mbofu* and *Arabian Scotch* was revived. The costumes were spectacular but the dancing was dull'.[1]

There is some dispute in Lamu oral testimony about the dating of the end of Beni. Some say that this 1961 competition was the last occasion of full Beni pomp and that with the movement towards Kenyan independence everyone was too interested in politics to bother about Beni. Others say that Beni was danced on Independence Day 1963 though not in full dress, and that it was lack of sympathy from the new government which brought the dance to its end. This and other differences of opinion can probably be accounted for by the fact that there were many different levels of Beni activity. The elaborate processions might end and the dance itself go on; the dance itself might cease to be danced but the songs might continue to be sung or the big drum continue to be used. There are still many traces of Beni to be seen in Lamu – a man, now elderly, whom everyone still calls *Kingi* because he was the famous and athletic leader of the *Scotchi*; the big *Scotchi* drum which is still used at weddings or in the victory celebrations of football teams; the participation in marches on Kenyatta Day of groups of men who in the past marched together in Beni. But for all intents and purposes we can agree with Adam Ismail, nephew of Abdalla Zena and of Abdalla's sister, Salima Zena, who inherited the family interest in the *Kingi* association. 'Salima Zena died in August 1963, three months before Independence. By that time everything was finished.'[2]

But why was everything finished when Beni had been so strong in the 1950s? On this there was more disagreement in Lamu oral testimony than on any other question. Some said that the colonial government had banned the dance just before independence; others said that the new Kenyan government had refused permission for the bands to practise and had criticized Beni as time-wasting folly. But the colonial authorities certainly did not ban Beni and it seems that the Beni impulse was dying before independence.

The real reason seems to have been the changing attitudes of the next generation of young men. By the time the Dutch sociologist, Prins, carried out his fieldwork in Lamu in 1957 Beni had come to depend almost entirely on what he called 'youth culture'. Prins found that the public opposition of the two moieties of Mkomani and Langoni was still going on but that the members of the big families

[1] Lamu Annual Report, 1961.
[2] Interview with Adam Ismail, Lamu, 23 October 1972.

had withdrawn from this competition. The ancient dualism was still expressed, Prins thought, in the processions of *Kambaa* and *Scotchi*, but 'it may well be that the observed or inferred "total social fact" of dual organization may soon become a thing of the past, the many spheres in which the binary principle had been active dwindling to the sole sphere of song-and-dance so characteristic for present-day Lamu youth culture'.[1]

In fact Prins was observing in 1957 the last days even of Beni song-and-dance as an expression of the old locational rivalry. The youth culture was changing. The middle-aged men who used to dance Beni in the 1950s, and who were my informants in Lamu, view this change without pleasure or approval. Young men have had fancy ideas put into their heads through the school system, which has developed rapidly in Lamu district since independence. Young men do not wish to bother to put in the time and the effort that was required to make a success of Beni – they would rather merely put on a record and dance with a few friends. To organize a successful Beni society required managerial skill, discipline, a desire to function in the total community. Young men today are lazily individualistic.

These denunciations of the new generation ring ironically like the denunciations which the Reformist Islamic elders once levelled at the Beni generations themselves. In the high days of Lamu Beni there was a constant generational tension as the young men shouldered their elders aside impatiently in order to seize control of the associations. The indictment of youth by a former Beni generation for lack of interest in the dance is a very clear sign that the Beni *ngoma* is at last dead in Lamu after sixty years of vigorous life.[2]

The last days of Beni in Mombasa

The present situation of Beni in the other towns of the Kenyan coast is much the same as in Lamu. At Malindi the competition of *Kingi*

[1] A. H. J. Prins, *Didemic Lamu: Social Stratification and Spatial Structure in a Muslim Maritime Town*, Groningen, 1971, p. 54. Prins visited Lamu in 1957, 1965, and 1968 but remarks that in his book 'the time lapse between the visits is disregarded'. This means that his book, published in 1971, still speaks of the Beni societies and their competition as if they remained an active part of Lamu life.

[2] None of my informants in Lamu, of whatever generation, gave the opinion that Beni had been a bad thing because it was too 'European' or displayed a colonial mentality. However younger informants tended to stress that locational rivalry in itself had been a bad thing; had diverted the people of Lamu at a time when they needed unity; and had diverted energies from development. Expressions of rivalry continue, however, in football matches, in competitions between schools, and so on.

and *Sultani* has ended; the brass instruments are 'finished'; but the big drums of the two societies are still used at weddings and to lead processions on public holidays.[1] At Mombasa the memory of Beni is still vivid and some of its symbols still have meaning but the competitions have ceased and organized societies no longer exist. Yet, just as in Lamu, the period after the Second World War was a period of spreading influence for Mombasa Beni as well as a period of eventual decline.

The story is well told in George Mkangi's summary account of his research on Beni in Mombasa. Mkangi emphasizes that before the Second World War Beni in Mombasa was a matter of prestige rather than of profit and that the leaders of Beni were prepared to spend great amounts of money. During the Second World War there was great activity in Mombasa port and much prosperity in the town. But 'after 1945 an economic wind of change blew'. Mkangi describes what followed:

> People could no longer launch lavish *Gwarides* without incurring heavy debts. Consequently *Kingi*, *Skotchi*, and *Sadla* changed their non-economic stance. Instead of competing for popularity only, they took to playing Rhumba and Jazz music and literally threw themselves into the open market for hiring. With this new trend they strove to win as many adherents as possible outside Mombasa. A revolution had taken place, and they were now the *Kingi* Jazz Band, the *Skotchi* Jazz Band, and the *Sadla* Jazz Band . . . These new Jazz Bands came to be known as 'Brass Bands Jazz' or *Brasso*.[2]

As a result of this spread outside Mombasa and of the development of a Jazz style, the Beni tradition came into effective contact with other dance traditions for the first time in the late 1940s and 1950s. One of these was the Christian tradition of *dansi*. In the Mombasa hinterland *dansi* was no innovating novelty, as it was in Ulanga district in the 1950s. It had been established among the Christian communities for several decades, and it had developed a fierce internal rivalry.

'Joining Kayamba's *Weruni* Dancing Club in Kaloleni,' Mkangi tells us, 'was a voluntary affair. But as time went by opposition to it sprang up and the rival clubs came to represent different groupings,

---

[1] Interview with Swaleh Ali bin Swaleh and Khamis bin Athman, Malindi, 24 October 1972.
[2] George Mkangi's summary of his interview with Samson Kayamba, October 1968, and his overview of 'Beni Research', 1968.

just as the old *ngomas* had done. Another Dancing Club was formed
in Kaloleni by Henry Harrison, called the O.K. Club. To meet its
challenge Kayamba changed the name of his to Good Hope Club
in 1935. The two clubs fought for popularity and for nothing more.
They had no economic motives. They let people in free of charge.
What interested them mostly was which club would entice more
dancers and more spectators. In fact it was the organizers who incurred debts but they were well compensated if they pulled in bigger
crowds than their rivals.

There was plenty of rivalry between Good Hope and O.K. An
open contest for followers ensured in 1935 . . . The Kayamba group
called the Harrison group *Adzakudza*, literally 'those who came',
since Harrison and most of his followers were descendants of the
freed slaves of Freretown, Rabai and Ribe. Kayamba and his followers called themselves *Enyenji*, the Aborigines. The contest between *Adzakudza* and *Enyenji* became tense and spread to Ribe and
Rabai. In those places all those who were descendants of freed slaves
followed and supported Harrison, himself a freed slave. The rest
joined Kayamba.

This division was mostly emphasized by Kayamba and his party
as a propaganda device intended to isolate Harrison from the
majority and to ensure support for Good Hope. This technique
worked and in 1935 an open contest was held in which Kayamba's
Good Hope Club attracted a larger audience than Harrison with
his O.K. Dancing Club. This defeat made O.K. disband.[1]

But Kayamba was not without rivals for long. Soon the Harrison
supporters formed the *Hawii* Jazz Band Club. Something fresh was
needed to re-assert the dominance of Kayamba's followers. The something new was Beni, or *Brasso*. Kayamba made contact with Mombasa
Beni only in the 1940s. He did not join any of the societies but was
able to take advantage of their new desire for profitable arrangements.
He hired out the *Kingi*, *Scotchi*, or *Sadla* bands, which scored a great
success in Kaloleni and triumphed over the *Hawii* Jazz Band.

Kayamba's motive in hiring Beni was clearly still that of prestige.
'He went on organizing free dances, even though the cost of bringing
one of the *Brasso* bands from Mombasa was about 150 shillings, including transport, drinks, and food.' Now that Beni had at last arrived
in the Christian settlements of the Mombasa hinterland, it was thought
of as 'smart and modernizing . . . of higher social status'.[2]

[1] George Mkangi's summary of his interview with Samson Kayamba, October 1968.

[2] George Mkangi's summary of his interview with William Richard and Chamanje
George Mkangi, October 1968.

But the cost of hiring a Beni *Brasso* band, and the eagerness of people to hear one, combined in the late 1940s and 1950s to introduce a much stronger financial element into the dance contests of the hinterland. The *Brasso* bands themselves were in the business frankly for the money, and by the 1950s it cost more than 200 shillings to hire one, with extra expense for the Baluchi dancers – 'brown women with long wavy hair and very beautiful' – who had become a great attraction and a necessary fashion, since 'the more an organizer brought them the more prestige he got and the more people paid their entrance fees'.[1]

So the hinterland clubs began to charge entrance money to meet the cost of hiring. Soon they began to realize a profit for themselves. Beni, or *Brasso*, became much more merely an entertainment or a show than it had ever been before. But the Beni mode itself still had power to attract. The founders of the *Nyika* Dancing Club, for example, modelled themselves on Beni; they had a King and a Queen, whose arrival at the dance hall was greeted by a cessation of all activity and by the playing of 'God Save the King'. 'In the 1940s branches of *Wana Kingi* or *Wana Scotchi* sprang up in the countryside. These branches were known for their fierce rivalry and even fights.'[2]

It can be seen that these developments neatly drew together all the threads of the band situation on the coast. But the vigour of Beni–*Brasso* in the 1950s was deceptive. Beni was in its last days. George Mkangi gives a socio-political reason for its decline in the 1960s. Beni, he writes, had always been 'a youth movement'. In the early colonial period young men had been 'much impressed by the colourful militaristic life of the British Navy and Army', and, later, by the 'swaggering walking ways' of African ex-servicemen. But in the 1950s and 1960s young men on the coast began to face up to realities. There was an economic squeeze. There was a growth of ideological consciousness; an interest in nationalism and in Pan-Islam; a growing sense of the disadvantage at which the coast found itself in relation to the rest of the country. 'The futility of Beni became evident. It was this change which forced the dwindling of the movement; but it had already done an irreparable damage to the coast and to Mombasa. For while they danced the rest of the country was developing educationally and in agriculture. Beni has made the coast remain as the backwater of development.'[3]

[1] George Mkangi's summary of his interview with William Richard and Chamanje George Mkangi, October 1968.
[2] ibid. [3] George Mkangi, 'Beni research', 1968.

There is a good deal of truth in this idea of the disillusionment of youth with Beni. Yet the festive and factional life of Mombasa, and the musical life of its young men, as it exists today suggests that this sort of radical Puritanism is not the only explanation of Beni's decline. Bands are still popular and associated with the competition of football teams. What seems to have happened in addition to the repudiation of Beni extravagance by politically conscious young men, is that a shift of fashion and style took place. Beni had become less and less an expression of essential locational or group rivalries and more and more an entertainment. As an entertainment it was vulnerable to changing musical styles, and a military-style brass band was not perhaps the most effective combination for following the latest developments in African urban Jazz. The development of the radio and of the recording industry meant that the youth of the coast became familiar with South African township Jazz or with modernized Arab music or with Congo Jazz. Mkangi records what happened, in a manner which shows a transition from Beni to other forms rather than an abrupt demise of Mombasa competitive band music.

In the mid-1950s a younger popular band sprang up – the Union Jazz Band. It was an amalgamation of many players from the various Bands. The old ones, like *Kingi*, could not stand the competition and were disbanded . . . From the 1960s on *Brasso* in any form has been losing its appeal enormously. It only plays at Gatherings of older people who like to recall the nostalgia of the Beni era and of their youth. *Brasso* has been overtaken by the happy, noisy, twanging, electrifying, guitar-playing youth.[1]

The last days of Beni in Dar es Salaam

The oral material available to me for Beni history in Dar es Salaam says little about the 1950s and 1960s. I do not know whether there was a period of revival after the Second World War, as in Lamu and Mombasa, or whether there was a renewed diffusion into the city's hinterland, though I doubt it very much. But it is plain that by at least the late 1950s Beni was dead in Dar es Salaam. J. A. K. Leslie's vivid survey of the life of the city, mostly written in 1957, makes no mention of Beni at all, though it has a good deal to say about dance modes of other kinds.

[1] ibid.

As in Mombasa, the central place which Beni had occupied with modernizing youth had been assumed by Jazz Bands. This shift from Beni to Jazz is neatly symbolized by the story of the family of Kleist Sykes Plantan. Kleist had served in the First World War and had taken part in Beni; then he had moved into the African Association, and later into the Muslim Association and the African Retail Traders' Association. It might have seemed that Kleist had left bands of any kind far behind him. But he had sons and these sons served in the Second World War, and when they returned to Dar es Salaam after the war they were as restless as their father had been before them. For an old problem he found an old remedy, though in a new guise. 'By 1948 Kleist's health was dwindling. He then spent fewer hours on the business, and during his private time he listened to music. Incidentally, he had opened up a Jazz Band for his sons, particularly because he had to find a way of keeping his son Ally in Dar es Salaam. Ally, who was very much interested in music, had previously run away from Dar es Salaam to Nairobi to study music. Though his father did not appreciate this incident at all, he had at least appreciated Ally's interest in music. Therefore, in order to have Ally back in Dar es Salaam, he had to open this Jazz Band for them. He gave them a house which was their club and helped them a great deal materially, in the buying of instruments for example. As his health was dwindling, Kleist spent all of his evenings listening to the music being played by this band during their rehearsal, and whenever they performed Kleist would get a free attendance as a patron of the band.'[1]

The Jazz Bands played many of the same roles as Beni. Leslie wrote with reference to the late 1950s that 'Jazz clubs . . . have their social side and the members often stay together for years . . . there is a struggle for leadership among the organizers, and constant permutations, not unconnected with money; for the bands are beginning, the best of them, to enter into comparatively big money.'[2]

The songs of the Jazz Bands had the same salty topicality as the old Beni songs. Describing the Dar es Salaam elections of 1965, Daudi Mwakawago writes:

> Jazz clubs and other social organizations tended to mould opinion – largely in Kondo's favour. Here the football club of which he was

[1] A. D. Sykes, 'The Life of Kleist Sykes', Student Research Paper, Dar es Salaam, JAN/HIST/143/15, September 1968, pp. 13–14.
[2] J. A. K. Leslie, *A Survey of Dar es Salaam*, London, 1963, pp. 101–2.

a member was an important channel for information, and it was rumoured that it provided an unofficial campaign organization for Kondo . . . This club was one of the leading ones, but has always played an influential role in public affairs, being one of the roots from which TANU sprang. Leslie also notes the importance of 'football' or 'jazz clubs' . . . as 'marts for news'.[1]

After his departure from Tanzania into political exile, Mr Oscar Kambona was accused of having spent considerable sums to reward the Morogoro Jazz Club for their consistent propaganda support.

Finally, for all their greater commercialization the competition between Dar es Salaam Jazz clubs has much of the same atmosphere as Beni:

> Tanzania's pop music fans today are solo crazy, [wrote *Now in Tanzania* in April 1969]. Every song played at the various city halls these days has a solo . . . A solo is an instrumental piece performed by one person, usually the guitarist . . . It is the solo that makes or breaks a song, since it is the piece that evokes the most spontaneous reaction from the floor. Often a song with a good solo is greeted with shouts, whistling, howls, or claps. Dancers will shout 'encore' four, five, and maybe six times on the basis of what the solo does to them. All dancing becomes uninhibited during a solo . . . The musicians themselves are happy when a solo 'kills' . . . Many times a group of young men would dance together in a line or a circle, and during the solo, arouse themselves to a state of great excitement. 'It is an act of faith dancing a solo played by your favourite band'. Tanzania's favourite solo players are in Nuta, Dar es Salaam, and Morogoro Jazz Bands . . . These bands, notably Dar es Salaam's, have a hard-core following of about 100 people who attend every dance their favourite band plays . . . When the bands have outside engagements . . . this hard-core of fans is sure to be there. Bands use very sophisticated techniques of ensuring that their following stays and grows in number. When dancers have lost all self-consciousness and are dancing freely and expressively, as happens during a solo, at this critical moment, when the dancer is defenceless and open to sugges-tion, the band leader shouts 'Dar oyee' or whatever the name of the band may be. The dancers, grateful that Dar Jazz can make them feel so much more, and satisfied that DJB are musicians of note, reply 'Oyee, chukua, siwako, unaua, wewe'.[2]

[1] Daudi Mwakawago, 'Dar es Salaam: Two Urban Campaigns', in *One Party Democracy*, edited Lionel Cliffe, Nairobi, 1967, p. 219.
[2] 'Solos "Kill" Jazz Lovers', *Now in Tanzania*, no. 7, Dar es Salaam, 1–15 April 1969.

155

But despite these parallels the triumph of the Jazz Bands swept Beni away in Dar es Salaam. There *is* a Beni dance group which performs in Dar es Salaam today; at least there was one in 1968 when Mr Chijumba carried out his research on Beni history in the city. But as he soon found to his disappointment, this Beni group has no connections with previous city associations. 'When I interviewed the leader who is hardly thirty years of age he knew virtually nothing. His group has no name; there is no hierarchy of office in it; none of his dancers know anything about past Beni groups.' In short, this Beni team was an importation into Dar, brought by migrant workers from the south-east, where the dance in much modified form had become 'traditional'. The dancers held a stick or a green handkerchief and danced to shouted commands. Little enough was left of the elaborations of Beni and the group attracted little public attention.[1]

The decline of Beni in the rural areas

The development of individualism, the increase in the scale of communication, the secularization which under-cut Beni throughout eastern African in the 1950s had, of course, much wider cultural effects. As Hartwig makes plain in his discussion of Kerebe music, Beni survived these changes in Bukurebe at least rather better than did other forms of competitive dance.

> The dance era could not endure indefinitely . . . though the contest was very much in doubt until 1940. After this time young men acquired a new sense of direction that doomed the existing order . . . When asked about the future of their games, members of formerly prestigious groups readily acknowledge that their day has past. Young members, whose presence insures the game's future, are very few in number. Most are either too engrossed in acquiring an education or, for those whose education has terminated, they are too busy earning money. The interest of the youth for this form of music has been dissipated. Their idea of good music is what they hear over the radio and small groups flourish throughout Bukurebe in imitation of contemporary pop music, though they retain the use of the drum. Their dance is no longer Kerebe. From the singing of the hunters to the sedate performance of the *enanga*, from the demanding era of the game to the occasional weekend dance, the role of Kerebe music has continually altered to the prevailing social

[1] B. J. Chijumba, 'The Beni Dance – Research Report', October 1968.

needs. In each instance the sense of community has increased until it has now reached the level of the nation and beyond.[1]

By contrast with the decay of some other cultural forms, rural Beni, while in itself in decay, has shown some resilience. 'Though presently in decline along with all games,' writes Hartwig of Beni, 'its demise will be more gradual because of its modern aspects . . . It remains popular in the eyes of the educated youth in contrast to other games that are regarded as being sadly out of date.'

Thus Beni and its mutations survived in many parts of Tanzania in the 1960s but in so fragmented and varied a pattern that it is very difficult to make any generalizations. And since it is impossible to set out to describe the state of the Beni mode in every Tanzanian rural society, the best way of catching the flavour of the most recent period of Beni seems to be to take a cross-section. I propose to move across southern Tanzania from east to west, describing the state of Beni or its mutations in each area. One advantage of selecting southern Tanzania is that I have already had occasion – in the account of the struggle over Beni in Masasi and in the account of the rise of *Mganda* in the villages of the Tanzanian shore of Lake Nyasa – to write of Beni developments there in the 1930s and 1940s; another advantage is that this stretch of southern Tanzanian territory borders on both Malawi and Zambia so that we can see something of the interaction between the Beni history of the three territories.

Beni was still danced on the southern coast in the 1960s. Indeed, it seems that in the smaller coastal settlements generally, from Pangani in the north to Lindi in the south, Beni continued to fit into a surviving competitive factionalism. I was told in 1968 that 'very smart young men' danced Beni in Lindi. It was young men from the Lindi–Mtwara hinterland who kept the dance alive in Dar es Salaam in the 1960s, though by the time they got there they no longer appeared 'very smart'.[2]

Moving westwards away from the coast, however, the impulses which Beni in Lindi had once radiated out into the interior had died away by the 1960s. Beni only survived in the interior where it had developed into a local dance and had ceased to be one of a series of changing fashions.

The contrast between Masasi and Umwera districts is instructive

[1] G. W. Hartwig, 'The Historical and Social Role of Kerebe Music', *Tanzania Notes and Records*, No. 70, 1969, pp. 55–6.

[2] Interview with Archdeacon C. Kasoyaga, Assistant Bishop M. Soseleje, and Father Aidan Bakari, Masasi, 25 September 1967.

here. In Umwera Beni had become assimilated under the name of *Chikosa* and was still danced in the 1960s. In Masasi neither Beni nor any mutation of it was danced by that late date. Informants are unanimous that this had nothing to do with the missionary prohibition. 'When the missionaries banned the dance,' asserts a Moslem elder, 'it had already got roots. People continued to dance, particularly in the villages. The ban only became effective around the mission stations.'[1] Beni is remembered as having been especially popular in the Chiwata neighbourhood during the 1940s despite missionary opposition. But thereafter it declined and was replaced by other dances. Teachers and schoolboys followed the fashions of 'modern' dance and jazz music; villagers followed a series of dance fashions, some of which the missionaries opposed as they had opposed Beni. 'There was another ngoma, known as *Jole*, which began in the 1950s,' remembers a mission teacher, 'and this was even worse in so far as it was mostly danced by youngsters and the product was the destruction of the girls. I think the church was justified in banning the dance.'[2] It seems improbable, though, that the ban was any more effective in the case of *Jole* than it had been with Beni.

I have no information, unfortunately, upon the general history of dance in the Masasi district over the past ten years or so. I do not know whether it has paralleled the developments in Bukurebe and seen the end of the era of dance or whether there have merely been changes in dance fashion. But one additional element can be observed at work both in Masasi and in other rural areas. An attempt is being made by the Tanzanian Government to prevent the abandonment of 'traditional' dances; such dances are encouraged at secondary schools throughout southern Tanzania; striking regional dances of the Makonde and Yao are performed on state occasions. I would hazard the guess that the effect of this activity will be comparable to the missionary efforts to sponsor 'traditional' dance as a defence against Beni, and that it will have relatively little to do with the essential patterns of cultural change.

To the west of Masasi another situation exists. The district of Tunduru is occupied by the people of the great Yao Sultans, who moved into Tanzania after the First World War. The Yao of Tunduru have remained fiercely Moslem and impervious to mission influence. They have ignored allegations of backwardness, secure in their own sense of their past superiority. In this environment, Beni has taken on

[1] Interview with *Mwenye* Amwanyese Mzee, Nakole, 30 September 1968.
[2] Interview with Raymond Jumla, Mkomaindo, 28 September 1968.

some of the characteristics of a Yao 'national' dance. The dance is now called *Magova*. One of my informants, a young Makua from the Masasi area, said that the only place he had seen Beni danced 'was at Tanga when I was working in one of the sisal plantations. There it was con-conducted by migrant sisal workers who came from the Tunduru district.'[1] Just as Beni was kept alive in Dar by migrants from the southern hinterland, so in Tanga, the original Tanzanian home of the dance, the only men who performed it in the 1960s were migrants from remote Tunduru.

This connection between Beni and the Yao recurs in Songea district, further west again. In 1968 Mr Ndomba interviewed a number of Yao migrants from Malawi and Mozambique. These men, now in their forties, had come into Tanzania for medical treatment at Morogoro and Litisha leprosariums in the Songea district, and at the leprosariums they performed Beni. Beni still retained some of its old elaboration in these leprosarium performances; men were elected as 'kings'; flutes and drums were played; songs were in Swahili. The performers re-gretted the old days when Beni was danced on a competitive basis, pitting village cluster against village cluster and clan against clan. As migrants to Tanzania, they all felt a common identity so that they now danced Beni as an expression of Yao-ness, rather than as an expression of clan membership. Still, it was important for them to declare their oneness and Beni retained a vitality in the leper settlements that it had long ago lost in the villages of Songea district in general.[2] The Swahili songs performed at the dances no longer boasted of the virtues of one clan or mocked the deficiencies of another, but commented on topical events – 'independence, economic upheaval, the Arusha Declaration, etc., etc.'.[3]

These Yao lepers were all Moslems. Their persistence with the Beni mode points up the continued commitment of the villages on the Tanzanian shore of Lake Malawi to 'the great Christian *Mganda*'. But further round the lake, in the country of the Nyakyusa, the situation was a more complex one. Mr Mwambene thus summarizes the results of the research he carried out in 1968:

> It is said that what was called the 'Parade' by the Army in the first world war was copied afterwards by the villagers. The first

[1] Interview with Saifi Abdala, Mchawala, 18 September 1968.
[2] Interviews with Hashim Mohamed, Hussein Abdalla, Jawadu Salehe, Mwalimu Abdu, Sheik Hassan Ali, *Mzee* Osman Bakari, September 1968.
[3] Interview with Rajub Athumani, Morogoro Leprosarium, 25 September 1968.

centre of its origin was Malawi, and then it spread outward into Rungwe district. There was an actual imitation of the army parade with a leader holding a stick, followed by other people behind him. Later some modifications to suit African demands were introduced. The dance then branched out into many types of dances, known as *Min'goma*, *Mapenenga* and *Mipalano*. Each of these types of dances has a recognized leader who is accepted by all the followers. Smartness in all these dances is greatly advocated. Those who infringe the regulations are thrown out of the society. In the *Ming'oma* dancing societies there is a leader commonly called the 'King' . . . Sometimes there is inter-group competition and some people act as hosts of the visiting group. Before the removal of the chiefs by TANU, each chief had one or all of the dance teams mentioned and there was competition between the dancing societies of one chief and those of another chief.[1]

Furthest to the west of all, in Sumbawanga and Ufipa districts, Beni itself had enjoyed an atypical popularity immediately after the Second World War. Mr Khamsini, who did research in the area in 1968, describes the episode:

> The Beni dance was called *Mbeni* in Ufipa, and it seems to have been a current dance all over Ufipa . . . Immediately after 1945 there was a Mbenimania in the area. One club or group from one village visited a number of neighbouring villages, sometimes as guests of the village headman, to display their art. The inhabitants of the host village joined in, and it was not unusual for a dance to go on through the night. The dancers were rewarded soundly. They were given flour, various crops, goats, sheep and even cattle. Next time, it was the turn of another village, the one that had previously played host, to visit the surrounding villages . . . And so the whole thing went in circulation. Apart from these visits the *Mbeni* groups performed at weddings and on feast days . . . Young boys and girls were not included in the groups because of the long distances which had to be traversed when the group went on its tour . . . Personally I saw the dance in its last stages, in the late 1940s and early 1950s.[2]

Ufipa had been the centre of an earlier, much more elaborate, competitive Beni in the years after the First World War. This later revival came from outside, carried by 'the Bemba of Zambia', by way of the Wanyanda, 'people who live on the boundary between Zambia and

---

[1] Interview with Reverend Lazarus Mwanjisi, 26 May 1968.
[2] O. R. Khamsini, 'The Beni Dance', April 1968.

Ufipa'.[1] By the early 1950s this wave of Beni was over, and the dance is not danced in Ufipa today.

Clearly there are some special factors operating in the Beni history of this southern belt. Interactions with Malawi and Zambia have been especially important, and correspondingly the recent restriction of movement between Tanzania and Malawi has disrupted, among many more important consequences, a natural dance 'zone'. But the complex state of Beni in this southern belt is more or less characteristic for rural Tanzania as a whole, and the drawing of another east–west swathe through central or northern Tanzania would produce a similar sort of picture.

What comes out, of course, is still a picture of unevenness. Though Hartwig is right to stress the increasing 'scale' of the musical participation of the young as they move away from specifically Kerebe, or Nyakyusa, or Yao dances and join in a national, or continental, or global popular culture, there are still many people who need particular forms of dance to express their particular identity. In some cases Beni, which itself stood in the past as an indication of enlarging cultural scale, has come to play this particularizing role.

The survival of Mganda: an exception?

It is always more difficult to explain why something comes to an end than to explain why it originates. I have felt a particular tentativeness in writing this chapter. One cannot be certain, for example, whether the absence of Beni in many Tanzanian rural areas is due to the fact that the dance no longer has anything of relevance to offer such areas or whether it is due to the fact that there do not seem any longer to be centres of creative Beni vitality, radiating out the mode at periodic intervals. Moreover, though the explanations offered by Larson and Hartwig and myself are in general convincing, there is the fact of the continued vitality of *Mganda*, which seems to counter some of our generalizations.

Of the fact that *Mganda* does still flourish there can be little doubt. Even in Dar es Salaam *Mganda* is the only offshoot of the Beni tradition which can command attention. Leslie recorded *Mganda* performances in the 1950s, danced by 'a union of emigrants from the Mbaha area of the Nyanja tribe of Songea District'. He pointed out that these

[1] Interviews with Thomas Chasuka, Damas Rogato, Dominic Rogato, Zachary Rogato, Father Otto Sangu, etc., April 1968.

migrants were 'mainly the more educated who seek clerical or artisan jobs . . . As they are all from the same village, and to some degree related, they do in fact receive from each other practical help . . . they tend to live in groups of two or three, particularly bachelors, and if they can they get three adjoining rooms in a Swahili house, thus forming a small homogeneous enclave in an alien community. With this mutual support they are able to organize a Sunday entertainment, usually the dance *Mganda* in one of several different styles, where one or more teams of dancers will perform, for the enjoyment of themselves and of by-standers of other tribes – for this very modern-looking dance, danced in modern clothes by obviously educated young men, has not the disadvantage of seeming old-fashioned and "backwoods" as other traditional dances have.'[1]

As well as dancing *Mganda* the Mbaha migrants of the 1950s struck some other authentically Beni-style notes, among much else running a football team under the name of *Navy*. But they kept themselves self-consciously aloof from Swahili society and Leslie reports that 'many hardly succeeded in learning Swahili in a three-year tour'. It was an ironic return of the Beni tradition to the coast.

Mganda is still vigorous in Dar es Salaam today. In the late 1960s there was an *Mganda* dance team at the University College, composed of the domestic servants from the lakeshore. One of their number was elected as 'King of the *Saba Saba Boma*', and he inspected them during their dances, wearing his badges of royal rank. They danced at fêtes organized by the *Umoja Wa Wanawake Wa Tanzania*, the national women's organization. On these occasions the booming of the big drum, the rasping of the gourd *kazoos*, the danced drill of the lines of 'soldiers', all summoned up the largely vanished Beni style. On at least one occasion an *Mganda* competition was held in the Students' Union of the University, in which two teams danced against each other before an appreciative audience. One team was made up of workers from Dar es Salaam; the other was composed of students from the lakeshore. It is hard to imagine such a competition taking place in any other 'traditional' dance style. Alone among the Beni mutations, *Mganda* retains its prestige with the educated.

Mganda is danced still in the villages of the Tanzanian lakeshore. It is danced still in the secondary schools of that area. And it is danced still all around Lake Malawi in the area which gave it birth. One of the pamphlets published by the Malawi Publications and Literature

[1] Leslie, op. cit., pp. 54–5.

Bureau after national independence was Koma-Koma's glorification of *Mganda*, from which I have already quoted. In 1965, when the pamphlet was published, Koma-Koma had no sense of writing about a passing style. His whole account is in the present tense; he quotes a letter from the Adjutant of *Bwaira Boma* to the Adjutant of *Koleji Boma*, written in January 1963, challenging *Koleji* to compete with *London* and *India Bomas* and reminding them 'to bring enough trumpets'; and he quotes songs in praise of Dr Banda. And he ends affirmatively: 'Mganda is a very nice dance. It makes one travel e.g. Bomas from Likoma or Chizumulu islands can be invited to go to Tanzania (not now) or Portuguese East Africa. Also one makes a lot of friends whom one can visit.'[1]

I have the feeling that the difference between *Mganda* and other Beni mutations is in the degree of confidence of the local cultures to which they have adapted. The areas which sustain *Mganda* still feel a cultural self-confidence, despite their relative lack of economic development. In Malawi they feel at the core of the new nation. In Tanzania they feel proud of their educational advantage – even though this is today being rapidly overtaken – and of their success in the towns of eastern Africa. For them *Mganda* is a modern and progressive dance no longer because it is in any sense European, but because they are themselves self-confidently modern and progressive men.

[1] W. P. Koma-Koma, *M'ganda Kapena Malipenga*, Malawi Publications and Literature Bureau, Limbe, 1965, pp. 25–6, 35. Here, as throughout this book, I am quoting from the translation of Mrs Catherine Chipembere. The text of an *Mganda* song in praise of Banda is given on page 33.

Conclusion

In the last resort, then, the Beni *ngoma* has turned out to be rather surprising. A dance mode which seemed so obviously derivative and parasitical has proved to have been deeply rooted, creative, and versatile. I think that in this respect the Beni *ngoma* can stand as a metaphor for many other features of twentieth-century eastern Africa which are normally explained in terms of Europeanization. Nothing could *seem* more European than Beni, it is true. Yet the brass-band tradition itself had extra-European origins and some of these influences were still active in nineteenth-century eastern Africa; apparent exoticisms, like danced drill and mimic combat, were in fact derived from the long-standing competitive dance traditions of the Swahili coast; and in the later days of Beni the desire for so-called European clothes could more sensibly be regarded as a desire for convenient clothes or for 'modern' clothes. With or without direct European influence the African societies of eastern Africa would have responded to the impact of the modern world and it is surely important to disentangle their own creative responses from the responses imposed or induced by direct European agencies. And this remains true even if African creative responses could not be 'free' but were bound to be constrained by what was available for them to make use of.

Seen from this point of view, Beni appears quite clearly as a creative African response, though in some ways a constrained one, rather than as an imposed European idiom. Europeans did not set out to produce Beni; did not produce Beni; and did not approve of it when it was produced. Moreover, because the brass band and the military parade and the other 'exotic' features of Beni were so firmly fixed in the context of African social self-help and competition; because they became an expression of African communalism; their significance was quite different from the brass bands and parades of Europe.

This essentially African musical and dance form lives up to its promise as a source of commentary and as an articulation of the varying levels of popular concern during the colonial period. Much more could be done in the systematic collection of Beni song texts, but those which have survived and been recorded reveal a variety of emotions – the emotions of the men caught up in the First World War, the emotions of the Lamu populists in the 1920s and 1930s, the initial responses of southern Tanzanians to the Arusha Declaration.

The most exciting of these texts express African resentment of or opposition to colonial rule. But Beni was not *essentially* an oppositionist phenomenon. It was too profoundly assimilated into African societies for it to be exclusively or even mainly concerned with the externalities of opposition. Hence the Beni texts and Beni history more generally also reveal significant tensions within African societies, and significant aspirations. Beni as a competitive dance tradition mirrored the tension between ex-slaves and freemen in Islamic Ujiji, just as *dansi* mirrored the same tensions in the Christian villages of the Mombasa hinterland. Beni mirrored the tensions between Swahili and non-Swahili, between 'posh' and 'vulgar', between young and old. During the nationalist period, with its emphasis on unities. Beni was blamed for these divisions as if it had created them rather than mirrored them. But to the social historian of eastern Africa, to whom the reality of internal divisions is of the utmost importance, Beni turns out to be a good decoder. My own experience in Lamu was that people could not or would not talk in general terms of social change but through the concreteness of a topic like Beni one could reach the reality of the retreat of the town aristocracy from locational competition and the reality and significance of populist feeling.

Beni mirrored aspirations as much as divisions. It expressed at various times and places the aspiration of the young Swahili freemen who wanted to take the lead in modernization; of the young men in the countryside who wanted to be given the respect due to their experience in migrant labour or at the battle-front; of the Bemba underground miners who wanted to create a decent life in the industrial towns.

These aspirations lead us back to the theme of protest. Protest was so often generated by denial of aspiration. It is true that within Beni both the aspirations and the protest was symbolic – a matter of claiming the right to share in the use of certain symbols, such as clothes, and badges, and ceremonies. But the fact that aspirations were symbolic made them no less threatening to Europeans. A man like Vincent Lucas, Bishop of Masasi, attributed supreme significance to the realm of symbol, and spent his days seeking ways in which Christianity could capture the symbolism of the African peoples of southern Tanzania. He did not underestimate the significance of Africans who were claiming to capture and use 'European' symbols. And it can be argued that this was a perfectly sensible way of regarding the colonial relationship at the core of which was the successful manipulation and control of symbols. For this reason the clashes between Beni dancers and missionaries, apparently so trivial, in fact touch on some of the central issues of colonialism.

I believe that all this can be claimed for the study of Beni. Yet as this book has proceeded I have become more and more aware that Beni history is merely one thread in a very complex pattern of eastern African cultural history. It is a brightly coloured thread and easy to disentangle but not necessarily more important than any of the others. To understand fully the issues raised in this book we need to have many more studies of local cultural history such as Hartwig has given us for Bukurebe. We also need studies of dance modes which were as widely diffused as Beni but very different in origin and nature. We need to study, for example, the fascinating story of the way in which the masked initiation dances of Malawi were spread in the nineteenth century to the East African coast and in the twentieth to the industrial towns of Central Africa. We need to study the diffusion of dances which were originally characteristic of the eastern Congo and as far afield as Zanzibar. In this way we shall learn much more than we know about the processes of diffusion and adaptation in eastern African cultural history over the last hundred years. In this way, too, we shall be able to learn more about the particularities of Beni and to discover how far the story told in this book is indeed a very special case and how far it is part of the general history of eastern African culture.

Appendix

THE ROLE OF WOMEN IN DANCE ASSOCIATIONS IN EASTERN AFRICA

Just as I was about to leave Lamu after collecting oral material on Beni I realized that I had seen no women informants. Very belatedly I made inquiries in Malindi about the specific role of women in dance associations. Later, as I went through the interviews carried out by students in Mombasa and Dar es Salaam and in many rural areas I realized that they had not interviewed women either. My several dozen informants on Beni history were all male. Faced with this disturbing discovery I rationalized away most of its significance. After all, in the coastal towns the essence of Beni lay in the public procession in which only men had taken part; the participants in Beni in the new towns of Central Africa were male migrant labourers, few of whom had brought their wives with them. No doubt, I thought, we had all been directed to male informants because Beni was a male affair.

When the manuscript of this book was finished, however, two pieces of research on women's history came to my attention. Both concerned dance associations in the towns of eastern Africa and both proved that I had overlooked in my own research a most important dimension.

Margaret Strobel worked in 1972 and 1973 on the history of women in Mombasa. In August 1973 she gave a paper to the annual conference of the Historical Association of Kenya which traced the development of women's associations in that city.[1] Reading her paper was an uncanny experience. Where my footnotes referred only to interviews with male informants, hers referred only to interviews with female informants. While I talked about Beni associations in Mombasa, she talked about Lelemama associations. Gradually it became clear, though, that for much of the time we were talking about the same thing. I called the associations by the name Beni because this was the musical style and the dance style performed by the men; she called the same associations

---

[1] Margaret Strobel, 'From Lelemama to Lobbying: Swahili Women's Associations in Mombasa', Annual Conference, Historical Association of Kenya, August 1973.

Lelemama because this was the name of the dance performed by the women. In the memories of her informants the other half of the life of the Mombasa associations was revealed; they remembered the names of the women patrons and leaders, the triumphs of one team of women dancers over another.

But there was more to Margaret Strobel's account than that. The history of the Lelemama associations in Mombasa was not merely the history of the 'hidden' half of the Beni associations. In some ways and at some points in time the Lelemama associations diverged significantly from the Beni development. While many non-Swahili men took part in the Beni parades, for example, the Lelemama dances continued to be performed exclusively by Swahili and Arab women. Moreover, some women leaders were not content merely to command the women's division of *Kingi* or *Scotchi*. As Ms Strobel writes:

> The earliest *ngoma* associations – *Kingi, Kilungu, Scotchi* – had a male *beni* or brass-brand contingent as well as a female *lelemama* section. These three, drawing from the Old Town élites and their followers, were most prestigious and most able to afford feasts and competitions . . . In the mid-1920s Fatma Mwaita, the daughter of the *Sheha* of *Kilungu*, left *Kilungu* to join the rival *Kingi*, and then began her own *lelemama* association. In taking the name *Ibinaal Watan* the Arabic for 'daughters of the city', she imitated a men's regiment within *Kingi*, called *Ibn Watan*, 'sons of the city'. Shortly afterward she quarrelled with *Ibinaal Watan* . . . and started a rival group, *Banu Saada*.

These two new associations were much more loosely linked with the male-dominated Beni associations. Ms Strobel emphasizes the contribution which they made to the lives of women in Mombasa:

> For weddings *lelemama* was one of many days' entertainment, with several hundred women attending, showing off their new clothes, cheering the dancers on, visiting with one another, and awaiting the latest rumours and antagonisms to be revealed in song . . . Besides the specific occasions, a *lelemama* could be organized whenever the members gathered enough money for a feast in the shambas, either for themselves or as part of a competition. These dances helped break up daily routine as well as accent important days. The dances must have been exciting occasions both for poorer women, who worked long hours each day, and for the élites, who traditionally were allowed out of the house only to attend weddings, funerals, and these gatherings.

As time went on the women of *Ibinaal Watan* and *Banu Saada* began to break away from some customary restrictions. During the Second World War their members paraded in the public streets, just as the male members of Beni had always done, wearing costumes 'imitating the British Air Force, Army, and Navy, complete with hats, uniforms, bellbottoms, and carved wooden guns'.

One can detect a note of rebellion as well in the daughters of *Kingi* and *Kilungu*. Formerly, women of high status gave financial support but did not dance. However, the IW–BS generation of *waungwana* mounted the bench alongside the others and danced in front of male spectators without *buibuis* . . . At one point the older men of the community threatened to go to the mosques and pray that their daughters drop dead, if the latter continued. But the daughters were already married, and if their husbands did not object, they continued dancing.

In this way, and as Margaret Strobel develops the story at fascinating length, the history of Mombasa dance associations turns out to provide an admirable way in to the distinct history of women.

And this turns out to be true for the new towns of Central Africa as well. Malira Kubuya-Namulemba has written a study of women's associations in Lubumbashi.[1] She is especially concerned with the associations formed by 'single' women – widows, deserted wives, women traders, prostitutes. To begin with their history once again coincides with the story of the associations formed by men. She shows, for example, that 'single' women were especially valued members of the early Beni and *Kalela* associations of the 1920s. They were always free to attend the *ngomas*; they were usually able to contribute financially; they turned out smartly and lavishly dressed. But 'women found themselves ill at ease in these mixed associations and frustrated by their secondary role. They had no word to say about their organization or direction. Nevertheless they too desired to benefit from the advantages of association. Little by little they developed the idea of forming their own groups.' By the late 1920s and early 1930s associations of single women emerged, which organized their own dances with great success and profit.

Margaret Strobel's work raises all sorts of questions which it would

[1] Malira Kubuya-Namulemba, *Les Associations Feminines de Lubumbashi* (1920–50), Mémoire Présente en vue de L'Obtention Du Grade De Licence En Histoire, Année Academique: 1971–72. Université Nationale Du Zaire, Campus de Lubumbashi.

be fascinating to ask in Lamu; Malira Kubuya-Namulemba's work raises all sorts of questions which it would be fascinating to ask on the Copperbelt or in Kabwe. It is a pity that such questions are not already asked and answered in this book. But the revelation of this whole new dimension indicates that the lengthy treatment given them in this book by no means exhausts the interest of the dance associations for social history.

Index

NOTE: Wherever possible references are given some explanation: thus, *Ngoma ya Kingi* has the words (Dance of the king) included. This will differentiate between place names which will generally be of one word only.

Non-Christianized Africans have names like Hamisi bin Mustafa, frequently omitting the word 'bin', which means that the person's name is Hamisi while his father's is Mustafa. African names therefore appear by the first word, unless Westernized, as in Magubane, Bernard.

The titles *Mzee* (revered one, or mister) and *Mwalimu* (teacher) are not used in the index.

Tanganyika has been used in preference to the modern name of Tanzania for historical reasons. Otherwise countries are indexed by the name known today, i.e. Malawi.